Dear Katherine

All these stories are designed to ignite in you that inner spark and courage to live your best life.

Love Rosaly

Ignite Your Female Leadership

Thirty-five outstanding stories by women who are inspiring the world through feminine leadership.

FOREWORD BY

JB Owen

Founder and CEO of Ignite

PRESENTED BY

Alex Jarvis, Alina Christina Buteica, Alison Jessica Weihe, Allyne Henesey,
Andrea Cairella, Andrea Gontkovicova, Ashley Avinashi, Barbara Santen,
Catherine Malli-Dawson, Helle Brodie, JB Owen, Joanna Mercado Peters,
Dr. Judy Gianni, Judy Lynn Sutton, Kari Chiappetta, Kim McDonnel,
Kristina Mänd-Lakhiani, Lizzy Koster, Madalina Petrescu, Marnie Tarzia,
Nadia La Russa, Narelle Gorman, Nitasha Sarin, Phyllis Roberto, Rachel Hayek,
Riikka Ylitalo, Rosalyn Palmer, Rusti L Lehay, Samantha Ridley, Sandra Smart,
Tanya Donahue, Tara Pilling, Taranum Khan, Ph.D. CCS, Trish Mrakawa,
and Ulrike Stahl.

Published and printed by JBO Global INC.

Dedication

This book is dedicated to women all over the world who lead in all ways that makes sense for them. Women lead by working, mothering, guiding, coaching, providing, supporting, teaching, nurturing, organizing, administering, directing and even governing. How you show up in your life as a leader is up to you. You are the author of your own story. We want the women in this book inspire you to step into your power and to find your vision and voice. We hope this book gives you permission to care for yourself in the same way you so selflessly care for all those around you. Our wish for you is that you live your life with purpose, passion and perseverance – taking steps each day to advance favourably in the direction of your dreams. By the end of this book, we hope you feel ignited to take action to become the CEO of your own life. — **Marnie Tarzia, MA and Best-Selling Author.**

Ignite Author's Testimonials

"The Ignite journey is incredible. Writing and sharing my story has been a great challenge and an immense pleasure. It is one thing to get words on paper – a release in itself. When combined with the editing skills and their leading questions, inspiring the author to put more of themselves on the page, the experience is transformational healing. I am grateful that I said yes to this amazing opportunity. My deepest desire is for readers to be inspired to write their own stories, so they too experience healing and live their most authentic life."
— **Phyllis Roberto**

"The collective energy, compassion, integrity and love in this forum of incredibly brave and gifted women keeps you coming back for more. I can honestly say it has been an honour and privilege to have been a part of this eclectic group of leaders. We are free to be ourselves with instant acceptance with no judgement and there is tremendous encouragement to speak our truths. I have healed parts inside I didn't even know needed healing and am proud to have witnessed others undergo the same. The sharing of these life experiences has forever changed me to be more of who I am."
— **Samantha Ridley**

"If you've ever dreamed of writing your story and getting it published, this is the way to do it. By working with the Ignite team I'm realizing my dream and had excellent support to make it happen. From the weekly writers' nests that helped me get into the groove of writing, to the mastermind sessions where a safe space was created to share my thoughts and my initial paragraphs, myself and the other authors were supported every step of the way. I was also challenged to go deeper into my story and share more than I thought I had to give through the remarkable editing processes. Women supporting women is recipe for success."
— **Sandra Smart**

"This process of writing my story has been one of the most internally fulfilling experiences ever! I feel so grateful to have had this precious gift of the opportunity to express my heartfelt message and what I felt on paper with the world. I feel so thankful to be in this anthology."
— **Madalina Petrescu**

"Together we are so much more ingenious than we are on our own. I believe this was proven in this IGNITE community of outstanding women, writing this book. Sharing my story made my head and heart connect. I am so grateful for having found such a professional and dedicated platform, pushing me beyond my limits in a safe and nourishing environment."
— **Ulrike Stahl**

Publisher's Note:

We are delighted to offer the second compilation book in the IGNITE YOU series. Our mission is to produce inspiring, motivational and authentic real-life stories that will Ignite You in your life. Each book contains 35 unique stories told by 35 exceptional authors. They are of the highest caliber to offer engaging, profound and life-changing examples that will impact the reader. Our mandate is to build a conscious, positive and supportive community through our books, speaking events, writing workshops, ignite experiences, podcasts, immersions and a product marketplace. We welcome new authors onto our platform and new book ideas. Should you desire to be published and featured in an Ignite You book. Please apply at www.igniteyou.life/apply or reach out to us at suppport@igniteyou.life.

Published and printed by JBO Global INC.

5569-47th Street Red Deer, Alberta, Canada T4N 1S1 - 1 877-377-6115

ISBN# 978-1-7923-0665-5

Ordering Information: Quantity sales. Special discounts are available on quantity purchases by corporations, associations, and others. For details, contact the publisher at the address above. Programs, products or services provided by the authors are found by contacting them directly. Resources named in the book are found in the resources pages at the back of the book.

Printed in China.

Ignite
Your
Female Leadership

JB Owen and Catriona Le May Doan

FOREWORD BY
JB OWEN

Founder and CEO of Ignite

Known as the fastest woman on ice, Catriona Le May Doan is a three-time Olympic medalist - winning two golds and a bronze. She has participated in four consecutive Olympic games and broken 13 world records for speed skating. She is a formidable athlete, dedicated individual and her numerous achievements undoubtedly prove that. One is easily impressed by her multiple World Cup Championships. She also is an Officer of the Order of Canada and has been inducted into the Canadian Sports Hall of Fame. Looking at Catriona's accomplishments, she is nothing short of spectacular. Few, if any, have achieved what she has in her sport and reached that level of success.

If you meet Catriona, you will first notice her smile, then her legs! Her dynamic grin is infectious and instantly warming. Her four decades of training has sculpted and molded a pair of legs as perfect as one can get. Athletics has taught her discipline and devotion, and you can see that in her personality and physique. She is a woman to notice. She is a true female leader and a champion through and through.

Yet, like all leaders, she faced obstacles and endured tremendous setbacks. At the 1994 Olympics, she fell, crashed into the side wall and finished a disappointing 17th place. In front of the world and with millions watching, Catriona slipped on her blade and ruined all chances for any medals.

Decades of training, untold amounts of money, endless hours of sacrifice by her and her family were eradicated in an instant as she uncontrollably slid down the speedway to a crumpled stop. It was a devastating fall and as Catriona describes, one that could have debilitated her spirit and ended her career.

That moment could have defined her. She could have gone home and accepted failure as her fate. But, like all females born to lead, she got right back on the ice and kept training. She committed to competing in the next Olympics four years later, and that determination won her the Gold and the Bronze! Of course, she didn't give up there. She went on to attend the next Olympics in 2002, becoming the first Canadian individual, and only female Canadian, to defend a gold medal at any Olympic games.

Catriona's accolades are outstanding, and her achievements are nothing short of impressive… but it is her open heart and unwavering commitment to others that is even more inspiring. After hanging up her skates, Catriona continued working with athletes and devoted herself to helping others. She was asked to be an honorary coach for Team Canada and traveled to the next Olympics opting out of winning and opting into giving. She used her skills and experience to help prepare the new athletes for the stresses they were about to undergo. She focused on their internal well-being, positive mindset and emotional stability. She knew being a success was not only about performance but about attitude, connection and self-determination. She used her leadership skills in the mental, emotional and physiological support of others.

That is the differentiator of a true female leader. They don't use full grit and guts as their only leadership style. Female leaders dive deep into the internal structures that make us who we are. They factor in the person, the atmosphere, and all the variables to do their best so everyone is served. They guide with a gentler hand and use their feminine graces to ease-in and get great results. Female leaders push less and encourage more. They battle for the cause not the individual. They by-pass their own egos and prefer mutual collaboration. They set aside their personal needs to serve a higher purpose. Female leaders lead from the heart. They include their emotions and factor in how they feel. They use that to consider others and find how to make as much as possible, a Win/Win for everyone.

Learning to Lead

Through this book, you will read countless stories of true female leadership. They may not be the hard-hitting, stratospheric tales found in movies or sensationalized news reports. Instead, they will be the quiet giants, the heart-centered, mindful stories of women in everyday situations, finding their skills of leadership. They will use the gentler side of leading because that is what women do. They use their talents, skills and inner knowing to guide them forward. They listen to their inner voice and trust their intuition. They look around themselves to include as many people as they can and they learn by leading, bringing others with them to all rise higher.

There is a collective energy in the way women do this. This book is filled with many examples of how it has been done. It is layered with authentic examples of every aspect of inherent leadership. It shows how being a female leader takes not just strength and perseverance, but self-worth and self-conviction. How knowing oneself and honoring that is the true reflection of valuing all. Leaders lead most effectively by example. Female leaders amplify that. They step up first, give full out and always have a helping hand available. The new paradigm of leadership rests in the heart of women and IGNITE Female Leaders is a book destined to inspire all women stepping into and embracing that gifts of feminine leadership.

Enjoying Your Leadership

In the upcoming pages of this book, you are going to read many stories of women leading themselves and leading others. You will see the 'triumphant' leader and the 'solo' one. You'll be witness to them impacting many and additionally see their own determination to intrinsically impact themselves. There is no common way to lead when it comes to women. Many in this book have hit tremendous pain points and been torn apart at the very seams. Others have been pushed, challenged, disgraced, ignored, dismissed and even shot at to ignite them into their leadership role. All have had to struggle and get back up from hardship. None were simply given the keys to any throne. They worked to become leaders. They preserved to push through anything that might have held them back so they could be at the forefront of their own life.

While curating the stories for this book, we noticed an amazing commonality. The pages were not filled with grandiose and flagrant examples of dominant control. The messages were not centered around accolades or achievements. Few, if any, bragged about awards or recognition. Most, if not all the stories, shared the common theme that Female Leaders lead in a different way. They go inward before they go outward. They think before they leap, weighing in all the options before making a clear decision. Most importantly they MUSTER. They dig deep and find their inner strength.

They search within and ask nothing they are not willing to do or give of themselves first.

We also noticed that photos with hands on hips, in power suits, behind a big mahogany desk was a stereotypic persona few related to. The new vision of a Female Leader was showing up in dresses, high heels, and fuchsia colored lipstick. They wear grins on their faces, a smirk behind the eyes or a full-out gayful show of laughter, instead of a furrowed brow or stern demeanor set up and contrived. Our leaders were vivacious and feminine. Fun and free. Beautiful and brilliant and their pictures broke the mold of what a female leader "should" look like.

Destined to Lead

That began an even deeper exploration into what leadership truly is. What does it mean to lead the female way? What is true female leadership? What constitutes leadership in general? You are about to find out…

My wish is that when you read through these stories, you are deeply transformed by the examples of guiding others through guiding oneself. I hope that your mind opens, and your self-awareness awakens to how powerful you are on your own leadership path. That you feel the strength within the sharing and the supportive intentions behind it. Each author wrote her story so that you may relate to her heroine's journey and see a bit of yourself in it. Every story is designed to lift you up in your own leadership discovery. Written to encourage you to grab your steering wheel in life and not only hang on, but ride it full out, with your foot on the gas and not looking in the rear-view mirror.

We all know it is one thing to lead under necessity and strife, it is another to lead with love, compassion, and focus. You will see throughout this book that self-determination is the common theme. Caring, empathy, and collaboration are constantly present. Intuition, personal care, integrity, and purpose are the four corners of the lives each one of these women have created. Their leadership is in leading themselves first before they ever felt they could lead another. That is what makes this book so unique and unprecedented. They have lived it. It isn't a theory. They do more than talk about it, they have become it, and now they have written it to share it directly with you.

As you turn the pages, you will find each story begins with a Power Quote. It is like a mantra or a battle cry. I believe we all should have one. That sentence that pushes you to do even more and makes you think a little deeper. It is what your bumper sticker would say, or what you'd write on your office wall. Each Power Quote is designed to remind you of what you have inside – exceptionalness. Power quotes are that sentence or phrase that you say when the tears might be flowing both in hardship and in reward.

Then, you will read their Intentions. These are the author's goals and aspirations of what they wish their story will do for you. It is a personal message, filled with meaning, and purpose. They want to Ignite You to begin living your most exceptional life and they share it in their divinely unique way. Their intentions set the tone for their story and are designed to both awaken and inspire you.

The story then follows. It is an account of a woman stepping into leadership and embracing the Ignite moment that fostered that. We all have Ignite moments in our lives that change us, define us and set us on a new path or trajectory for life. These stories are those moments, told in the most genuine and enduring way. They show that all of us have those moments and they not only define us but transform us.

Once you have finished their heartfelt stories, you will find an inspiring 'Ignite Action Step' (or Steps). These are the doable and tangible things they did to support and expand themselves. Each author explains an easy-to-do, practical idea for you to close the book and implement immediately. They are the processes and practices that worked in their lives. Each one is different and unique just like you are and proven to yield magnificent results when done consistently.

We all know actions speak louder than words and never is that more accurate than in leadership. Action IS the key. To move the needle forward in your life we encourage you to try one new action step each day or pick the one you like and do it consecutively for thirty days. There is no way Catriona held any of her Olympic medals without constant practice, work and effort. She didn't just think about it, she did something each day in her desire towards it. Her leadership in overcoming her own setback is what became so admirable around the world. She could have quit. She could have succumbed on her first disappointment and let define her for the rest of her life, but instead, she took action. And if that action didn't measure up, she shifted and took another. That is why we have offered you thirty-five different action steps to try. Each one is potentially the step that could change your life forever. Start with one, just pick that one that calls to you the most and follow through to see significant and lasting change in yourself.

Please remember, others may be looking to you for leadership. Your kids, siblings, friends, neighbors and even spouse may be watching to see how you lead so they can emulate you. This is your moment to step up on the podium of your own life and make it golden. You get to decide how you run your race and how you will speed skate through your life. Make the most of it and let these stories remind you that you can do anything, be anything and accomplish anything you choose. You can gallantly charge forward and run down the hillside into the bliss and enjoyment you have created. It absolutely can be wonderful on every level; you just have to blow the bugle horn and do it.

Lead with Heart

We know that many people read compilation books to be inspired. If you feel that your story is still unfolding, or you're trying to figure it all out, we are with you. We have all been through hardships and go through them numerous times in our lives. Our stories may show our successes, but we still waffle like everyone else. We just have practiced and re-practiced using our leadership muscles. The greatness behind of all these female leaders is behind you. We support you full-out and will cheer you on as you find yourself. We all extend our hands should you need a bit of support, some advice or a shoulder to cry on. We offer ourselves should you ever want to reach out because something we said really resonated or what we shared was exactly what you needed to hear. Please know we are all accessible and eager to connect so please feel free to find us.

Leaders need to stick together. We need to support one another as we rise and flourish. We need to help each other along the way even if that means for a moment someone might surpass us. For everyone to benefit, everyone must help. In your road to leadership, you will be challenged and confronted, but if you are true to your inner knowing, those challenges will be met with the purest intentions. A leader is someone who takes a chance, follows their heart and overcomes obstacles along the way. Seek out all that you need so you can make beautiful decisions about your own life. Focus on you, your aspirations, and talents. Accentuate your gifts and shine your brightest light. Give all you can to your expansion because you are worth it.

I am ignited by the idea of you turning the next page and reading a plethora of wisdom, intertwined in a cornucopia of knowledge. I am excited that you are about to step up to the podium of your own experience in life. It might be measured by awards and trophies or minutely counted by a stopwatch. It might mean the whole world knows your story or you happily stand in the background and let others shine. However you reach your pinnacle is sure to be filled with some goosebumps and some hairs up on the back of your neck. That's life. That's what makes it juicy and exciting.

It isn't all or none, it is how you lead yourself through and emerge on the other side.

The stories you are about to embark on are all our stories. They supercede race, culture, age and even gender. They are the human story, the experience of being a Being on this earth. They touch at the very heart of belonging, connecting and sharing. They are raw, real and unrestricted… that's what makes them so amazingly engaging. They cut through all the 'stuff' we want people to see and shine a light directly on the heart of who we were born to be.

Ignite was created to ignite others and impact humanity. Our mandate is to do more, share more and spread a conscious positive message to as many people as possible. We believe in the human connection and that power comes from being heard, being seen and belonging to something greater than one's self. We invite you to Ignite others. To let your story be heard, share your experiences find your voice. We pride ourselves in bringing people together, offer a solution, give back and do something good for the planet. That is the mission and purpose behind IGNITE. There is power when one person touches the heart of another, and a spark begins. Be it inspiration, love, support, encouragement, compassion or belief. We all can be a leader in living a kind and gracious life.

May you have many ignite moments that transform your life into the amazing person you were meant to be. – JB Owen

Please know that every word written in this book, and every letter on the pages has been meticulously crafted with fondness, encouragement and a clarity to not just inspire you but to transform you. Many women in this book stepped up to share their stories for the very first time. They courageously revealed the many layers of themselves and exposed their weaknesses like few leaders do. Additionally, they spoke authentically from the heart and wrote what was true for them. We could have taken their stories and aimed for some 'brule' defined perfection, following every editing rule, but instead we chose to leave their unique and honest voice intact. We overlooked exactness to foster individual expression. These are their words, their sentiments and explanations. We let their personalities shine in their writing so you would get the true sense of who each one of them is completely. That is what makes IGNITE so unique. Authors serving others, stories igniting humanity. No filters.

JB OWEN

"It is better to be known for who you are
than known for who you are not."

It is my intention to write a story that will not just move and encourage you but will touch your heart in such a profound way, you will be inspired to listen to it, follow it and do right by it. I hope from reading these words, you will feel compelled not to do what others choose for you, but what you choose for yourself. To be always guided by YOUR heart and lead from that place that is authentically YOU.

LEADING IN-BETWEEN

At a summer camp for budding creative girls, each cabin was asked to put on a comedy skit for the final weekend when the parents came to take us home. I organized a fashion show where each cabin-mate strutted down the makeshift runway wearing her pajamas and carrying the stuffy she had brought from home. As Emcee for the event, I colourfully described every flannel nightgown and frilly pink-flowered p.j. set. I had to coax the shy ones and cajole the few that refused to participate, as the crowd laughed and cheered throughout the hilarious event. I felt like a leader, coming up with the idea, mapping it out and executing it without a hitch. The bear-head slippers and back-door pajamas had the crowd roaring hysterically. My leadership skills were born.

I saw my mother be a leader in our family business and at home. She ruled very sternly, both from her Russian upbringing and her years of self-survival. People in our town often commented on my mother's work ethic and personal drive. She was forever going, doing and completing. She liked to be busy. Unlike my friends' mothers, she never wore an apron. She never baked cookies for the bake sale or wore a reflective vest as one of our crosswalk monitors. When I was young, her working was an oddity. Most of my friends enjoyed the traditional working father with the stay-at-home mom. Both my parents ran our business and deep down I was proud of my mom for not having a sing-song voice as a lunchroom helper or waiting aimlessly in the food court as my friends and I shopped around the mall.

To me, my mom was a not just a leader but a BOSS!. She ran a company, had staff and made decisions on a dime. She was fair, honest and could barter a deal with anyone. She was shrewd without being rude, always letting the other person speak, before she gave her answer. In public, she was formidable to me. I wished she would have showed up for my school programs and drama plays, but deep down inside I was proud she was stronger and more independent than the other mothers. I watched her coordinate and delegate and those powerful skills struck a chord in me. I never wanted to be perceived as weak, so I followed her lead, and strived to one day become 'The Boss'.

Although I *felt* leadership in me, it took awhile for me to utilize it in a good way. For much of my school years, I competed always striving to be the best. I didn't enjoy athletics, so I flourished in art, drama and debate. That meant always winning against my opponents. Always wanting the lead roles in the school play, pushing to have my art in the school newspaper or as the cover of the yearbook. I even pressed to redesign the school crest to prove myself.

Leading was mixed with getting my way and convincing others. It took me years to mature, to get it right. I spent countless moments fine-tuning and working on ways to lead with the heart, lead so others felt supported and lead in a way that had everyone winning. Only, there weren't a lot of role models emulating these kind of strategies or moms like me, running my own business after my kids were born. Business owners were primarily men and I felt odd not doing what they did. However, I wanted fun in the workplace and heart in our company. I made it more like a family and less like a job. My staff were like my extended family members. Each one needed their own special attention. Maybe it was by commenting on a new outfit or asking how their training for an upcoming race was going. I gave them nicknames like Flash and Megatron based on their work habits. We'd do lunches as a group outside when the weather was nice and I'd leave colored stickies on their computer screen with words of praise. Acknowledging was key and I found encouragement got me way more than traditional overriding, bullying and demanding.

I was happy building my business at a doable pace. I had two small children under the age of three and they needed me as much as possible. Except, the business was doing exceptional. Sales were up, stores wanted our products and we were being heavily sought after by major retailers. When I started my company in my basement, I knew it was going to go big. Within six months I was on a plane to China to source suppliers, manufacturers and factories to work directly with me. I didn't know the language, the culture or the game. Showing up as a tall blonde in a male-dominated country was difficult. Many times, I was mistaken as the assistant stepping in for the boss. I was denied courtesies shown to male business-owners traveling abroad. I was an Amazon woman to them and they told me. I even had one factory send a car to pick me up from the airport with bikini-clad girls in the backseat. They thought I was a man and that is the way business with foreigners was done. My name didn't indicate I was a woman. I was often referred to as Mr. Owen in emails and on signs drivers held while waiting for me at the airport. If ever I had a male interpreter, all questions were directed at him and not me. A factory tour would be cut short once I arrived and they saw I was female. I even had one factory owner show me utter disdain once he found out I was a woman and left me on the side of the road, refusing to return me to my hotel.

None of this deterred me. I was on a mission and determined to make a huge success of my business despite the prejudicial treatment I received. I stayed focused and grew my company to a million dollars in revenue in under four years. It was hard but worth it and my pride was running high. I felt like a leader. I was driving the entire business from concept to conception. I was creating a hundred and eighty new designs each season. We had expanded into four separate divisions that all had a unique market share. Larger companies were taking notice and competitive companies were becoming more combative as my company moved in on their territory.

Things were great... until my husband quit his job and came to work for my company. I don't know how it happened, but I lost all forms of my leadership autonomy. Looking back, it was a recipe for disaster. I didn't want him to feel emasculated by working for his wife, so I handed over power to make him feel valued. It was a lethal and slippery slope. He kept taking more. I kept giving it up. Soon enough, waking up and talking about the business while brushing our teeth was ruining our mornings. Hammering out staff issues before going to bed decimated our love life. Everything became a power struggle. To keep the peace, I acquiesced continually. I gave in when he brought in new male staff and replaced my loyal part-time moms who worked from the heart. I looked the other way when we ordered more stock than we needed because he said it made us look like heavy hitters. I signed checks for bigger salaries because he assured me it meant better people. The company I had built was changing quickly and everything moved from creating what I love – to only what made money.

As the dynamics shifted at the office, they also did at home. My leadership skills were ignored, overruled and placated. It eventually obliterated our marriage and I was left back in charge. Only, this time the company had grown to three times the size, with four times the payroll and close to a million dollars in product, moving in and out of our newly obtained warehouse. As I stepped back in, the staff wasn't used to my management style and havoc took over. Product was being stolen, workers were showing up late and a few even arrived intoxicated. Vendors weren't getting paid and products soon fell into back order. I had been diminished in front of the staff so many times they thought it was how they should treat me. They started acting out. None of them saw me as their leader. The staff had turned over so many times and only a few were loyal to me.

I tried desperately to keep it all going. I used my feminine charm to get extensions. Negotiated better payment terms creatively. Made promises I knew I couldn't keep while scrambling to keep everyone paid and happy. In mid-February, the utility company cut off the heat at my house. The bills were in my husband's name and he had left them all unpaid. The bitter winter weather made the house so cold and I was using every blanket we owned to stay warm at night. Then the Sheriff came to repossess our car with the only two car seats I used to drive my kids to daycare. My husband was supposed to be handling that. I had to terminate an insubordinate worker for showing up drunk numerous times. He turned spiteful, vengeful and began threatening me. Following me home and standing across the street from my office, staring in my window, sending menacing texts to me.

No matter how hard I tried, I felt as if I was on a sinking ship. Nothing I did was working and the few staff that were left started conspiring to push me out and bring my husband back. I started to liquidate to stay afloat. I began selling off the product so I could pay for the new product that was about to arrive. Word of my desperation spread to our investors. My husband brashly grew the company by bringing in hundreds of thousands of dollars of outside money (from people who do not work at the banks) to raise capital to grow even larger. 'Private investors are better', he told me, and I gave in. All that time I was tempering my leadership skills and dumbing myself down, shares were sold and contracts were signed. We owed some pretty big money to people who do not work at the banks.

Knowing I was drowning underwater, those investors showed up. Just like in the movies they even brought some muscle. They demanded I hand over the keys to everything, take only my purse and walk out. They actually *strongly* recommended it in the best interest of myself and my children. That was probably my ignite moment. Faced with possible harm versus trying to salvage the fragmented pieces of a crippled business made it easy to choose, but I wasn't going to reveal my giving in to them. I stood up for myself and threatened them back picking up the phone to call the police if they didn't leave immediately. I wasn't going to be bullied by anyone for a moment longer. I was fighting back in full strength like only a true leader would do.

I distinctly remember my feelings when facing them down. I wasn't fighting for my company; I was fighting for my dignity. I was standing up for me as a person, a woman and an intelligent business owner caught in an uncontrollable mess. I wasn't leaving with my tail between my legs, nor was I surrendering my company because a bunch of men thought a woman couldn't do it. Everything, all these horrible circumstances kept spiraling due to my own self-doubt and insecurities. I knew for a long time that things were moving opposite of what I wanted but I didn't stand up. I saw the changes taking place, but I quelled my concerns. 'All those men must know more than me.'

One month after that frightful day, I walked out of my business, my home and my office. None of it mattered anymore. I left everything behind. I took my two kids and drove away, moved to a new town and started over. I was deeply in debt, humiliated in every way and gossiped about all over town, but I was free.

It took me close to two years to heal from that. I was on the brink of something big, really big and leaving all that withering like a fish gasping on a cement dock, was debilitating. I no longer felt like a leader. Everyone tried to keep me focused on all that I had accomplished. They attempted to soothe me, but I was downright mad. Furious that I had let it all slip between my fingers. Irate that I hadn't been stronger, smarter, wiser and more assertive. All I could see was what I had lost. In a way, my business defined me and letting it fail when it had so much potential was like a death.

It took me a few years to get my courage back. To once again step into the arena of leading a team and building a business. In truth, it's hard to hold creative people back. Entrepreneurs are a strange breed. They will go out on a limb time after time, believing in themselves. They have great ideas and a fury of passion. They know what they want and are happy to lead. But many self-made business owners like myself have never been to university, studied economics or business algorithms. Instead, they lead from intuition and follow their heart. They know what works and what doesn't from trial and error. They put in the hours to get the results they need and let purpose rule over profit.

Not having a degree behind my name limited my thinking. I thought those that did, knew more. I had built my business to a great success never giving myself any credit because I did it through trial and error, not projections and analysis. It took me a long time to see the value in that. All I really needed to do was turn my attention back towards my mother. This year is her fortieth anniversary in business! She has won numerous awards and has been awarded Business Woman of the Year multiple times. She serves on many boards of directors, chairs committees and is still The Boss, full-time at seventy-four years old. She never went to university, yet she has built many successful companies. She mastered in the school of hard knocks and thrived on trial and error. She let desire and ambition be both her teacher and her lessons. She showed me that being a leader is less about being taught and more about becoming. There is no right or wrong way, there is only the way that serves the greatest amount of people in the best way possible while maintaining your integrity.

When I started my next company, I created a living charter of important objectives and clear values. I defined the corporate mission so that every member had the vision of where it was headed. I wrote out our key directives and put them on the wall for everyone to see. If any new employee scoffed at them, I knew they weren't a good fit. I added fun and flare into the company culture and only hired like-minded individuals with a with heart-centered point of view. I also made supporting women my number one mandate. Be it with products, my initiatives, or anything the company did, it was to uplift and empower women. I made it my purpose to encourage and inspire women to reach and take hold of their dreams.

There are many ways to be a leader. I suggest whatever yours is, make it about living *your* life and do what *you* enjoy. When we think about leading, we sometimes take charge or rule over others. Traditional leadership is often seen as rallying the troops or commanding many to follow. True leadership is a journey of one's self. An unwavering idea that allows nothing to get in your way and no one to diminish your vision. That kind of leadership leads you to victory, with no one being left behind. Persevering on your own path and picking yourself up when you must, is the sign of a leader taking a position that no one can outflank.

On your journey into Female Leadership, let it be with full heart and constant grace. Allow your individuality to shine and your uniqueness to lead. As a woman you have amazing skills; understanding, compassion, sensitivity, inclusion, intuitiveness and a nurturing heart. Use those to your advantage. Amplify each of them and allow them to be a bigger part of your work. Feminine Leadership is all about enjoying the skills and qualities that define us as women. We laugh and cry. We rally and rage. We can be all over the map and at the same time be clear, specific and centered. Instead of shying away from any of that, shine a spotlight on it. Be you, in all your feminine energy. Let your leadership reflect the kind of woman that you truly are.

IGNITE ACTION STEPS

Creating a personal charter: In starting a new business it is important to know its Mission, Objectives, Vision and Values. I recommend you do that any time you begin a new endeavour or form a company of any kind.

Knowing your *personal* Mission, Objectives, Vision and Values will help you define not only the kind of business you will run, but the kind of leader you will become. Uncovering this information about yourself will empower you to only seek projects or employment that is in alignment with that. Having this key information at hand when stepping into or formulating any new collaboration will help you know if it is a good fit and sustainable. Take the time to write down the following, so you have a clear understanding, and always remember.

What is my Mission? What do I want to do in the world? Be known for? Contribute to…? What goal(s) will get me out of bed everyday happy to work? What Objectives am I trying to reach? What tangibles are in alignment with my mission? What markers will show I have obtained my mission? What is my vision of myself and my future? Who do you choose to be 1 year, 5 years or 10 years from now? What values are most important to me so that I feel in alignment with my vision and can reach my objective?

JB Owen, Founder and CEO Ignite You, Lotus Liners and JBO Global.
www.igniteyou.life

ROSALYN PALMER

"Lead from your heart. Inspire from your actions."

I'm sharing with you what I now know to be true: your authentic value is the glue that holds you, and others, together. Leadership is having the vision to know when, and where, to apply that glue and the courage to do so. Then, it's in reapplying that glue and holding the centre, the truth, the love and the decency together – always.

AWAKENING MY LEADERSHIP DNA

It was the anger that took over; something pure that tapped into a primeval instinct for survival. "Now you have ruined my new dress, you bastard." I had chosen my best summer dress. The multi-coloured flowers suited the sunny June weather; its gaiety reflected my mood. I was in my hometown, to meet important sponsors for the Theatre production launching that evening. My parents were invited to the after-show party. My generous boss assigned them front row seats. I took to my job like a duck to water as I loved the theatre and adored working in St James's Square in the heart of London. Long hours, awful pay and I loved every minute.

So the chance to take one of our successful London productions on a nationwide tour was thrilling. Yet, here I was on the cement floor of a multi-story car park, covered in petrol and grime and fighting for my life at 2:30 PM on a midweek afternoon.

The man sprang out as I opened my car door to go to the pay machine. He was huge and pushed me down into the passenger seat footwell. As he turned the keys that were still in the ignition, my mind went into overdrive. Movies had taught me that being abducted was not a good thing. "You can have the car. I'll just get out." I heard my own detached voice say, "You'd better be quick. Here's my boyfriend!" I raised my crumpled arm to point out the driver's window. The man spun to look, I grabbed the ignition key, jabbed at his eye and with a superhuman surge of strength, pushed him out. He pulled me out with him by my hair. I had only one thought: "I'm not going with you!" He threw me on the petrol smeared and grimy car-park floor and that's when the anger kicked in. I fought like a wildcat and escaped.

When I saw his face on the cover of The Sun 14 years after the attack, my blood ran cold. There he was. The UK's most prolific serial rapist who abducted his victims and became increasingly more violent towards them. I rang 999. Scotland Yard confirmed I was one of only two victims who escaped. I recalled the details so vividly they knew it was him.

Yet even before that confirmation, this experience instilled a belief in me, "I am a survivor. I have the inner wisdom, drive and determination to survive against all odds." The lens of 'get on with it and push on through' became how I saw the world. I found it empowering. I knew I wasn't invincible, but it brought me through challenges such as breast cancer, financial loss, divorce and redundancy. It awoke my leadership DNA.

The seeds of that grit and self-determination were sown when I was born as a grocer's daughter. My early years were spent living above the shop in a run-down suburb of Nottingham. The dilapidated buildings were later torn down, depriving my parents of their livelihood. My enterprising father went on to purchase land where new housing developments were planned and created a thriving business.

The first shop was an Aladdin's cave of food and hardware. Huge apothecary jars were filled with sweets and unknowns. Huge hams would be cooked and sold by the slice. My father, and his mother before him, prided themselves on their delicatessen products. My grandfather kept pigs and chickens in a huge farmyard and cured his own meat.

To the locals it was the social services of its day. My parents knew whose husband gambled his wages away. The women, heads down to hide blackened eyes, opened threadbare purses as tears rolled down their cheeks. My mother would raise a finger to her lips, shushing them, while passing them wax-wrapped packages. I remember the women clutching my mother's hand and the 'looks' exchanged. My parents didn't call themselves leaders. They led by example. The seeds were sown while witnessing this compassion in action. The DNA reinforced. Later, I became a self-employed woman in business and currently work for an international charity serving the most marginalized people in the world: the Leprosy Mission.

I read no books on leadership, business or marketing. I lived it. Pocket money was earned weighing out 56-pound bags of muddy potatoes into smaller brown paper bags. It was my job was to cut huge blocks of cheese, with a large wire on a marble block, into small predetermined packs. *(I hardly ever need to weigh anything as I estimate so well. My mental math is brilliant.)* My father would create special offers: buy one, get one free, 10% off... etc. He'd create leaflets run off a Banda machine that I would post through every letterbox in the neighborhood.

In our living room, we had two huge Indian vases (I still have them in my home today). The vases, cobalt-blue with gold paintings of smoky hills, were always stuffed with money as the banks closed before our shop. Every day I saw the physical reciprocity for hard work and the toll it took on my father. Exhaustion and migraines on Sundays forced him to bed. He found it hard to delegate. Early seeds were planted for another lesson: let go of leadership responsibility to others when you can.

Life-lessons drove me. As early as a 7-year-old, I pushed until I was a Brownie Guide pack leader. In school plays and operas, I always went for a starring role. At 16, I was chosen as the Girl Guide from Nottingham to meet the Queen. All schools in the county came together to create companies in a business competition called Young Enterprise. I stood to be elected as the MD (CEO). Me... the girl from a state school who debated down the boys from the best private schools, and 'I' was voted in. However, our enterprise fared badly. Those boys resented me. I felt unsupported. I didn't understand the leadership lesson at the time. Laying the blame on gender, I went off to university. I loved English, writing and words. Over the course of three years, I focused on being a journalist and applied for a masters degree in Fashion Journalism at the prestigious London College of Fashion. After rigorous tests and interviews, I was accepted but the money was not to be had, so I angrily took work in retail management with Mothercare. It was brutal.

All my teenage retail experience shaved 17 months off the management course which fast-tracked me to become a deputy in one of the UK's busiest stores. The graduates and older staff resented me; I resented not training as a Fashion Journalist. I found no joy at work but it toughened me up, teaching me time and staff management, money and stock control. It taught me to get up even when I wanted to run away. It also taught me how unkind people can be to each other when they are not valued or heard. I would enter the staff room and hear ageist comments: "Get rid of her, she's barely out of Uni." "They should let her go, she's past her sell-by date." My opinions offered to the area managers were met with derision. I got out of that position and into a theatrical management PR role but a disastrous production led to bankruptcy. Next I went to work for the leading theatre programme publisher in the UK.

A publishing job entailed driving to every theatre in the UK to negotiate print contracts. All the theatre managers were men and they invariably saw me as some pretty 20-something to be intimidated or flirted with. I came away with the contract and my knickers always stayed firmly on. It seasoned me but it eroded my soul. When the company stalled, I was made redundant.

This fault-line in my glittering career path led me to think: What's next? The PR industry was taking off and Lynne Frank's PR agency was THE agency, so I applied and thus began two years in a world where trips on the Orient Express, breakfast with movie stars, launch events with the Rolling Stones and seeing leading fashion designers at close quarters, were all regular occurrences. I cut my teeth on leading-edge PR, ran an account that was named as one of PR Week's Top Ten Campaigns of the 20th Century. Consequently, I just 'walked' into my next two jobs. Two years later, I started my own highly successful PR agency – RPPR, which won the coveted PR Week Award for Best Small UK Consultancy. The quote from the head judge was about our attitude towards staff development: "RPPR has a large company attitude to staff care and development but still has a small friendly feel." That same year, I was runner-up in the 'Women into Business' Awards. The year after, I sold the company when it had a £1.3m turnover. Thanks redundancy.

In our second year, when we were barely breaking even, I'd attended a strange weekend course with a huge, intimidating American man – Tony Robbins. Checking out his media profile, I decided that I'd be the one to handle and improve his PR in the UK. As we headed towards the firewalk at the end of the crazy weekend, I found myself walking along beside him. I pressed the note I'd written, clearly explaining why he needed my company's services, into his hand. A week later, the phone rang and my company became his UK PR representatives. Overnight, his staff had my husband and I enrolled in his University and on a flight to Maui, Hawaii to attend Wealth Mastery. I was beyond excited. Here I was representing, arguably, the world's leading personal-development guru, and I was also going to learn how to be rich.

After a long day, frustrated at not being able to meet personally with Tony, I skipped part of the seminar, to watch the sunset from the outdoor hot tub. The pink-hued sea was amazing. A large bear of a man was already in the tub, smoking a cigar and wearing a green army cap. His dog collar said who he was but his face was more familiar to me than nearly anyone's in the world. He looked tired. I decided not to mention the Gulf war and instead spoke about the sunset. Somehow the conversation led to my company, upbringing and values. I asked him: "If you had any advice for me as a leader what would it be?" General Norman Schwarzkopf laughed. "You are the first person I've met who didn't ask about war but instead asked about what is really important, that of how to be a leader in a situation where men and women don't want to be. The trick of being a leader, is to get those people who are afraid and tired, to follow you willingly; to trust you with their lives. You do that through taking personal responsibility, finding your own courage, leading by example and allowing them to be their worth and potential." It was worth the whole trip to hear those words of wisdom.

That conversation ignited a company that was run on values. We introduced a values contract that staff had to sign. Everyone was given a day off each month to engage in personal development or to give their time to charity. A sign in the office read: 'Questions Are The Answer'. We encouraged thinking outside the box and to even question the need for a box. But when I started to employ staff better educated than me, I started to feel inadequate. I had a business turning over half a million pounds and clients telling us that we were the best hearts and minds in the PR world but I seriously thought I should study for an MBA: to go home after a 12 hour day and then get books out to prove that I understood business and leadership.

Thankfully I remembered the young woman in that car park and my mother's mantra of 'True to thy own self be thou'. I re-ignited in myself that trust in my inner knowledge, in the school of life that had brought me to this place, in knowing that all I needed was already within me. I became good at making decisions after Tony Robbins taught me that the word 'decide' is from the Latin words for de - 'off' + caedere - 'cut', meaning to cut off. So, once you decide, you take action immediately. At this point providence, or God, does step in and, more and more, I trusted this inner leadership. To me, it was crucial to run a successful business without losing my sense of self; my very soul. I wanted business to be fused with love and fun and to value my worth, and that of others, in something more than just monetary terms. Indeed, I barely looked at the numbers. My then-husband handled all the financial and administrative side of the business. Life was fast. My ability to make decisions? Honed.

For me, business was more than a means of making money or a way of feeding my ego. I didn't really classify myself as an entrepreneur or leader; I wanted to make my parents proud and to honor the service to the community that my grandparents had given. I employed a driver too old for other jobs and a cleaner who had been in prison and couldn't find work anywhere else. They were loyal, brave and kind. The cleaner became my nanny, looking after my children as if they were her own. I trusted her totally.

I learned to trust my instincts but question my prejudices. After interviewing an excellent candidate, as she left I overheard a member of staff say to another: "She's great. It's a shame that Ros won't employ her as she is so tall." What?! What could they mean? It troubled me deeply and I sat with it a while. Yes, it was true. At 5 foot 3 inches, I felt intimidated by tall women. I had unwittingly been prejudiced against them. So… I hired Tracey. She didn't have relevant PR experience but she did have courage, humour, insight and a thirst for knowledge. She proved to be one of my best hires ever.

Tracey and others of my team also taught me about self-care. I was so driven in business that I felt that all should be sacrificed for it and that collapsing on the sofa after a long day, clutching a gin & tonic, while mindlessly eating pasta, was OK. My fragile immune system had other plans so I learned to embrace a host of self-care strategies to balance out the stress, sleepless nights, alcohol-driven media-culture and meals on the run. Just about. My path to wellness was, and still is, carefully trodden.

Now as an emotional wellbeing expert, I find myself in the business of healing others in body and mind. Women in leadership are one of my key client cohorts as they face up to how stressed, exhausted and overwhelmed they've become and finally turn to therapists who are wellness-warriors. True wellness like leadership starts from within, being open and willing to share with others is key. I see it as my new leadership role to liberate those trapped in painful patterns of emotion and behavior. To speak publicly about mental health and challenge the systems and beliefs that hold us prisoner. There is a new softer, more emotionally intelligent form of leadership and self-leadership emerging. This book and other positive forms of advice about Female Leadership are designed to ignite what is already within you. Trust that. Embrace that. Own that. Nurture that! Listen to your inner leadership wisdom. Learn what makes your heart sing.

IGNITE ACTION STEPS

It is vital that everyone in your team or organization feels they have a voice and can invest in and contribute to your vision and values. As an empathetic and open leader, it is important to ask for feedback and also to make changes based on what you receive. To overcome many people's reticence to share their feelings, an exercise I have run many times before is detailed below: I've included a few examples of some of the more spirited answers in italics!

The focus is on individual ideas so ask each team member (if you are a leadership team of one or a solopreneur then ask yourself):

- What would you say our values are? *(honest, loyal, intelligent)*
- What three words would you use to describe us/our company culture? *(united, dedicated, sound)*
- What three words would customers use to describe us? *(professional, connected, value for money)*
- What three words would competitors use to describe us? *(maverick, results-based, smart)*
- If this organization were an animal, what animal would it be? *(leopard, dolphin, duck billed platypus)*
- If this organization were a colour, what colour would it be? *(red, royal blue, yellow)*

The answers are often amusing yet revealing. For example, people who might hesitate to admit that they are frustrated with the company being slow to change, may be open to describing it as a tortoise. You can ask why they have chosen their answers.

Finally, also ask:
- On the basis of what you have written above, sum up the company in one paragraph. *('We are a new style organization with old fashioned values.' 'We are a united task force of strong, smart and well-educated individuals'. 'We make it our business to know our business and that of our clients').*

Rosalyn Palmer
Rapid Transformational Hypnotherapist & Coach. Author. Broadcaster.
www.rosalynpalmer.com

RIIKKA YLITALO

"If you want to save the world, save yourself first."

You are the love of your life and worthy of love just the way you are. Love is your birthright. Through witnessing my story, you are offered a life-changing opportunity to truly be who you are and courageously start following your own path. Lead the way my friend.

MY QUEST FOR LOVE: SELF LOVE

I have found the biggest gifts in the worst experiences of my life. Have you noticed any repeated lessons in your life? I have discovered, the same lesson keeps coming back harder and more forceful, until you get it. In the beginning, it might be a tiny whisper or a gentle brush of a feather but, in the end, it'll knock you out completely. It's up to you to get back up and keep on trying. It would be lovely to get the lesson the first time but the story wouldn't be as interesting or colourful. At first I was brushed by the feathers, then hit by pillows. When the one-sided pillow fight against me didn't hit home, it was time to move because the competition had started. I felt like I was getting punched and knocked-out by life. Even then, a knock-out wasn't enough. Rocky Balboa must have been my idol.

I know competition well. The air is thick with excited expectation and clouds of chalk powder are floating around. The warm-up area is buzzing with female athletes and their coaches wearing their national colours; a symphony of red, blue, white, yellow, green, and black. Short conversations in different languages can be heard. Sweat is glistening on brows below harsh lights.

Weight plates loaded on barbells are crashing, clanging and sending waves of vibration against the floor as lifters are doing the final warm-up reps to get ready to figure out the best powerlifter in the world. By now, the competitors have completed the lifts of squat and bench press on the stage in front of the international judges and audience. The total of the best accepted lifts, one out of each discipline, will determine the end result and placements in the competition. On regular intervals, one can hear cheering and clapping from the crowd. The tension keeps rising among the lifters and silence falls, as the last round of deadlifts is getting closer.

One of the competitors does not seem to be excited. Her face with classically beautiful features is set on a determined expression and the brown-green eyes framed with black eyelashes are focused on the wall. She throws her long, blonde braid a bit irritably out of the way to her back with a sharp neck movement, while one of the team's coaches is helping her to get ready by adjusting her tight, black lifting suit. Another team coach and a few team members are hovering around her. They are doing their best to let her focus and give her space to collect herself, while being supportive.

That determined competitor is me. I was wearing a lifting belt loosely around my waist, so it's easier to breath. It will be tightened just before the lift. I have black, knee high socks and wrestling shoes on. The front of my bare thighs is covered with white powder to help the bar slide without unnecessary friction, the gravity is a mighty enough opponent as it is. I am competing in the 75 kg weight category. My body is lean and muscular after strict dieting and countless hours of lifting weights and doing cardio.

The results have not happened overnight. Active even before I could walk, I have done various sports such as: baseball, ballet, judo, self-defence, functional training, cross-country skiing, shot-putting, sprinting and volleyball, already before and during elementary school. Working out at the gym started at twelve years old. Sports were highly regarded in my family. I have grown up by competing in anything and everything with my big brother and always kept pushing myself towards winning. Deep down, I knew I was trying to compete for attention, approval, appreciation and love mostly from my dad (and partly from my big brother). I felt those were things I had to earn and I learned to demand a lot from myself, more than anyone else did. I brutally beat myself up whenever I failed at something or couldn't reach my expected goals. Rarely did I celebrate victories or achievements. I had a nagging feeling and a constant demanding inner voice in my head; that something could have been done better.

Ever since I was a little girl, I have loved strong female characters in the movies, TV series and books; those who could take care of themselves and even others. This included situations where the strong female lead was the one saving not only herself but also others from tough situations. It didn't matter if the opponent was an unjust villain or a pack of vampires. Sure, I went through the princess phase and loved pink but my Barbies played with my big brother's He-Man figures. Our dad taught us to carve wood with knives. It was more exciting than boring needlework. I put an absolute minimum effort into knitting and crocheting in elementary school. Thus, the first socks I knitted were huge and ugly but my grandma loved and wore them anyway.

I looked up to my big brother; climbing trees, playing with plastic guns, wooden bows, slingshots and swords with him. My dad taught us to shoot with an air rifle when I was seven. I'm still very good at shooting on a target. I almost applied to Special Forces after high school, following in my brother's footsteps. I wanted to become a fighter jet pilot. Three of my mom's uncles had been fighter pilots during the Second World War between 1939-1945. I felt that regular Army was not a big enough challenge for me to take on. Discouraged by a friend of mine, I never applied for Special Forces. Instead I travelled to the USA to work as an au pair for a year, to see the world. I wanted to improve my English, self confidence and become more independent. During that year, a new and thrilling chapter began in my life: powerlifting found me.

As I dove into powerlifting, people kept saying I was very talented and I must have won the gene lottery, but the reality is that I had earned my place among the very best of the world by dedication, discipline and hard work. My vision had been clear for years: to win the gold in the World Championships of powerlifting. Naturally, I am thankful for my genes, but I have made sacrifices to get there by living the life of a top athlete, while still studying and working. There hasn't been much time to hang out or party with friends, or even date anyone seriously; getting ready for competitions always came first. My lifestyle is, and has been, powerlifting for years. It has allowed me to represent my Nordic country, Finland. Life is about choices and I made mine.

Ten years ago in St. John's, Newfoundland, Canada, is a day I remember like it was yesterday. We kept hearing announcements from the platform that was behind a wall next to us. My time was almost up for the last lift of the World Championships of powerlifting and my mental game was cracking at its very core. The scared little-girl within me felt exasperated and the adult-me made no effort to filter it out from the team. All my energy was directed at fighting against the angry tears. I had just been informed that if I were to lift my last deadlift successfully, I could get a bronze medal at the Worlds. "How fucking shitty can they possibly be?!" I thought. "If I could win bronze after performing so poorly, what does that say about the other athletes?"

The truth is, it was supposed to be a happy occurrence. I was poised to win a medal. All hope wasn't lost and the coaches of Team Finland were trying to cheer me up. But I was too far gone and already in survival-mode, just trying to struggle through the competition until the bitter end. I realized the gold was lost already after my third competition lift, when I was done with squats. I had been trying to cling to the hope of compensating with bench press, but the gap between me and the ones in line for the gold and silver was too wide. Deadlift was my speciality, but I was already drained mentally and physically. All I felt was that I was a complete failure and worthless for not winning gold. I had screwed everything up by overtraining prior to the most important competition of the year and, as I later discovered, of my life. Overtraining is a burnout for athletes and I was underperforming because of it. I had done my absolute best, but was still blaming myself. I felt I had let everybody down: my coach, my family, my teammates, my friends, my first coach in the USA, my original team in Seattle, Washington and my home country, Finland. It was a heavy weight to carry.

My vision had been to get the payout for all the sacrifices I had made along the way and finally reap the fruits of my labor, by getting a personal-best and winning gold. Instead, I felt I was being ridiculed or even insulted by actually still having the possibility to get a bronze medal. My goal had been to win gold with a total weight of 650 kgs and nothing less. Silver is the first loser, bronze was even below that and the rest of the placements had zero value. I was not able to wrap my mind around the concept of being excited to participate. I was there to win, but to me, I had failed.

I was called to the stage and had done my best to collect my head. I psyched myself up by listening to aggressive metal music, slapped myself on the cheeks and marched to the stage with a mentality of getting ready to murder the bar. I took a deep breath and started to pull the last deadlift from the ground, even though my body was screaming its objections. I knew my teammates and the audience were cheering me on, but I couldn't hear anything specific except some blurry wavelengths of different voices. It's interesting; the extensive mental conversation you can have with yourself during one single lift. Mine was a brutal one with zero empathy. I left myself no other option than to give it all I had one centimeter at a time. I was able to pull the bar up and lock it into the final position. The head judge gave the 'Down!' command and I knew the bronze was mine.

The crowd went wild, as I lowered the bar on the ground and was straightening myself up. I forced a smile and a wave for them but in actuality, inside, I was having a temper tantrum. The little girl within was scared everyone would be disappointed and I had let them down. Or worse, I wouldn't be loved. All I felt was unworthy.

At that moment, I began my personal calling, I just didn't know it yet. It was my first strike-out. More were to come.

After the Worlds, my central nervous system was on overdrive. I was unable to sleep without sleeping pills. If I tried to train even three times a week, which was way less than normally, I got sick and caught a cold. My body forced me to rest, since my mind was too overpowering to give in otherwise. It took years for me to see that competition as anything other than a failure. The way I was trying to get over it, was to prove myself worthy at the upcoming National Championships. My identity and self esteem was based on me being a successful athlete. Without it, I didn't know who I was or if I was worthy. I needed to be acknowledged to feel I was enough.

My second strike-out came some years later and the blow was much harder. I had not learned the lesson yet. I had quit powerlifting, graduated with a Master's degree, started martial arts and was competing nationally. Working as a production supervisor in a factory was far from my dream job; closer to a nightmare. I felt nothing was good enough. I got yelled at in morning meetings in front of everyone. My boss and I triggered each other and were in a constant battle for the alpha title. It was very hard for me not to use my strength and power to stand up for myself.

During that time, I also had injured my knee in the final match of European Championships in submission wrestling. Sports were my therapy but with an injured knee, I was unable to train and couldn't even walk properly for a couple of months. Since I couldn't follow my training schedule, I started to do more and more overtime and sometimes even worked two shifts in a row as well as weekends. My previously healthy diet got unhealthier and I didn't seem to have the energy to see my friends. My life started to feel joyless. I was on the edge of a burnout. My fixed term contract was ending and I wasn't offered a permanent one. I felt like a failure again. I had given everything I had and more, but still wasn't winning.

I had to start taking better care of myself, put up some serious boundaries and get my energy back to enjoy life again. My big brother pushed me to continue my self-development journey. It hurt to be forced to face the unwanted turn my life had taken, but it woke me up to see the unpleasant realities that had to be changed. I was not happy with the way I was existing. I'm thankful he forced me to use his additional ticket to a business seminar in Tallinn, Estonia. It was for entrepreneurs and I got the fire to become one. A spark had already been there, but now it was lit. I loved learning, improving myself and getting to be with like-minded people. I started to think of business ideas and felt my future was bright and full of possibilities. Only, I felt I wasn't ready to take the leap just yet.

My third strike-out came while working in a software company. I became the only project manager assisting in sales and on-boarding new employees. I had to start creating and developing the processes of the department from scratch. My overworking nature had me on the verge of burnout in less than two years. I stuffed it down and kept going. Dancing around exhaustion, cutting corners and negotiating remote working-days and days off, I took a short sick leave and later resigned. Before my departure, I actually had tears in my eyes. I felt like I was suffocating and had felt like it for a long time. That was the moment I knew I had to STOP!

The employee in me had to die before I was ready to begin my entrepreneurial journey. It was finally time to go after my own dream. I named my company Themiscyra. Based on a Greek myth, it was the capital city of legendary Amazons. Some of you will remember the beginning of the movie Wonder Woman – on the beautiful island where the Amazons were training their warrior skills. That utopia inspires me to build a team of female leaders around me. To create an amazing network of female solopreneurs and entrepreneurs and together we'll make miracles happen. Only now I am ready to unleash my true strengths and there is no stopping me. I am still afraid at times and feel insecure, but I'm learning to dance with my fears and tap into my inner warrior queen. I feel my calling is to empower women in business and life through self-love. My mission is to help them live wholeheartedly and be true to themselves.

I am thankful for all the struggles I have had, since they have made me who I am and that much stronger in life. Because of them, I am able to help others on a deeper level. I got the bronze medal, so I could win the mental gold. In comparison to the gold medal at the World's, that is priceless.

I have earned several nicknames from the men in the powerlifting and martial arts circles, such as 'Viking', 'Alpha-Female' and 'Amazon'. They were meant as compliments and later on in life, I was able to take them as such. On some level, my ego liked them because it made me feel worthy and admired. On another level, I felt insecure about my femininity, since I had been told that men are afraid of me. It hurt to hear it because I hadn't embraced my feminine and sensitive side entirely. It was painful because I didn't love myself unconditionally and wasn't ready to reveal the true me behind my safety armour.

I have learned to be open to the lessons. I encourage you to do the same in your life. Zero in on the pain-points and you'll start seeing the right direction to move forward. Self development is the key. Take responsibility in your own life, happiness and relationships, instead of blaming others, situations or circumstances. Discarding victim-mode might be difficult, but it truly is empowering. There is no limit to how high you can raise your bar. Remember that every day, for the rest of your life.

You are enough, you are worthy, you are beautiful inside and out and you can do anything you set your mind to. Put the oxygen mask on yourself first and let's conquer the world together. With love, Riikka.

IGNITE ACTION STEPS

You are worthy of love without having to earn it by overachieving. If you lose the safety armour, a wonderful, new world opens up in front of you. Live with passion. Love yourself and your life. Become unstoppable. If there is something you don't enjoy in your life, change it or change your perspective of it. Find your path or create a completely new one and start following it courageously. Live fully and eliminate regret.

Start practicing self-love every day.

• Look into a mirror, directly into your eyes, smile and say: I love you. Remind yourself that you are enough and worthy of love, just the way you are.

• Start noticing if you are beating yourself up over something you did or didn't do. What you think about you, is the most important thing. If it is self destructive, work on changing it. Silence your inner critic and talk to yourself like you were your best friend. Ask, what does the little girl or boy within need right now?

• Put up boundaries and learn to say 'No'. If it isn't 'Hell Yeah!', it should be 'No'.

• Make yourself a priority in your life and take care of yourself lovingly. Pour your cup of self-love and let it spill over. Share from there, and keep refilling it.

• Ask for help from a friend, family member, coach or therapist, when struggling. It is a sign of strength to show a weakness and courageous to be vulnerable.

Be you. No one can do it better.

Riikka Ylitalo, Founder and Amazon Queen of Themiscyra.
themiscyra.fi

CATHERINE MALLI-DAWSON

*"When you have the power to impact others' lives
– do it with love, compassion and be gentle."*

My intention is to help others understand that there is a compassionate way of managing transformation put upon you. When you are on the receiving end of life altering decisions made without your input, you have three choices: 1) fight the decision, 2) accept the decision and 3) embrace the opportunities that open up for you.

THE HATCHET MAN

I was a tool. An instrument of the machine in which I existed. I was the vehicle for the organization I worked for, to carry out their objectives without getting their hands dirty. My boss asked me to help get things back on track and "evaluate the team" they had at the business office in Alaska. When I heard that statement in our meeting, *"Evaluate the team,"* I glanced sideways at my reflection in the highly polished mahogany table. I felt the need to check in with myself. "Had I heard that right? I'm suppose to 'evaluate' the operation team? What do I know about this team and who am 'I' to assess them?"

I looked up from my notes and glanced around the boardroom table at the other executives gathered there. It had been stated as flatly as if they had asked me to pick up the pen laying in front of me. Intuitively, I knew what they meant. They said 'evaluate' but I knew it meant 'eliminate'. I wanted to hear them say it. Out loud. In public.

I boldy, asked..."When you say, 'evaluate the team', can you clarify what exactly I'm evaluating them for? Is it performance, structure, skills?" I got 'the look'. A cross between incredulous and disgust. I didn't feel it was directed at me specifically, more towards the fact that now they had to verbally acknowledge what my intuition was whispering to me.

In perfect CFO fashion, the polished answer was; "The team in Alaska has always been a bit on the fringe of the organization. They like to think they are unique. While it may have made sense at one time for them to be stand-alone, I don't feel that is the case now that we are all on the same system. We'd like you to evaluate their performance. More importantly, we'd like you to review their current structure to determine how and when we might be able to consolidate the teams into the central office located here."

There it was. Out in the open. Absorbing the gravity of his comments, I simply nodded and returned to my notes. It was then I realized – *I was their hatchet-man.*

My mind raced back to the time when my father had been laid off. I was in my early twenties, sitting at a much smaller, simpler table in my parents kitchen. The wood was fake and had little chips on the edges. My father sat across from me in his light-blue, short-sleeved work-shirt. He punched the buttons on his calculator with growing frustration. Then he stopped; his head shook and dipped a little. I sat quietly chewing on my fingernails. He slowly raised his head to look at me through red-rimmed, glistening eyes. "My brain just doesn't work as well as it used to."

To say that my heart broke for him doesn't describe the helplessness, sadness and fear that I felt running through my body. At college, having my own school work to complete, I knew there was little I could do to help him. After putting all his energy into being the best machinist he could possibly be, his skills were no longer needed. The work had moved to China or somewhere else, where the labor was cheap. He had spent the last five years working at various machinist roles that only paid minimum wage and rarely lasted more than five or six months. Now at 56, he was back in school studying for an exam that would allow him to change his trade and move into the up and coming industry of water treatment. He was desperately trying to remember math calculations so that he could pass his latest exam. I watched as his shoulders shook, his cheeks glistened. He pushed away his papers and laid his head down on his crossed arms. I slowly stood up and walked around the table, wrapping my arms around him giving him the only thing I could, a hug.

Seeing the impact of that bureaucratic decision on my father and ultimately my life, I wondered if they knew who he was. A diabetic, who had an unskilled and helpless wife. Who had three growing kids still at home. Did they even care? Someone who didn't even know us or our situation, desecrated our lives. In that very moment, as I watched my father struggle, I vowed never to allow myself to become so dependent on a job or employer. I promised myself that I would always have a solid foundation and a backup plan so I could fully take care of myself and family.

"Catherine, when can you schedule to be up in Alaska?"

Drawn back to the meeting by the mention of my name, I looked around again at the dispassionate executive faces, realizing they were asking me a question, "I'm sorry, I was making some notes. What was the question?"

Knowing I was no different than the person who had once decided my father's skills were no longer needed, I vowed in that moment that I would not hide behind the executioner's mask. Always staring, never caring whether the victim was guilty or how his actions would affect their families. I promised to know each person's story and give them options that had never been given to my father. I wanted to face them, unmasked and speak honestly and truthfully about the situation. I pledged to sharpen my hatchet blade to be as fine as any surgeon's scalpel and only make an incision when absolutely necessary.

"I can be there Monday morning," I replied, when they repeated the question.

That January, I arrived in Anchorage, AK near midnight with temperatures at -18F. Climbing into a tiny Ford Fiesta, freezing my ass off in spite of the winter clothes I had purchased for the trip, I set off for the hotel, bumping and sliding along the frozen roads with the 20 foot white-wall tunnels created by the snow and ice. I felt as if I were making my way down the long hallway leading to the executioner's chamber. I pictured the axe high above my head, swinging, descending, slicing through the air; swiftly as it would for an outstretched neck. My hatchet may come in the form of a pen, but I knew it would hurt just the same.

Settling into my hotel room, I thought about the task that lay ahead of me. I had been through many reorganizations and redundancy programs in my career. The main difference being, I was typically on the receiving end of the changes. I had never been part of the front-line planning team. I felt dirty and subversive. Is this how spies feel when they first go into the field?

The difference is they get a lot of training before being released into the warfare. There were no drills or civilian scenarios that could prepare me for what I was about to face. I honestly didn't even know what training I needed for what lay ahead. While I could adjust for the weather, I had no idea what I was walking into the next day. I had been told to expect resistance and resentment from the current leader whom I had been sent to 'help'. How I dealt with her was up to me. My bosses trusted my judgement.

"I appreciate you coming up here and helping me with this project," Carolyn said as soon as we met. Her body language gave away the lie that hung in the air like stale smoke in a bingo hall. She had been the leader of the Alaska team for over 17 years and was nearing the end of her career. She was clearly not happy about having an interloper in her midst. Especially someone from the 'lower 48' and 'corporate'.

Resistance. Resentment. I had just experienced both and this was only our first meeting. We discussed the history of the project and her team's work to address the issues. I met the staff, had a tour, made my notes all while keeping the bile, growling in my belly, from making an appearance. There had been several previous attempts to combine the teams and Carolyn knew that my help was really a disguise to try again. As I had vowed transparency, I shared with her what I could from the directive I had received.

"I know 'why' you're here." She spat at me in one of our meetings. "They've tried several times to shut down our operations up here. But they don't understand all the challenges of the Alaskan processes. There are so many regulations here that they don't have to deal with in the lower 48. (I cringed at the dismissive reference to the continental United States). Every time we've tried to combine the teams or share responsibilities in the past, it ended in disaster and significant revenue-loss. I can't see how this time will be any different."

Despite our differences, over the course of the next quarter, we held meetings, made action plans and took corrective steps. I held to my promise. Within three months we had addressed a multitude of issues, re-engineered several processes, cleared years of backlog and celebrated Carolyn's retirement.

Then, I found myself responsible for this ragtag band of Alaskan misfits who had grown on me in the time I had been there. Abbie, with her luxurious red hair, multi-colored inch-long nails and permanently pursed lips that hid a sharp intelligence, only occasionally allowed out for others to see her brilliance. Michelle with her razor sharp wit, had a love and commitment to family and natural remedies for all ailments. Joey's quiet and contemplative persona hid his deep, analytical way of thinking which allowed him to play with numbers like a magician. They all chose to live in Alaska, undoubtedly one of the harshest places to scratch out a living. Some were running from something, while others were searching for the romanticism of the Alaskan Frontier. Whatever their reasons, they all had one underlying theme. They all wanted to leave a mark on their world. They all felt deeply about making a difference. They were all brave in their own way and they all had a story. Here I was, their official hatchet man, come to slice and dice everything they had worked so hard to create.

While many guessed at the ultimate outcome of my work, I could sense most of them felt a certain amount of relief when I was given responsibility for the team after Carolyn's departure. Whether it was because they liked my leadership or they thought the worst was over, I don't know. I moved everyone forward, encouraging cross-division training with the teams down south. They seemed to enjoy the opportunity to travel to the other offices and get to know their counterparts. Where once there was animosity and sniping, now there were birthday wishes and thank you gifts exchanged through interoffice mail. We continued to streamline processes and started a job-sharing program between the two offices. Revenue was now flowing smoothly and log jams were removed. While the occasional stick of dynamite was needed, most of the new processes were adopted with little resistance.

At six months, I delivered my report with options for the future. Although I knew what the ultimate goal was, I felt compelled to present the two options equally. The two teams had proven they could work well together. Everything promised was delivered: increased revenue, efficient processes, cohesive team. There really was no compelling reason to change anything else. Except...

That was not what the execs wanted. So it was Option 2 – Consolidation. When I accepted this assignment, I knew this was the ultimate goal. So while I was streamlining processes, redefining functions and recovering revenue, I was also working with Human Resources to understand what the options would be for the team should this be the final decision. I pushed boundaries and drove some of them a little crazy with my demands to care about the workers. In the end, we developed a program that addressed the majority of people's needs. We had options for those who wanted to stay in the organization in Alaska. New opportunities for those who were open to relocating to other locations, and compensation packages for those who felt it was their time to try something new.

In the end, the majority of the team decided to take roles within the organization, many of them relocating to the southern offices in Washington and Oregon. One woman decided to complete her nursing degree that she had put on hold because she needed to raise her kids. We were able to find her a part-time position that allowed her to continue working and get education assistance. A few decided it was time to retire, travel and spend more time with their grandkids. Another woman chose to take control of her career and set up her own business as an independent consultant.

We cried, we laughed. We argued, we celebrated. After 18 months, the Alaskan office was completely disbanded and the work was absorbed into the centralized departments. I'm still in contact with several of the team members who I delicately sliced with my scalpel of efficiency. When I connected with two of them a few years later, they told me when I had first arrived, they hated and feared me. Yet, when they moved on, they thanked me for releasing them into the next phase of their lives.

Nobody likes change. Breaking up a division could have created and left lasting trauma. I hoped my approach, in the end, helped people better understand the 'why' behind the "bureaucratic" decisions. I helped remove the victimhood and enabled them to seek out opportunities they may not have done if they stayed in their unique Alaskan wonderland. This experience and the choice to remove my hood and gaze upon my victims' faces with love and compassion, taught me about valuing humans and not just 'human capital'...

Beginning on this path, I prayed that no one on my Alaska team would find themselves five years down the road, frustrated and feeling forced to learn a new trade when they should be retiring and enjoying their time with grandkids. I prayed that each one would look back at this time and see this transition as a gift that helped them move on to a new phase of their lives.

A few of them still touch base, reaching out to me occasionally. One of them calls me when she faces a major decision, including whether she should marry her now husband. I'm glad she did, they make a lovely couple.

I made sure that while numbers were important, the impact on human lives deserved consideration, if not greater attention. Being a female leader, I was able to bring more compassion into my approach and made people more important than profit.

Now when I'm asked to be the hatchet man, I happily decline the rough-edged hatchet in favor of my finely-honed scalpel. I encourage you to approach similar opportunities with a new found sense of encouragement. Take the time to help people let go of old patterns. Think of how you can explore new ideas or rediscover old dreams that were buried out of the necessity of living day to day.

IGNITE ACTION STEPS

Regardless of how ready you are for change, change is never easy. Some of the lessons I learned from my first restructuring project have helped me redefine what that process looks like and how it impacts people's lives. The following are some of the steps I incorporate into my approach for transforming others.

Compassion – First and foremost, when making any kind of transformation initiative, I imagine myself in the recipients' place. Being able to understand what their fears, concerns, hopes and dreams are, helps me better communicate the impact of the decisions. I ask myself three questions: How would I react to this? What is the best that could happen? What is the worst that could happen?

Transparency – It doesn't serve anyone to be subversive or dishonest. While I may not be able to reveal everything in a given situation, being honest about that fact and sharing what I can, helps others feel more at ease. This builds trust and the belief that I am working in their best interest. I ask myself the following questions whenever I share information that may impact someone's life: Is the information I'm about to share public knowledge? What is the worst assumption that could be made from the information? Am I prepared to answer questions related to the information?

Collaboration – When making sweeping changes, engaging people in the problem-solving helps them understand the process. They will see things more objectively and make more rational decisions. When they are included in brainstorming the solution, they are more willing to accept the outcome and final decisions. I ask myself the following three questions when driving collaboration efforts: What is the benefit for each person involved? What will happen if they don't want to collaborate? How does this contribute to the bigger picture / longer term / overall strategy / greater good?

Catherine Malli-Dawson
Founder, CEO of LifeWhys LLC
www.lifewhysllc.com

MARNIE TARZIA

"The best leaders leverage our strengths
so our needs become irrelevant."

I hope my story provides you with an opportunity to reflect upon the contributions that your most memorable mentors have had in shaping the evolution of your growth. I believe this tribute to my mentor demonstrates that there are always pivotal people who help us navigate our path. I hope my story invites you to think about the lessons you've gleaned from all those that have helped you along the way.

LEADERSHIP LESSONS MY MENTOR TAUGHT ME

Alan Mirabelli was a master leader, brilliant social scientist, consummate speaker, talented photographer and invaluable mentor to me for eleven years. A prominent social scientist for over three decades, Alan had a reputation for excellence in his field. In many ways, our professional working relationship felt like a father-daughter friendship. Professionally, he was the wise advisor prominent people turned to when they needed advice, mentorship and support.

I received a text message from Alan on a beautiful summer day. "Hi Kiddo," (his nickname for me as he was 24 years my senior): "Call me when you have a minute? Not an emergency. News to share. A/"

Intuitively, I knew something was wrong and instantly shot back a reply: "You don't text me unless something is wrong. Is everything ok?"

Alan responded immediately, "Relax kiddo & stay out of your head." My heart sank. No reassurance that everything was fine, confirmed my suspicion that something was wrong. I never heard from Alan outside of our regular work-related emails. Once he retired, I rarely heard from him unless I took the initiative to contact him, which I did from time to time seeking his advice with work related matters or when I needed his endorsement on jobs that I applied for.

After teaching my class, I hurried back to my office and called Alan immediately. . "Hello Marnie: Are you sitting down?"

My stomach clenched, "This can't be good." Out loud, I ask, "Yes... Why?"

"I'm sorry to tell you this Kiddo, but I have terminal cancer. The doctors said I have 3-6 months. I will have physiotherapy so my legs are functional throughout that period of time, but it won't change my diagnosis." That was Alan. He was rational and pragmatic at the best of times and even in speaking about his terminal illness, he never faltered.

I went mute. I said nothing. There was silence on the line. Tears streamed down my face. I could not catch my breath. I could not find any words of support. There were no words I could express to make this better. I felt devastated and helpless. All I could get out was: "I'm so sorry to hear this news Alan. I don't know what to say." I was shocked and it was tearing me apart inside and yet he seemed calm and at peace.

Alan replied: "There is nothing you need to say. Your tears are my prayers. We will talk again soon." He sighed heavily, "I'm tired and want to go. And Kiddo: I'm sorry." He hung up.

I sat back in my chair and wept. I could not believe that this all-around great man who epitomized strength, was dying. For the entire time I had known him, Alan seemed larger than life. He had a media voice that was kind of a cross between James Earl Jones and Michael Douglas. Alan spoke about the research on Canadian Families when he lead the Vanier Institute of the Family (which is the Canadian Research Institute on Canadian Families) and he spoke at professional conferences across North America to educate all sectors: education, health, municipal, provincial and federal levels of government, economic forums. The audience he spoke to were professionals but obviously they had families of origin/creation. He also spoke at Family Conferences.

When he was at the podium speaking at conferences on Canadian families, he was as polished and refined as some of the great orators of our time. That is no exaggeration, he was that good. He had "it", as in – that special brand of excellence that produces a type of charisma that is magical. He had looks that grabbed your attention, an intellect that challenged your mind and a magnetic, compelling personality.

In his final public speech, mere weeks before his death, Alan said; "Euphemisms [about death] keep us from focusing on what really matters. We have a culture that will talk about children and how much goes into the beginning of life, but we never want to talk about the other end of life."

A brilliant communicator, Alan received a Masters Degree in Communications. Words mattered to him. He used words intentionally and sparingly. He told me, "Listen more; talk less." Before he died, he said he didn't believe in the metaphor of war as it relates to cancer. He made it clear he wasn't battling cancer – he was dancing with it. In his eulogy, when his friend spoke about him, she shared, "Alan insisted, 'After I'm gone, do not say I passed. When I go, say I died. I did not pass... I did not pass away... I certainly am not passed! You pass a Sunday driver. You pass the salt. You pass gas. You don't pass – you die!'"

Before he died, in every conversation I had with him and in every text message he sent to me, he communicated clearly, concisely, coherently, right up to the end. I called Alan to celebrate accepting a new position with our provincial government. He always sounded strong. He congratulated me on the leadership capacity, encouraging me to leverage my strengths with public speaking and writing. I reassured him I would still pursue my dreams, in addition to filling this leadership role.

In our last call, Alan shared that his latest photography exhibit was a success. He was truly touched by friends who had shown up from all over the country to support him. He mentioned his friend, Peter, had taken pictures of the event, which he cherished. Alan went on to tell me he'd be doing a final talk in his community for the palliative-care hub hospice. It was his way of expressing gratitude to the staff there, as they had essentially been like 'friends on call', working to support him at home so he could avoid an institutional hospice-type setting.

Alan was adamant that he did not want to burden those he loved in caring for him. He told me he was determined to have the same authority and autonomy over his life as he had always had. One quote he stated made me feel vulnerable as I knew I would have to go forward without his support: "I've lived my life as a run on sentence. Getting the call that I had a terminal cancer diagnosis was as though somebody had put a comma in that sentence. I was left asking myself what I was going to do after the comma and before the period." That hit me.

I could tell Alan was saying 'goodbye' without saying it. Instead he said, "Kiddo, you will go far in life, because you have a bright mind and a generous heart. There are two primary emotions in life. Love and fear. Decisions rooted in love are best. Everything you need to succeed – you have. Trust that you know enough. I must go Kiddo." Then he was silent. That was it. Our last conversation.

I had never been in a space with Alan where he wasn't the most articulate, intelligent, powerful man in the room. Not even once. He was the alpha male in the boardroom and everyone knew it. He was scary-smart, had a quick wit and could talk circles around anyone that challenged him. His strength at work made me feel safe and cared for. I had never experienced that kind of a male authority figure in my professional world. I was used to good-old-boy clubs and bullies. Alan never diminished me because I was female. He taught me how to be a great leader. From him I learned how to be assertive and speak my truth, especially at work.

I found myself mentally walking through our eleven-year mentorship. He was there for me throughout every step, every trial, tribulation and triumph in my professional journey. He coached me through it all. His terminal illness was a huge blow. I kept asking "How could this be? Why him? Why now? Why this? Why would God do this to such a great man?" I felt cheated and robbed of the mentorship I needed and valued.

Then I heard Alan's voice chiming in my ear like a school bell, "Stop asking questions there are no answers to, Kiddo... It is never helpful. 'Why did this happen?' Because it did!"

It took me a long time to adjust to my world without Alan in it. He was my top reference for every job I had ever applied for, endorsed me to get into graduate school, coached me when I was studying for interviews. He happily supported me in solving every complex professional problem I ever struggled with. To say that I felt vulnerable in losing Alan as my mentor, would be a complete understatement.

Deep in my sorrow, before Alan's death I wiped away my tears and picked up my pen and wrote 'Leadership Lessons Alan Taught me:

Lesson #1 – The Tall Poppy Story:

Alan told me the tall poppy related to me as a professional. I was intrigued. I laughed, "Alan, forgive me here, but what does all of that have to do with me?"

Alan, with a twinkle in his eye said, "Kiddo, you just told me you can't understand why coworkers are making disparaging remarks about you behind your back. You are the tall poppy in the workplace."

Alan explained high-performing employees are often resented, attacked, cut down, strung up or criticized, as they are perceived by peers to be a threat. People operating from ego want to cut down the tall poppy in the workplace. Women in ego are acting from fear and worry of the tallest poppy outdoing, outperforming and out-earning them.

He urged me to take it as a compliment when women were threatened by me. When we are powerful through demonstrating significant skill and expertise in our respective fields, combined with high levels of social-emotional intelligence – it is a winning combination. He went on to explain that if people can't beat you on merit, they will often try to win by beating you down in other ways. From his mentorship, I learned not to engage in backbiting, to lead by example and to strive to demonstrate the behaviour I want to see in others. In addition, I've worked to surround myself with ego-less people ever since.

Lesson #2 – When Someone Shows You Who They Are, Believe Them:

I had an eye-opening experience with a colleague and friend who violated my trust. Without my knowledge, she reached out to my contacts to promote a program she had created to solicit their help in developing it further. It wasn't so much that she reached out to my peers without my knowledge that upset me. My issue was that her program contained information that I had shared with her from graduate school, from some of my course-work. What upset me was that my friend did not cite the sources of the information I had given her. She altered the information slightly to pass it off as her own. When I questioned my friend, she brushed it off, saying she wasn't sure where the information in her program came from. In that moment, she lied to me in and trust was broken. I reached out to Alan and said: "I want to believe my friend, but her actions tell me she is lacking integrity."

Alan shared his wisdom. "Kiddo, emotion is clouding your judgment. You have a tendency to think with your heart and feel with your head. She is no shrinking violet. This is your friendship, so this is always your call but be careful. When someone shows you who they are, believe them."

Wanting to sustain the relationship, I did the opposite. I continued our friendship. When similar issues surfaced a year later, I made the decision to walk away. In one of our calls, JB Owen, the co-author of this book shared with me that it is always in our best interest to notice patterns inherent within our relationships and to "never paint our red flags green." It was time I listened to my instincts. I've learned to stay honest and to stop making excuses for inexcusable behaviour even when I care for the person.

Lesson #3: Stay Curious and Be a Lifelong Learner:

Alan always encouraged me to stay curious and to be a perpetual pupil. This comes naturally for me as lifelong learning is one of my character strengths. As far as Alan was concerned, it was a sign of strength to express vulnerability and to reach out to people with talents in areas that I was working to develop. Alan shared: "Kiddo, always remain in an open-to-learning stance. Remember: We are all teachers and we are all students."

His advice came to mind when I felt the pull to start up my own consulting business. I knew that I needed advisement from someone who had a proven track record for excellence in consulting.

My most recent ignite-moment happened over a cup of cappuccino. I was speaking with Kari, a fellow-author in our Ignite Series, a woman I respect for the success she has acquired in her own consulting business. Like Alan, I also admire Kari's character; she is a person of influence and integrity. I explained to Kari that I believed I was well-suited to motivational speaking, teaching and coaching as these were mechanisms for inspiring and informing others. I believed that my gifts could be best served in these areas. The problem, once again, was that my fears arose. I went on to present a list of excuses as to why I thought I couldn't succeed in starting up my own business.

Kari called me on my negative mindset. Her words felt like something Alan would say, "Marnie, what would you tell me, if I gave you a list of my doubts?" Once again, as if Alan was in the room, she said, "Whether you think you can or you can't succeed –you are right and I know you can do it."

Wow. Talk about the perfect person showing up at the right time with the perfect message. Kari brainstormed with me ideas, strategies and networks I could tap into to get my business off the ground. I was beyond excited. Her words made me come alive. I knew I had to leap into starting my own business and trust that the net would appear.

Mentors, friends and those we trust have the ability to nurture and nudge us. They see past our limiting perceptions and focus on our possibilities. Don't be afraid to lean on them. We all need someone in our corner to share the difficult times. Our mentors witness our journey and hold space for us to succeed. I encourage you to seek out a mentor in your life. Someone older and wiser, who has walked a well-worn path. Or a younger version of yourself to remind you of what you can do. There is no such thing as a self-made person. When we succeed, it's because someone helped us along the way.

IGNITE ACTION STEPS

Let me be your mentor for moment. Whenever you have an idea and feel stuck in doubt, here are some action steps you can take to propel you forward:

Identify Your Strengths: We all have talents that we enjoy and skills that we are great at. What is that one thing you do well? Strengths are those things we excel in and also give us energy. Write down a list of your top strengths and how you can leverage your strengths in your own best interest and in the service of others.

Start Up or Join a Mastermind Group: The research is clear; in order to succeed we need a circle of support to help us to move forward in the direction of our dreams. We need people in our inner circle to hold us accountable for the goals we set for ourselves. We need support and accountability in order to achieve goals and a mastermind group is a means to that end.

Find a Mentor: Seek out someone who has strengths in areas that you are working to develop. Find someone you trust that will provide you with the psychological safety that is required to be vulnerable in expressing your needs. You deserve a mentor that creates ideal conditions for you to grow, thrive and flourish.

I know Alan would be proud of me for paying forward my leadership lessons by mentoring others just as he did for me. Alan often said: "Kiddo, I'm happy to help you in any way that makes sense." While Alan never got to read my books or see me become an author, I can't help but think he had a hand in all this. The first time the picture of me showed up on my mobile phone, captioned: "Marnie Tarzia, Best Selling Author", my car window was open. A white feather blew in the window and landed on my hand. I looked up at the white, feathery clouds in the summer sky, smiled and thought "I know, it's you Alan. Thank you."

Marnie Tarzia
MA Speaker, Leadership Specialist, Best Selling Author
Marnie Tarzia Consulting

ANDREA GONTKOVICOVA

"Be the pilot of your own life. Stay out of the passenger seat and enjoy your flight."

I want to help people to realise and appreciate the luxurious palette of possibilities and options we have in the 21st century. We have the right to choose what we want and how far we go. Full awareness accompanied by clear choices are the recipe for a fulfilling and happy life. May you own it and enjoy it.

PILOT YOUR LIFE OR SOMEONE ELSE WILL

The air was cold and the wind drove it directly under my skin. The trees around me were shivering too and while I could not see the picturesque Tatra mountains in northern Slovakia from the window of the house, I could smell and feel their cold proximity. I was in an oasis of peace, nature and life, while at the house of my grandparents. I remember my grandma as a tiny person with a strong body and mind. She worked hard around the house or in the fields. She didn't say a lot, but when she shared a joke, her eyes changed completely and flooded me with her joy and sparkle. Not much taller, my Grandpa didn't say much either. He carried the weight of the land and livestock on his shoulders, as the farm was quite big and the work was plentiful. He woke up before dawn to cut the fresh grass needed daily for the animals. When I got up, he was already back home from the field, enjoying his breakfast as if it was the best Sunday feast ever.

They lived on a farm. The front garden of the little cottage was filled with a huge pear tree; its roots were hugged by peonies and garden lupine. There was also space for vegetables, but it was hard to grow anything more exciting than potatoes, cabbage, carrots and cauliflower. Summers were short and cold. The soil was hard and ungenerous. The huge barn behind their cottage had a very tall gate, ready to welcome and give shelter to anything needed to run the farm. Good luck was provided by several families of happy black and white swallows in the nests under the roof.

I had been coming to this place all my childhood and knew each corner, path and hiding spot. Lacking proximity to other children, led me to be more sensitive and attentive about animals and nature. The sheep, hens, cats and dogs were all my buddies. I gathered eggs still warm from the hens' nests and carried drinking water to the sheep. The fields and woods around the house were my unlimited gym; no monthly membership required. There was just one radio station and an extremely small TV but the time to listen or watch was limited anyway. The work took priority. Thus, the chance to connect with the world and humanity while being here was extremely slim.

In spite of all the solitude and simplicity, I was always seduced by its magical sparkle. That is why I went there on the weekends. After an intense school week I did not mind farm work, helping my grandma. She also let me cook simple things, which I quite enjoyed. My favourites were pancakes and home made pasta. From mixing the dough up, to serving them as a meal. However, when I needed to prepare for my school exams or tests, I was exempted from the usual daily duties to purely focus on my study.

I remember one morning when I was having my favourite breakfast; a cup of hot cocoa and a slice of bread with butter and honey. As I was biting into the thick soft, sweet slice of bread, I was flipping through the pages of my history notebook to prepare for a test the next Monday. My grandma joined me at the table sitting beside me. She observed me silently for a few minutes, then asked what I was studying. I was going through the period of Maria Theresa and her 16 children and quickly summarised for my grandma the highlights linked to her ruling of Habsburg in the 18th century.

She was looking into my eyes and listening with all her attention. When I was done, she took a deep breath and gradually shifted her head to the side. Her eyes passed through me, looking into the distance misting over, as if covered with a blanket of experience and memories. She breathed again. Deeply. Slowly. Then she straightened her back, and took my book into her hands, flipping through the pages. "I am so happy for you. I wish I had the same opportunity when I was your age."

I did not understand the message she wanted to pass on. I was a "normal", healthy, self-involved 12-year-old. I did not see my having to spend lots of time studying and preparing for exams as an opportunity. Not at that time. Thus I asked: *"What do you mean grandma? Where do you see an opportunity in me going through all this hassle?"*

She looked again into the distance and answered: *"As soon as I could read, I fell in love with books. I read anything and everything. Books, newspapers, pamphlets, any material that smelled of paper and was covered with black small letters. For me, this was an open window out of the little house of my parents. It was a path leading me into the world and allowing me to see how things work and why. I was curious and hungry. I had big dreams about my school and my life. But my parents had planned it differently. I was the oldest daughter and they needed me to take care of younger siblings as well as help them on the farm. Time spent at school or going through books was not considered to be a priority. That was given to taking care of the family, animals and farm. Cooking a meal, cleaning the house, growing potatoes, cutting the grass, feeding animals or washing the floor. All of that was perceived as much more valuable in that place and time. One saw the result immediately. Unlike with the consumption of words and letters.*

Fortunately, my class teacher was completely in my camp. Already in the year 1925 he understood the importance of children, especially girls, continuing with school studies, trusting this was essential for allowing them to move on successfully with their lives, professionally and personally. He even came to our house to share this view with my parents, hoping to convince them. He did not succeed. I finally had to leave school at age 10 and all my big dreams faded like spring flowers in a vase. My childhood was consumed by the neverending and repeating pattern of cleaning the house, cooking, washing dishes, taking care of my sisters and farm work. While constantly surrounded by people and animals, I was actually very lonely. I did not have a friend, I did not have anybody to talk to and express my views and feelings. The chances of meeting my soulmate in a small village were extremely limited and daily duties made it even more difficult, as there was little time left for anything but work. However, I still needed and searched for empathy and understanding and it brought me closer to the spiritual life and belief in a bigger Power. I called Him God and I always remained thankful to Him. He kept me company and gave me hope and energy all my life.

When I chose my husband, my life did not change much. At those times, it was mostly about finding somebody with whom I could build my economic independence from my parents rather than an emotional or human bond. My husband was kind and caring. But, like the majority of men during those times, he was also of the view that work and duties had the highest priority. Taking care of the farm, household and the kids always came first. Everything else, including books and school, only came after."

I was speechless. I felt as if somebody swung a magic wand upon me and while I did not clearly understand what had actually happened there and then, I felt it was extraordinary. Special energy was flowing through my body and awakening every piece of me. It was a mixture of realizing all the duties she had versus the fun she desired. New understanding was coming into my brain. It was like getting a blood transfusion oozing into my mind. As I could not concentrate on my history studies any more, I closed the books for that day and went for a long walk. Alone, in body and soul, I was digesting those few important highlights of my grandma's life.

I lost track of time and the day progressed into late afternoon and evening. The village was quieting down. The sun was gradually hiding below the horizon and those few people who lived there were preparing or eating their dinner already. In some of the windows, the lights were turned on as day was coming to an end for many. However, my brain was fully awake, ploughing through every micrometer of its tissue.

The questions vibrating in my head were mainly about the level of independence and control we have over our own lives. Who is deciding what we do and how? Who holds the final key to the decisions we are making or do we only think we are making them? I wondered who sits in the driving seat and chooses the signals for the direction we go? Is it me who is selecting the steering path of my life or did somebody force me out of my driving seat? Did I abdicate it to somebody else voluntarily? Or, is there nobody in control and the car follows a journey of coincidences and free flow of events? Am I just an observing passenger bumping along? Is there any difference between how these things worked in the 18th century during the times of Maria Theresa, or during the childhood of my grandma in the early 20th century and... is it different for me now?

All this made me think of my lessons and education. I knew for a fact I had to go to school every weekday for the next six-plus years. Thus, I took it as a duty and a hassle, which ate a lot of my fun-time and energy. Until now, I thought I was super clear about this. Not anymore. Thanks to my grandma, I got a completely new updated GPS navigation system, which gave me not only the exact location, speed and track but also revealed much more of what was ahead of me, including the distance to and from important checkpoints. I could see so much further. Yet, I had many more questions.

What would I have been without the school "obligation" and "hassle" at this age? How would I have been spending my days, thinking about what and doing what? Is it actually a duty? If I had a free choice between washing floors and feeding animals every day and learning more about history and math, what would I naturally prefer and why? The puzzle pieces in my mind gradually started falling into place and with every step of my walk, I was clearer about the ultimate picture which was being built in my head. I finished with putting a thick wooden frame around it and vibrations in my brain finally calmed down. I was back at my grandparents and put the day to rest.

When I awoke the next morning I felt transformed, as if I became somebody else. I quickly checked out and discovered my body had not changed. My face, hair, hands and feet, all looked the same. Nevertheless, in my mind I felt older, taller, bigger and much stronger. There was new blood in my veins and the landscape I saw with the birds-eye view got bigger, the network of routes expanded, and options I could choose grew exponentially. Reasons why to move forward became clear and rock solid. Thanks to my grandma, I embarked on a completely new journey.

First, I changed my attitude to what life had to offer to me. I was so happy and thankful for my grandma. I realised that all the school, studying and tests, which I had previously considered as bothersome, were actually a big perk, (which the generation of my grandmother did not have). I lived in a time of luxury that I had taken for granted. Now, with this new understanding and transfusion of gratitude, I viewed all the knowledge available at my fingertips, from a completely different vantage point. Whether it was in the area of history, math, languages, physics, chemistry, biology… I became fully aware that the information I could grasp was limitless. Sources of where to find it were abundant: books, libraries, magazines, TV documentaries and most importantly, school teachers who were actually paid for passing that knowledge on to us often unappreciative and spoiled kids.

These thoughts had an immediate impact on my next Monday morning. My body walked into the school as if nothing had happened. The same clothes and shoes as before, the same rhythm and movements. Not my brain. My brain was much more excited than any day before and attuned to all it was going to hear. There were my favourite topics, such as poetry, geometry and history, but also those which excited me less, such as the composition of the electric circle, functioning of a lever and the logic and purpose of the periodic table. They all got consumed and registered with a high level of attention and appreciation. On that day, everything changed.

I realised the power in my hands, body and mind was comparable to that which created the universe. It became completely obvious to me that I myself had to grasp it and choose with the full authority and freedom how much of this knowledge I wanted to absorb and integrate. I had that same hunger in my blood as my grandma but I had not been attentive to it. Now I decided to follow my instincts and open the gates of my mind so that it could get what it desired.

I did not want to live a life like my grandma who never had a chance to take the reins of her horse and buggy into her hands. It was not that she had not made her choice or did not have the energy to fight for it. She did. She wanted those reins in her hands badly but she was completely overruled. She was mercilessly pushed aside to take the passenger seat and observe silently where the buggy took her. She was denied deciding and speaking, which turns to choose, how fast to go and where to stop for food and drink. Fortunately, nothing very sad happened to her on her life journey and she survived. However, she absolutely did not thrive and she definitely did not contribute to humanity with all her abilities and appetite. How could she?

I would not have this happen to me. I would always be the only engineer of the car of my life and the only chauffeur driving it. I had all the readiness and strength to steer my journey. It was only me who would decide which direction I choose, how far do I go and, most importantly, how far do I really get. I switched from 'must do' to 'I choose' and 'can do' mode. This was revolutionary and frightening at the same time as there were no more excuses and hiding behind anybody's back. As of this moment, my life became my own personal responsibility. I put myself, barefoot and naked, on life's theatre stage. I felt cold, exposed, fragile. Still it seemed to be the best thing I could do even with the risk that I might tumble or even fall. But I also had a chance to win if I played with all my talent, energy and will.

I was impatient and wanted to start my game immediately. My first acts were small ones. I swapped my music lessons for evening English classes, started regular swimming trainings and so on. I was happy how it made me feel. The next big crossroad came when I was choosing my secondary school at the age of 14. My parents and teachers had doubts about my abilities and drive and wanted to push me towards an easier route where I would have a craft in my hands at the age of 18. But my commitment to hold the steering controls told me differently. I followed my intuition and chose the more difficult path, a grammar school. I became one of the few students passing with honors to the surprise of many.

I wanted to do this to pay back the generation of all our grandmothers. These ladies were as smart and determined as we are and still they did not have a choice. Many of the paper sheets covered by little black letters, remained beyond their reach. These days, we can decide and have the steering controls in our hands. The amount of information and knowledge available is much bigger than we can physically absorb in one lifetime. We just need to choose to act upon this and benefit from it.

I also want to pay forward the idea of my grandma's magic wand. There are so many talented people around the planet who, for various reasons, doubt either their abilities or don't see the palette of options the world is unfolding in front of their feet. I would like to offer the same gift my grandma gave to me, to you, to encourage you to make time and go for a long walk to think your life flights through and get ready for the thick network of routes and cross-roads before you put the next day to rest. Those walks will be your moments of blood transfusion and instincts awakenings. With every step, your puzzle will be more complete, until finally ready to be framed.

IGNITE ACTION STEPS

Open your eyes wide and be conscious about what is going on. Look at your life map. See the abundance of crossroads and routes you can choose. Embark. Take the yoke in your hands. Start the engine. Switch on your GPS and keep your sight on the display. Check on your other directional flight controls regularly. Monitor your location, altitude, speed and track but very importantly, look ahead and keep choosing your routes. Never leave the engine on, if you are not holding the controls tight in your hands. Do not let the autopilot define your direction. If running out of fuel, take a break. If in doubt, follow your intuition much more than your brain. Do what fits you best, not what others are telling you. If needed, unplug the headphones and mute the noise of the world.

Moreover, be aware that you will share parts of that journey with your loved ones, a partner, kids or friends. Make it a pleasurable and fun experience for them too.

Remember the life of my grandma. But choose the life you want. Enjoy your flight!

Andrea Gontkovicova
Business Leader, Philip Morris International
www.pmi.com

ALEX JARVIS

"Dare to lead – she who dares, wins!
Lead with LOVE & LOVE to lead!"

My story is about living an invigorating, joyful life, giving myself permission to 'dare to lead'. My intention is to excite, inspire, and empower you; to ignite the belief we are all capable of showing up as a leader. It is to step into the space of awareness, by awakening the ultimate gifts we have within. I encourage you to have the confidence to 'never say never' and instead, 'dare to lead'.

WHAT'S YOUR POISON?

It has been said if you are bored with London, you are bored with life! Samuel Johnston (1709-1784) said it first, claiming when you tire of London you are tired of life. I wasn't sure in my heart of hearts, if that was totally true, but something was bugging me. There was a nagging voice in my head that put it down to boredom. Can you believe it!? I was actually living in the dynamic city of London yet, still feeling a bit drab inside.

My life from the outside was somebody else's dream in more ways than one. Endless invitations to all-night parties with a huge group of friends. We were actually hanging out with '*The Bold and The Beautiful*' … excuse the pun! Dodging the paparazzi felt normal night after night. Truth was, we were more like '*The Young and the Restless*'. We drank, danced and partied hard all night long. In fact, every time I hit the town, I rubbed shoulders with the rich and famous! More invites, more parties. Loving and living life to the fullest. But, sometimes I wondered was that the true reality? Was I *really* having a great time?

I hatched a plan to escape the monotony of what I believed my life had become. The movie hadn't yet been made but I felt my life was like *Groundhog Day*. I was caught in a time loop! The more I thought about it, I realised I was stuck in this ongoing circle and more of that life just kept showing up.

I was armed with many qualifications under my belt, but I never really felt complete. I made a decision to travel to the other side of the world in search of change. In retrospect, it was to reinvent myself. To finally be free, to be playful, in my joy and to be rich in life. To be me, not just going through the merry-go-round of monotony.

You see, for my entire life, I tried to live up to somebody else's expectation of me... only, sometimes there were no expectations. None. A big fat zero! Surrounded by intelligent siblings, I began to behave in a way which fitted into the role I thought I was expected to play. In many ways, I dumbed myself down.

At a very young age, I felt different and not sure whether I was just odd, didn't fit in, or was '*special*' by having a deep kind of insight. As a child, I developed a belief that '*authority figures*' around me had very few expectations of me. That, they may in fact have thought I might be stupid instead of curious. After speaking to my mother many years later, she told me that a lack of intelligence was far from the truth. She simply didn't know how to cope with my overt curiosity or how to answer any of my incessant questioning. Her only option was to ask me to be *quiet*!

I also believed adults knew what was best for me. Better than I did for myself. It was this subconscious desire for approval and acceptance that over the years, led me to forget who I truly was. BECOMING what I thought people wanted me to be, not being aware of who I could be and certainly not showing up as my authentic self was my habit. Which at that point in my life I realise, was because I didn't even know there was another way to be.

After many years, that emotional burden became a load too heavy for me to carry. It created an issue in my right shoulder – literally 'carrying the weight of the world on my shoulders' caused a health problem. It grew too hard to live according to everyone else's rules or projected opinions. My shoulder protested.

That injury was only just the beginning and sparked a feeling where I knew I wanted change. Dramatic change. There was a feeling of urgency, so intense, that I needed to shift gears, not soon, but NOW! I realised for things to change, '*I have to change*'. For things to get better, '*I have to get better*'. For things to improve, '*I have to improve*'. When you expand and grow, everything in your life expands with you.

Saying my goodbyes at the airport to my immediate family was sad: a lot of tears and unspoken words. I had every intention of returning to the UK within a few years. I dreamt of earning enough money to buy a property in London and return as the 'NEW' me. These were my thoughts as I boarded the plane.

What a feeling! I finally felt free. I felt as if I could reach out and touch my liberation as the plane finally landed at Kingsford Smith Airport in Sydney, Australia.

The notorious long flight from London seemed relatively short, in fact it was a lot of fun. My travelling companions were five girls, all strangers, yet nurses on the recruitment program that I was a part of, immigrating to seek better opportunities in the land of OZ. It was 1986 in the years when flying was full of fun; when you could fall asleep wrapped in your blanket on the floor or in the aisle. With the help of numerous cocktails, we flirted and bantered with the Formula One Team. YES, *the racing car drivers*! They were on the same Boeing 747 as us. We all congregated at the back of the plane laughing, joking and smoking cigarettes.

The 'Lucky Country' was a term of endearment used by Australians for their beloved nation, despite being coined by a writer as a negative term. I arrived in this 'land of milk and honey', with luggage full of personal belongings and a trunk coming by sea, full of my psychological baggage. My spread-open heart was full of optimism. Most importantly, I had a future date with a Formula One team member.

For a split second, I held within me, the doubt and anxiety around 'daring to be me', 'daring to lead'. I mentally glanced back at what I had left behind and kicked myself for not having the courage and faith in my ability to study to become a doctor, while I was training at the teaching hospital in London. Intuitively, at that moment, I knew whatever I decided to do here, I would be extremely successful and the adventures would keep unfolding.

The mini bus with the six of us girls, had travelled 22 kilometres to a surfing part of town. I hit the ground running. The first night we played pool with generous males offering champagne, who we could not take seriously as they were wearing shorts and slip-on plastic shoes, which in England are called flip-flops, but there they were called thongs! Which, in my past understanding, thongs were 'a form of underwear that young girls and strippers wore'.

Stepping into my new life was like a step back in time – full-blown culture shock. I felt somewhat challenged. Though I didn't hold back, a few weeks later, my new look, the new me, dramatic blonde streaks and a new *disposition* of 'Surfy Chick' appeared. The day after my hairdressing appointment, the 'newly-discovered' me had my intake morning in the Hospital's Intensive Care unit where I would start my new job. Again the extreme change in culture raised its ugly head. To my horror, I was greeted on my first shift by male doctors wearing shorts, which were met at the knee, by long pull-up brilliant white socks. I knew deep inside, I would not be staying forever in this job or in this part of Sydney. Eight months later, I moved out of the staff lodgings provided, moving to the inner city hub with new feral friends.

Things seemed to happen at a blink of an eye, one minute I was in a uniform working shifts and the next I was jumping up and down in an elevator screaming at the top of my voice, "We've fooled them!" This was the belief we had, 'we' being my newly-found work colleague and so-called partner in crime.We had "tricked" a hiring committee into employing us. We were young and inexperienced and yet, the large international American medical company that was looking for ambitious employees gave us the keys to company cars. I had taken my driving test 10 years before and since then had never driven, so I was not sure I would even be able to! Adding to the joy, was a juicy salary as they just set us loose to sell medical products to doctors. My title was 'Account Manager' New South Wales and Australian Capital Territory (ACT).

I learned to live in the unknown with a level of uncertainty. Yes, I totally believed I was capable of anything in my new found persona. I felt I needed to radically shift my old view. To be able to cut through the fog of long-held assumptions and change the way I thought, lived, and breathed. I wanted to expand my mind to new levels and understand the role I now had in this world. I told myself that all I need, is what I have right now. Stop looking outward.

I encouraged myself every day to wake up with a purpose: to get out there and hustle! I realised I had to STOP '*crying*', and 'go and kick some ass!' (taking the words now right out of Lady Gaga's mouth). Thoughts kept swirling around in my head, positive words kept popping up. The words like, '*initiate*' and '*be present*' kept repeating. From this I believed I needed to take action, encouraging me to start doing what made my heart full and made me feel good! I was the creator of my life; I controlled my dominant thoughts. The more I changed within and saw the world through a different lens, the more it reflected in my outer world. Whatever I believed in seemed to show up. However I saw a situation, it seemed to present itself that way.

Don't get me wrong there were many times I kept saying to myself, "Stop promising, 'I'll do it tomorrow'", "I'll do this when I have more money" or "I'll start when I'm more settled." I realised this is 'not living' or 'being present!'. I had to STOP making excuses... start eating well, going out with friends more, book that trip overseas, join that gym, that sporting club, write that book, apply for that new position.

I met with a new job opportunity to go to another state and set up a business in capital equipment. I felt when it came to work I could achieve anything. I never held back. I was buzzed and felt high on all the new ventures. Work never felt like work. I lived in my joy; start-ups were my passion. Always working with a team in senior management roles, I believe 'we rise by up lifting others'. I noticed the more I believed in myself, the more it was infectious. The team also mirrored how I showed UP. The success had a ripple effect all around me.

Several years passed and I went after new exciting roles. I had no fear of 'Me'. I joined a medical-device distributor when there were only seven in the company! I changed my title whenever it took my fancy. Travelled all of America and Europe working with biotech companies, liaising with doctors; being a bridge between them and the developers. I had total belief that I deserved abundance and self-care was of the utmost importance to me. I was in a male-dominated industry. I went after roles where I often competed with numerous highly-qualified men. I was asking for a salary package three times higher than my competition, and YES I got the job!! CEO of an American company and travelled the world inside out.

I studied and achieved untold business qualifications. I was promoted endlessly. It came to a time when I made a decision to bring a child into this world. I told my group of friends, "This time next year, I will have a child," and like magic, that's what happened. My daughter is now twenty-two years old. Though I remained single, I could not have wished for a better daddy for my daughter. We both have an amazing relationship with her father. Over the last fifteen years, I have run my own successful business, which has evolved and taken many different turns and directions, from distributing medical products, cosmetic injectables, global projects on HIV lipoatrophy, facial feminisation, business strategy and risk management, interior design and the buying and selling of artwork. Whatever has unfolded, has all been meant to be.

I became more aware you don't have to be in a job to be a leader. I can be the CEO of my life, with my daughter, family, friends and extended community involving all aspects of my work and personal life.

I believe we are all leaders in life and as leaders we lead by example, I love just sitting in coffee shops sharing with everyone, 'we are all famous in our own communities'. Whether it be medical research, fashion or a mothers' group. We are guided by truth and the heart. We will inspire the transformation needed to create a new world that's deeply in love, stands in unity and flows with abundance. If your actions inspire others to dream more, learn more, do more and become more, you are a leader.

Now I embrace the unknown, enjoying the process, while being patient and recognising the bliss in the waiting, in the chaos. To be in the very moment and to expect the unexpected. To have the strength, knowing and courage to navigate through adversity. Creating a pathway to lasting inner peace, connection, joy and abundance. I enjoy being an innovator, pioneering in all areas of my life; general trends, being an influencer, loving communication and sharing my pearls of wisdom. To lead by example, teach by uplifting others, showing how effortless it can be to manifest.

Now I connect with myself more deeply than ever, by doing daily meditation, walking the Labyrinth and spending time in nature which helps keep me grounded, activating my inner leadership, learning to trust myself, fine tuning some of my most useful energetic tools and becoming more aware of who I am and why I'm here. Watching what shows up in any situation with ease. I am okay with feeling uncomfortable, okay with the challenge to grow. I have an open mind to new possibilities. My desire is to be a transformational leader in all aspects of my life. To be effective in creating, motivating, and managing the delivery of an ever-evolving inspiring vision of the future for myself and others.

Now, when I go back home to the UK, I return as the new reinvented ME, transformed and more ready than ever to show up and be the voice that is needed – be the change. My story is titled, 'What's Your Poison' because it is important to know what makes you tick, what is holding you back, what ignites you, what's causing you to not be who you are meant to be, what will propel you forward and how you are designing your life.

IGNITE ACTION STEPS

If you heighten your awareness, watch and notice what is showing up. While listening to your inner voice, take some action, give yourself encouragement to start doing what makes your heart full and makes you feel good! Be the creator of your life. Be dominant in your thoughts, change within and see the world through a different lens. It will reflect in your outer world.

'Stepping into your future'

Walking meditation is a very natural, easy process that can be achieved in everyday busy life. Insight, joy and serenity are available to you in every moment, whether you're sitting in silence or strolling down a bustling sidewalk in the city. The beauty of walking meditation is that it can be done anywhere without causing too much disruption to your schedule. It helps to induce clarity and have a clear mind in moments of adversity, stress, confusion or conflict.

With your mind in the present moment, there is a clear awareness of the reality around us. You could choose to be walking in the city or 'mindfully' in nature; looking at the flora and fauna, focussing on flowers, trees, colour and smells around you. The purpose of a walking meditation is to train the mind to stay present while the body is in motion. Each step is in freedom, peace, health, joy and self-liberation.

There is no right or wrong way to start the process of a walking meditation. You can begin by closing your eyes and repeat an affirmation. You can start with your feet close together, eyes open to the floor, walking in a line, one foot length at a time. Right hand holding left hand in front or behind your body. Using conscious breathing can also help. Breathing slowly in and out. Breathe in for a count of five, hold the breath for the count of five, breathe out for the count of five. Standing still with your eyes closed – helps you to become heart centred.

Be aware MAGIC is all around

Take the time to see the 'MAGIC' around you. Sometimes we bustle along and miss things that are literally under our noses. See the 'MAGIC' in everyday life and how the unexpected can change into a magical moment. Be in the moment, in the flow and expect the unexpected.

Alex Jarvis
Rose Alchemist, Speaker, Author, CEO,
Vanillaesthetics /JARVIS Interiors
www.jarvisinteriors.com.au

TARA PILLING

"Be the CEO of your own life.
The world needs you, all of you. Show up!"

My intention in sharing my story is to IGNITE you, to spark a light within you so big and bright that you will know how incredibly beautiful, talented and fabulous you are. Whatever you've been through, or presently going through, is nothing compared to the greatness that lies within you – you have everything you need to create the greatest life you could ever imagine.

MY ONE WILD AND PRECIOUS LIFE

Life can send us some challenges. Some of these challenges will be very difficult, perhaps unbearable. I promise one day you will see the opportunities and gifts. I truly believe that God/Creator wants you to win. I believe that there is no such thing as a coincidence. I have learned that everything, no matter how good or bad, is meant for you. Life is for you. The ones who thrive in this thing we call life are the ones who never give up but accept what's happened in their life. Despite the good, the bad and the ugly they create the life they want and impact the lives of everyone around them.

You are a lotus flower...

The lotus flower grows in the muddy, murky waters. The lotus flower, like you, in order to grow and gain wisdom, first needs the mud, the obstacles and suffering. The mud speaks of the common ground that we all share. Whether we have it all or we have nothing, we all face similar challenges; sadness, loss, trauma, illness, dis-ease, death and dying. A lotus is a survivor, a leader. It pushes its way through muddy waters and finds the sunlight opening one petal at a time – a great achievement. Often in our busy lives we overlook our smallest successes. Like the lotus, each petal that opens is an achievement of survival, life and opportunity. A lotus has strength and reverence as it can overcome all of its environmental obstacles and show the world its beauty.

Imagine you are five years of age in a hospital crib bed in a small-town pediatrics ward. There is not another soul around – for the first time ever, you feel calm and safe. There is only silence – no arguing, yelling, fighting or drinking. The nurses come in to check on you, to bathe you and take your temperature. You feel so loved and nourished. My ignite moments have happened in the arms of strangers who offered me love and safety. I recall the nurses taking me on their rounds, to look after their patients. "I want to be a nurse. They love you and keep you safe."

Imagine you are twelve and the only way to end the pain would be to end your life. I know others who have ended their pain this way. I am scared. I've contemplated suicide for as long as I can remember even at this young age. The pain is too great. The shame and fear of abuse, the pain addiction created and the hurt of mental illness and upsets were just too great.

Imagine. Your Mom is doing her best, but she's drinking, there are hurtful men always in her life and you miss your Dad. Horrible memories of crazy drunken nights, the physical abuse of men who hurt mom and us kids. There was nothing I could do.

Imagine a boy your age. Derek up the street, a nice boy in my class shot himself in the head. Killed himself. His suffering and pain are gone forever. I wish I knew he was sad, as sad as me. Maybe I could have helped him?! I overheard, "How selfish. His family is left with his pain." This really hit me. So, if I kill myself because I'm in pain – I'm selfish!? I was upset and confused, everything was just too much to understand. I run up to my room, this time I'm going to do it. I can't take this any longer. I'm consumed with tears, afraid to go through with it. Mom walks into my room, "Tara, I'm sorry things have been so bad. I'm sorry I've never given you good feelings about yourself. No one gave me good feelings about myself either or showed me how to be a good parent. Or how to love myself, so I don't know how to love you that way. I'm sorry. I love you." Her words were kind, so sincere. She did the best with what she had… Thoughts of suicide are immediately replaced by guilt. "How could I ever think of doing that to her?! She needs me…"

Imagine you are 21 years old. You've just returned from a new year's celebration. The phone rings; it's your Dad, "Tara, your mom is dead," a pause. "She's died in a house fire." I say, "I don't believe you, why are you lying? I was just on the phone with her." My mind flips to the phone call the night before. I remember thinking, Mom has relapsed, eight years sober; now she's drinking. A pit grows in my stomach. I am upset; angry. How could she do this? I tell her directly "Mom, call me when you're sober." a phrase she programmed in me as a child when dad called drunk. I come back to the call with Dad… My boyfriend answers the doorbell and calls me to come to the door. I put the phone down and see the police standing there. It's true. Mom is dead?! My heart was shattered into a million tiny pieces. No words, only confusion and an emotional impact too great to understand.

A day of travel later, I'm with Dad going through the fire. The TV is a solid puddle; the image burned into my mind. Her tiny handprints are on the wall and window next to the bed. She's gone. She's really gone. A silhouette of her body on the bed shows where she was laying and another one on the floor where she quit fighting for her life. I recall going through the motions disconnected from my heart. I think it was the only way I could be in that space without losing my mind.

There I am, going through her fire. The smell is horrible. That smell would stay with me for years. I am in so much pain, unbearable pain, I don't know how to do this?! This all must be a mistake. I don't want to be here. I don't want to talk to the police or fire chief. I keep thinking, "I want to be with you Mom. I am sorry I didn't take the time to talk to you when you called me. You were drunk, upset, you called to talk." I am ashamed in grief and guilt. Where do I go from here? I am once again that small child, afraid, ashamed and confused.

I spoke at her funeral. I have no idea what I said or how I managed to get through it. I clearly remember being upset that her coffin was open for viewing. I asked that it be closed. She was swollen and burnt and didn't want anyone to see her like that. My thoughts consumed me, "Is she in pain?"

My brothers and I left the funeral home. Visions of people's faces, sad and confused too. We followed close behind the hearse that is carrying mom's dead body. There are no words; I feel numb. My heart is really bothering me, my neck and arm are in so much pain. Where is Kim? My sister isn't with us. I feel us four should all be together. I remember Kim screaming in the funeral home. I will never forget that scream. How can this be happening? Kim, Richard, Nathan, what are we to do without her, she was our everything! "How can this be happening?"

Days come and go but I don't know how to move forward. I am consumed by grief. The boys have come to live with me. I took legal custody the day of Mom's funeral. Kim, my younger sister, is missing; Mom is gone. I don't know what to do or what to say. We are all broken. Every time I walk in Nathan's room, the youngest at 16, his sheets are saturated in tears. He can't stop crying and I don't know what to do for him. I don't know how to take his pain away. I feel helpless and broken too. Richard the oldest brother doesn't say much. I don't know what to say. Looking back, I wish I would have done things differently. We needed support and there was none.

I lost 30 pounds in three months. I wasn't well; my body was breaking down; I found out I had cervical cancer – the reason why I was wasting away. Thoughts of suicide return and won't leave me alone. "I can't do this any longer, I can't go on like this, the pain is too great." Sadly, my relationship with my boyfriend mirrors my childhood and yet, I convinced myself I liked it; it feels good in a really messed-up, but familiar and comfortable way. We both played our part in a painful cycle we didn't know how to stop. I couldn't live like that anymore. I sat at the foot of my bed looking outside the bay window, a vision of myself going through it, blood and broken in pieces. This time I felt, "I can do it." At that moment my brother walks in; he knows or he's sensing something. "Tara, Nathan and I need you." My heart breaks for them. I am ashamed I'd even attempt to end my sorrow only to leave them even more devastated. How could I ever do this to them!? They need me. Mom needs me to be strong. She always needed me to be strong and help her.

I think back about my mom, how she was always in survival mode. She got pregnant with me, her oldest, when she was 19. She left an alcoholic home life, married her childhood friend, also an alcoholic, so she could keep me. She had three more children before leaving my father when I was six. The drinking and abuse was too much. It was so confusing at that time.

Mom raised us four kids all alone, scared and struggled to make ends meet with little to no support. She did the best with what she had. She struggled with addiction on and off, attracted harmful relationships into her life and battled anxiety, depression, and agoraphobia. As children do, I made it all about me. I thought she drank because I stressed her out. I thought she loved the men more than us kids. Like me, Mom was looking for love and safety. I thought she didn't go to my school interviews or basketball games because she didn't care. If only I understood. I grew up projecting my anger towards her and yet she was my everything. It was her love I craved the most.

I am grateful to my mom and miss her every day. All the best parts in me are her and more. She loved us kids more than anything. Forever my greatest teacher. I love you Mom.

I spent the next twenty-five years of my life seeking. Searching for ways to release my pain. My body wouldn't let me hide it any longer as cancer appeared where my connection to my mother and to become a mother resided; my cervix, my womb. I was broken down physically, mentally and spiritually; there was nowhere from here but up or death. It felt like hitting rock bottom and death wasn't an option. Giving up wasn't allowed.

I dug deep within, connecting with the best healers, teachers, mentors. I studied as though my 'head were on fire' (a Buddhist saying). Through energy and vibrational healing, I released layers of pain and cancer. Yoga and meditation restored my mind/body to order. Nutrition and Ayurveda taught me how-to live-in harmony with myself and nature. I strengthened my will and intuition, experiencing incredible clairvoyant moments, even moments of astral travel. Conversations with Mom and others who had passed. I am grateful, I had the teachers and mentorship to help me develop my skills and affirm that I wasn't going crazy, a thought that crossed my mind from time to time.

These practices would impact my life so much that I would become a lifelong learner. Later, I would share these gifts with my students and clients. Experiencing incredible opportunities to heal the mind/body. I am forever grateful for these powerful practices in my life. But, I still wasn't getting the results I wanted. What else could there be…

I spent a year diving into self-development with Robin Sharma, author of The Monk Who Sold His Ferrari. Incredible work. Next, training and immersions with Tony Robbins, completing Mastery University, Leadership and graduating in Fiji at his private resort – pretty amazing! Then Bob Proctor called. Yes, Bob from the documentary 'The Secret'. I was a little resistant, but there are no coincidences – I knew I was ready. It's been an incredible journey with Bob that only gets better. Finally, results that stick!

If I can do it, so can you. Like me, you are a survivor. You are a lotus flower.

Today, I am grateful to share; I live in a healthy body, I have the most amazing husband and two children. I have incredible people in my circle. I have the best mentorship and I love what I do. My mind is calm and filled with thoughts of thriving. Living the best way possible. This doesn't mean my life is always easy or perfect, but I am the CEO of it. I have the tools to create my world, the way I want. I lead personal and professional life success consulting and show others how they can manifest their greatest masterpiece.

Life is filled with blessings in disguise. Hang in there. You are stronger than you know – you are a warrior, a lover, a fighter, a peace maker, a leader… you're a Lotus Flower… You have everything within you to succeed and create the greatest life you could ever imagine.

IGNITE ACTION STEPS

Never Give Up!

There are going to be times in your life when you are going to feel like giving up. During these times, it is most important that you do everything it takes to hold on tight; you are stronger than you know. You've got this!

Action Step: Never Give Up!

• Reach out for support. No matter how alone or lost you feel, I promise, you are never alone. Somebody always cares. I care. Please reach out for support.

• You have to keep moving forward, one step at a time, one breath at a time.

Forgive, Forgive, Forgive…

Forgiveness is absolutely essential if you are to create and live the life you want. Often times we hold onto old baggage and hurts at the detriment to our healing and success. When we forgive, we release ourselves and those who have hurt us and this creates space for change to enter. Forgiving someone doesn't mean we condone the behavior, it means we are willing to release the hold it has on us and our lives.

Action Step: Set yourself free – Forgive!

• Write out a list of all the people you need to forgive, don't forget yourself.

• It can be difficult to forgive those who have hurt us. Focus on any good qualities this person has. There is something good in everyone. What we focus on grows!

• Journal on the ones you need to forgive as often as needed. Write: I forgive…

Cultivate an attitude of gratitude.

A daily gratitude practice shifts our energy and being into a higher vibration. Each morning, write out ten things you are grateful for in the present tense. Write: I am so happy and grateful for…

• Place your hand on your heart and say each gratitude out loud from your heart.

• Give thanks 24/7. There is always something to be grateful for.

Self-Image, If I want to be free I have to be me.

If I want to be free, I have to be me. Not the me you think I should be, not the me that my family thinks I should be. Not the me my friends think I should be. If I want to be free, I've got to be me. Now, I better know who 'me' is.

What you see when you look in the mirror is not the real you. It's just a reflection of your physical being. While your physical body and appearance are important, it's the self-image that's locked in your subconscious mind that really counts. For this is the image that determines your success or failure in life. While the real you is perfect, boundless, and is always looking for ways to expand, the self-image in your mind is based on false and limited information that sets the boundaries for every area of your life. Create a winning self-image.

Action Step: Write out a Goal That is Worthy of You + Winning Self Image

• What do you really really want? Decide upon a goal, a big goal. Not a goal you know how to do but a desire, a dream.

• How do you need to think, feel, act? What habits would you need to cultivate?

• Stand in front of a mirror and act like this person and read out what you have written. See yourself already being the person that you desire. Do this exercise two times a day.

Action Step: Life Script

• Create a clear mental picture in your mind of the life you want to live, visualization. Write it out in the present tense with positive, powerful emotions.

• It is important throughout this process that you release any fears, doubts and worries... focus all your imagination on creating the life that you want.

• Read it out loud once a day with full faith that the life you desire is happening now, act as if...

This one wild and precious life is yours to create and live as you choose, you can create a masterpiece. You are the CEO of your own life. What are you going to create?

Tara Dawn Pilling
Proctor & Gallagher Certified Consultant,
Tara Pilling Lifestyle Consultant, Healing, Ayurveda, and Yoga
www.tarapilling.com

HELLE BRODIE

"Leadership is in ALL of us. We just have to allow it to shine."

We all have the gift of true leadership within us – to make a real difference in the lives of others. My wish for you is that you can uncover your gifts to truly shine. When you find your place as an authentic leader, you will reap the many benefits of leadership.

WE ALL BECOME LEADERS IN OUR OWN TIME

We all have a secret desire to make a difference. We all want to be significant. We all want people to love us. These are the wonderful rewards of leadership. And we are all capable of leadership. We just have to pull it out of ourselves.

As a teenage girl, I didn't feel like a leader. I wasn't the popular one; the one who everyone cherished. I wasn't 'that' girl. Maggie was.

We all looked up to Maggie. She was beautiful with long blonde hair, sparkling blue eyes, a beautiful body and slender legs. She was a smart, straight A student. Maggie was outgoing, she sang with a beautiful voice and played the guitar. And most importantly, (particularly at that age) all the boys were in love with her.

Everyone watched what Maggie did – the boys 'and' the girls. All the girls wanted to be just a bit more (sometimes a lot more) like her. We all wanted to be popular, smart, beautiful and perfect, just like Maggie. At the age of 15 in junior high, that was what leadership was all about.

What were the qualities that she had? What made her so special? As I think back on it now, I can see that she had a strong belief in herself. She was authentic. She was happy to stand out from the crowd as her true authentic self. She had that confidence in herself to be proud of who she was.

Maggie came from a loving and supportive family. She was praised for who she was every step of the way. It seemed her parents were almost blind to anything that might not have been perfect about her. I remember driving an hour to another city with her (without our parents' knowledge) so she could spend time with her boyfriend. It didn't matter that I was breaking the rules too. I just wanted to spend time with her so that I might be able to be more like her.

She was encouraged to step out on her own and had the support to do it. Most of us wanted to fit in. But Maggie was a leader. She set the standard and we all followed.

As a teen, I knew I was not a leader. I wasn't strong and assertive. I did what other people wanted me to do. I was the same as many other young women with strong parental figures, doing things to gain the affection and approval of our mothers/parents; and later in life, our lovers and our peers. I was doing what was expected of me and wishing I could be more like Maggie.

In high school, I got myself involved in a 'cool' peer group. If I couldn't be a goddess like Maggie, I would try something completely different. It led me down a dark road to daily drug use and plenty of disrespect for myself. There was rarely a day that I wasn't high as a kite at school. One day I was so high, I tumbled down a whole flight of stairs, sprained my ankle, had a huge lump on my head and bruises down my back and my legs. Of course, I didn't want to see the school nurse. I knew why I had fallen. The nurse would know too. I'm glad my parents didn't complain to the school. That would have been real trouble! I might have been found out!

My parents had no idea I was developing questionable habits. They enrolled me into a girl's private school because of a pending teachers' strike. They just wanted to ensure that I didn't miss out on the education I would need to lead a successful life.

I was about to lose my peer group. Everything that was familiar to me would change. This was going to be devastating! Surprisingly, it turned out to be a very fortunate event in my life. My saving grace was that Maggie attended this new school.

My new peers had no knowledge of drugs. In fact, they feared just the thought of drugs. Because I was a follower, I learned to do the things they did and more importantly, to stop doing the things that they didn't do, like drugs. I became a 'good girl' again, cleaned myself up and started to pay attention to what was going on in my life.

A few years later I went to University to pursue a career. I met my future husband there during the first week. Continuing my pattern as a follower, I did what he did, went where he went, thought what he thought. While this was a huge step up from my teenage drug-loving peer group, I still wasn't thinking for myself.

Shortly after University, I became a mother. Not because I really wanted to have children: because it was expected. You know, it's that biological thing. I was still a follower, without strong thoughts about anything for myself. If the man I loved had such strong feelings about having children early, then surely it must be the right thing to do.

I became a full-time mother and a supportive wife who allowed her husband to focus on his career and have the breadwinner status of the family. I was also running a little business 'on the side' so I could also be a professional; a career woman.

I was fulfilling everyone else's desires. I became the supermom that everyone talked about in the 80's. I worked full time, raised my children, kept house, was the faithful daughter and daughter-in-law and kept peace in the family. It was exhausting! But this was what I was supposed to do.

When this started to wear thin, I became frustrated. I still had to get up early so that I could get a few hours of work done before anyone else got out of bed. Then I'd make breakfast for my family, send kids off to school and my husband to work. After work, there was daycare, children's activities, homework and dinner.

I had it all, right? A small business, two incredible kids, a successful husband and a beautiful house! In the summers, we'd even go to his family cottage for the weekends to relax. Another house to clean, more meals to prepare, another garden to look after.

I get exhausted all over again now just thinking about it. I didn't realize that I was a single mom who was married and living with a husband. I know it sounds terrible! Yet there's another incredible silver lining in this. I was learning and gaining the skills and habits to make my own decisions to be able to look after myself and my two children. I had amazing kids, I could budget, I could prioritize and most importantly, I was beginning to think for myself. Looking back, I now recognize that I was quietly developing the traits of a leader.

Eventually I'd had enough, so I moved my kids and my business to another city where I had a lot more to learn: how to build the business so that it could support the three of us; how to buy a house on my own; how to make decisions about raising a family on my own. I recall praying every morning when I wrote in my journal, that I could pay the bills this month, provide for my children and raise them to be stable, loving, adults with a great sense of self-esteem – like Maggie.

I started into a major quest for knowledge. I read: self-help books to get through the emotional trauma of divorce; business books about how to build a business; books on finance; career growth; women in business. If it was out there, I had to read it. If I was going to do all of this on my own, I needed knowledge and guidance.

I was starting to see the world differently as a result of all this reading; starting to set my own goals; to follow my heart. I was reacting to my newfound knowledge. I was just doing what felt right!

I made all the decisions: the financial decisions, where we would live, what my kids could and couldn't do. I decided which clients to pursue, which people to hire (and when). I made all of these decisions. It was all new. I really had to rely on myself; there had always been someone to tell me what I should do.

I worked, learned and worked some more. I became smarter and stronger. Eventually people in my field started to take notice. I was so busy working and learning, I was oblivious to the changes in myself.

About 12 years ago, a young woman asked me if I would be her mentor. "Why", I wondered. "I was not really a leader. I was a follower. Why would she ask me to be her mentor? What did I have to offer?"

I did it anyway. I took on this new role. We talked about her career, what she could focus on, the skills that she should acquire so that she could climb to the top. Yet it didn't feel right. She just wanted to take, take, take all the time. If she wanted to become a leader, it would take more than just having someone else tell her what to do in three easy steps. She would have to think for herself. Like I had to learn for myself.

About a year later, another woman asked me the same question: would I be willing to be her mentor? I was wiser this time. I agreed. I wasn't willing to be her daily coach, providing answers to every question she had. If I was going to be her mentor, she had to be willing to do the work; to think about what she wanted and why. I could not give her a three-step guidebook with all the answers.

She was just starting out in business. So, I handed her a book to read, The Entrepreneur Roller Coaster by Darren Hardy. Here was a no-nonsense book that told of the ups and downs about being in business and about some of the things she would have to master. She gladly accepted the book and went off to study, grow and improve. This felt right!

'This' mentorship experience helped me to understand how I had changed. I had developed definite thoughts about myself, my values and how to live my life. Maybe I really did have some leadership skills. Maybe I really was becoming a leader.

People began to show up to ask for my guidance. Where were they coming from? I now understand that I had done the work of figuring out what was important to me and why. I was willing to stand out from the crowd, to be proud of who I am and where I have been. To live life on my terms. Others were beginning to see all of this and they wanted to be a part of it – the same way it was for me with Maggie.

I now realize that I started to become a leader on the day I moved out of my matrimonial home. I had begun to reject living up to the expectations of my mother, husband and peers. I now lead a business and a team 'my' way. I became an expert in my field. I am mentoring several people in the development of their own businesses. I now have confidence in myself. It took a lot of study, trial and error but I'm proud of where I am.

I have helped my kids to be leaders, thinking for themselves and setting their own direction. They are well grounded and well-rounded individuals.

Bobby, who worked for our firm a few years ago, had issues with his father. Bobby was never good enough and was always criticized by his dad, no matter how hard he tried or what he achieved. This issue really had nothing to do with the business or why I had hired him. I hired Bobby because he was a bright, hard-working, fun-loving guy.

Through several long conversations Bobby began to understand how his father's criticism didn't really align with the accolades he received from clients; how capable he felt at work; how he was looked up to by his peers. My job as a leader, was to help him to see past the criticisms and to believe in himself. When he did, his hidden talents and leadership gifts began to surface. Our team thrived.

Another of my team members, a young woman of 24 (we'll call her Jackie), broke up with her long-time boyfriend. She had been so invested in her relationship that she hadn't focused on what it was that she wanted out of life; what was important to her. This sounds like deja vu! I had been on the same page as she was about 25 years previously! After a few conversations, Jackie understood what she really wanted; what she believed; about her mission in life; about who she really is. It didn't take long for her to start trying new things and meeting new people. All she needed was someone to believe in her.

The conversations with Jackie were very therapeutic – for both of us. As we talked about putting her life back together, I looked back on my own life and became stronger through reflection. Jackie continues to gain confidence in herself, believing in herself and her mission. She too is beginning to develop the traits of a leader.

As an entrepreneur, I've had the great privilege over the last 30 years of leading, coaching and mentoring many people by connecting with them on a personal level. This has nothing to do with the business. It has everything to do with mentoring leaders who incorporate the attitudes to use their experiences to pass forward the support, helping to develop leadership and encourage confidence in others.

In the words of John Quincy Adams, "If your actions inspire others to dream more, learn more, do more and become more, you are a leader". It is the way of great leaders. There can be no greater satisfaction in knowing that you have been a positive influence in someone's life and inspired their greatness.

I used to think that leadership was about doing it alone, being strong and being on centre stage. These were my beliefs when I started on my quest for knowledge. I now recognize that leadership is about working with others and inspiring others while you allow them to inspire you – not doing it alone. The leader has the desire and vision to learn, grow and help others to improve, giving of themselves long before anything is asked of them.

I was fortunate to have two teenage children who helped me to become the leader I am today. They believed in me. They supported me while I was supporting them. We grew together. We reaped the benefits together. Today we are strong together. They inspire me to be better every day, just as I inspire them.

I am also fortunate to have a team who challenge me to be better. Rob, one of my staff, often asks, "Why do we have to do it this way?" On the surface it sounds like a challenge to my leadership. Yet I no longer feel threatened. I know that the asking of the questions will only help us both to be stronger and better. It will also help us to grow. As an entrepreneur, I've had the great privilege to mentor many people over 30 years. With each new team member, I have learned about myself and have become a better leader, helping others to gain confidence and belief in themselves.

The best leaders are open to learning from anyone. True that there are great things to learn from the most successful leaders like Tony Robbins, Robin Sharma, Coach John Wooden, Jim Rohn and many more. Read and learn and take in as much of their greatness as you can. But remember that some of the most important life and leadership lessons come from ordinary folks with a bit of curiosity. People who simply say, "please help me to understand". It's in the explaining of the why or the how that we really learn what is important to us. When we are compassionate with the people we are leading, we have an incredible opportunity to influence them.

My thoughts about leadership have changed over the years from outward beauty and popularity as Maggie possessed, to constant growth, compassion, belief in myself and a desire to inspire others to do the same.

You don't have to be outgoing. You don't have to be wealthy. You don't have to be famous. You don't have to be outwardly beautiful. And you certainly don't have to do it alone! True leadership lives inside ALL of us. Live by your own rules and allow the leader within you to shine!

Ignite Action Steps

- Work at becoming better every day. Never stop learning and growing!
- Embrace your authentic self; believe that you have all that you need inside you.
- Do everything that you can to inspire others to be better through your actions.
- Develop other leaders through compassion to build your own strength and leadership.

Helle Brodie
Brodie & Associates Landscape Architects Inc.
www.brodie.ca

ULRIKE STAHL

"Together we are so much greater than on our own.
Together we can achieve the most amazing things and thrive."

My story is about how I learned to look after myself and do it all on my own in order to get my parents attention and appreciation. This led to great success but also to isolation and burnout until I found my way to break free. It is my sincerest hope that my story will encourage you to fully explore the potential of collaborating and co-creating to make your life more vibrant and more successful.

IF YOU CAN'T BREAK THROUGH – BREAK FREE

It's December 1999. I'm sitting in my boss's office. Our daily meeting is coming to its end; I see how his attention is already moving to the next item on his agenda. "Come on," I push myself. "Tell him…," but my tongue felt glued to the roof of my mouth. My hands are ice-cold; my stomach crawls like an anthill. "Is there something else?" he asks a bit irritated as I sit there on 'mute' with my mouth open.

"Don't spoil his Christmas," a voice in my head whines. "He doesn't deserve that." I am about to give in but there it is again. This inner clarity that I can't wait another minute. That awareness this is not the life I want. That there is more than being a civil servant with a lifelong safe job. More than my career as managing director of this municipal administration with 30 employees. More than perfect performance, more than making tiny movements in a rigid corset of rules and regulations trying not to step on anyone's toes. I take another deep breath and set the words free, "I quit."

Silence, then: "That's not possible, you can't do that, nobody does that!" I answer quietly, "*I do. I just have to.*"

What brought me to this moment? For the previous 30 years, I had made my life hard, complicated through what I thought was 'living the right way'. I am the fourth child of five. My father, a factory worker, my mother a housewife, worked hard to provide us with a life better than theirs: higher education; learning an instrument; growing up in a supportive environment with plenty of space for everyone.

Large families were unusual, so people looked down on us. My mother spent much time and effort to dress us appropriately and insisted on good manners. My father was a very correct, honest and responsible man. He'd check every item on a shopping receipt and let the cashier know if he found an error – even when that meant paying more. For him, life was about sticking to rules, living responsibly. Law and order!

'First work, then pleasure.' The job wasn't there to please him, he did it to feed his family. Working in a bakery from age 13, followed by 40 years piecework in a factory, plus building our house in his free time, led to severe health problems. But as long as he could crawl to the doctor, receive a cortisone injection that let him stand upright, he'd go back to work. He died young, at 66.

Today I am truly grateful for all my parents did for us but as a child, what I really longed for was attention and appreciation. How to get that from my busy parents? I developed my individual strategy to please them: *I look after myself, I do not disappoint, I don't cause trouble.* This was challenging for a curious child who wanted to explore the world. Still, I tried hard to fit in AND get attention. This made me independent and successful, but it also led to rigidity and lacking the ability to enjoy life or indulge myself. Most of the time, I felt like a bird in a cage. I felt unseen and withdrew into an inner world. I learned to nurture my adventurous side by reading. Every Sunday after church I went to the library to borrow books, preferably adventure and detective stories. Not one or two. I hauled home four or five books and devoured them all in that week. The good thing about reading instead of living the adventure is: you don't get dirty, you don't do anything illegal, doubtable or run any risks.

I was not perfect in my endeavour of being the ideal daughter. In puberty my need to have new experiences increased dramatically and of course, the few times I tried to live out my adventurous streak, I got caught. My best friend used to climb out of her window to spend time with our clique. She never got caught and told me about all the fun moments she had. Finally, I summoned the bravery to do the same and asked my friends to pick me up one night. As usual, my parents went to bed at 9 PM; so did I. My friends showed up at 9:30. I carefully opened the window and jumped to the ground. We said hello and chit chatted a bit about what to do and where to go, when I heard a sound from the front door. I turned to see my father standing there, an unreadable expression on his face. Shockwaves ran through my body. I was paralyzed; it felt like an eternity. Then I scurried across the yard to climb the stairs to the entrance. He let me pass and closed the door. He didn't say anything; he just looked at me – unreadable. My mind was racing. To minimize the situation, I said we were just having a chat. He didn't respond; I had no idea whether he believed me or not. I didn't sleep much that night, worrying about what would happen. He never mentioned the incident again, leaving me with a profound feeling that I had disappointed my father. It was like a knife in my heart because I had tried so hard to be perfect and now I had spoiled it – just for spending some time with others.

A year later, hanging out with four friends, we decided to go to the cinema. Shortly after we sat down, the police came in to carry out an age check. I paid no attention to the age restrictions of the film; I just wanted to be part of the group, part of the experience. Suffice to say, I was underage and the police took my details. I asked what would happen, "The owner of the cinema will have to pay a penalty charge." If that was the worst that could happen, I decided not to tell my parents. Three months later, my parents hand me a letter from the child-welfare department. Again, that shockwave, then paralysis. It reports that I tried to watch a film I wasn't old enough for and accuses my parents of failing in their responsibility to supervise me. While I read, I think of ways how to explain how it happened. The reality? I wasn't even aware I did something illegal. That event had consequences. My parents imposed house arrest for three months.

Again, I crossed the line. Worse: my father seemed to talk less to me than before. As my father never talked much and my guilt prevented me from approaching him, we regrettably never spoke about it again, nor did I receive any absolution.

I tried to compensate with even more self-sufficiency. I did my schoolwork and prepared for exams without having to be reminded. I even started to get up in the morning on my own so that my mother could sleep a bit longer. I retreated further back in my inner world spending less time with others.

When it came to choose my career, I was unsure. I never had a dream job like others. My two elder brothers were civil servants; my sister worked in the hotel industry. They hadn't gone to university and I wasn't that keen on it either. My father always said that it is very important to have a job and stand on my own two feet before I establish a serious relationship. I already had a boyfriend, so it was time to have a job. The hotel business sounded interesting, but I followed my father's advice: "Civil servant is a safe and solid job." Why not, I thought, it's just a way to earn money. Diligently as ever, I excelled in my work and studies. I completed my degree 3rd out of 753 students in my county. I checked my market value and applied for treasurer position of a municipality. Even though I had zero experience in this particular field or as a manager, they offered me the job. So, I became a treasurer. My predecessor had left before I started, leaving me to find my way around and with hard work and determination. I did keep my head above water. One year later the head of administration position became available. I immediately knew I wanted the promotion. Afraid that the community council wouldn't want to find another treasurer to replace me and thus stop me from being promoted; I suggested that I could take on both jobs. Now I had one job I was just managing and a second one to get familiar with and do the work of two. Instead of three employees, I had to deal with thirty. I was 28 years old, nearly the youngest in the team and female. Not every employee was willing to support me and I had no peers to lean on. No worries, my childhood prepared me to do it all on my own and to fulfil my responsibilities. I worked even harder and managed it all.

Four years later, I broke down, unable to stop crying. Eventually, I pulled myself together, put makeup on and went to work. At the time, I did not consider why this had happened or try to make changes; I had no clue where to start. I'd taken on significant responsibility, said I could do it; now I had to stick to it. That was my conviction until I found myself at a United Nations' health conference in Cuba six months later to introduce a small German help organization. My boss, the mayor, had founded a private non-profit to support health projects in Latin America. He was invited to introduce his organization but did not want to travel, so he asked me to represent him. This was way out of my comfort zone. I wouldn't get paid or receive expenses for the trip, as it had nothing to do with my job. I'd have to do it out of the goodness of my heart, pay my own way and use my holiday allowance. I had the money and sufficient holiday days to do it. What held me back was fear. I had never been outside of Europe. On top of that, I would have to present in English. I had learned English at school but

I certainly was not fluent. With all these obstacles mounting, I was close to saying "no". I had to give my decision in 24 hours.

Sitting on my balcony, under a clear blue sky, the sun shining, I weighed the pros and cons of the trip, "If this were a friend's situation, what would I say?" The answer was crystal clear, "What an opportunity. This trip will be an extraordinary experience. You'll meet people from different backgrounds in a new environment. It's an adventure; you'll be safe as a guest of the United Nations. Why do you hesitate? Go for it!"

As soon as I touched ground in Havana, the fantastic feeling of Cuban life surrounded me. Angelica, my guide sent by the United Nations, picked me up from the airport and took me to her apartment. I was going to stay with her for two weeks. 'Her' apartment, since living space is scarce in Havana, was house sitting for a couple living abroad. It gave her somewhere to live, a place to accommodate me, practice her German and earn a bit of money. That is the extraordinary Cuban way of dealing with life. You do not get far on your own. Cubans could not buy much more than rice, beans, locally grown fruit and vegetables unsuitable for export and curd soap for daily hygiene. What a contrast to the world I came from, where 10 minutes of power failure created a flood of angry citizens, neighbours were suing each over an apple tree hanging over a fence – a society where people predominantly looked after themselves.

Cubans grab life by the throat and achieve great things despite scarcity and restrictions. You've seen those typical pictures of Havana, probably with a classic car. The owners use them as taxis, repairing them with the money earned. Beyond solving the problem of getting from A to B, it fills Cubans with pride. It is part of their identity. However, what was most impressive for me: their unrestrained joy of life. They don't take themselves too seriously. They are open and ready to find creative solutions. No money to go to the club? No problema, let's share a rum and coke, set up a CD-Player in the backyard and dance passionately. When facing rules and restrictions, they find a workaround. I wanted to see more of the country. A friend of Angelica had a car but no license to transport tourists. No problema, should the police stop and question us, we say I am his fiancé, so I saw and experienced much more than I would have as an ordinary tourist. We had so much fun.

Cubans are known for their *joie de vivre*, which I experienced in their free time and at the conference, which surprised me. Very different from conferences in Germany. The presentations themselves were standard. Afterwards, the audience made extensive use of the question period. They wanted to understand everything; to learn as many new ideas as possible.

Before they asked, they all made appreciative comments, pointing out something that impressed them. During breaks, if I approached a group, they involved me immediately. People came up to ask why I was at the conference, where I was from and my background. They showed genuine interest in me and offered support. Initially, it confused me, because I suddenly felt so 'seen'. Then, I felt inspired by the warmth of the connections and enjoyed the diversity I was experiencing.

This openness, tolerance and togetherness touched me deeply. I believed I had to do it all on my own, work first, then pleasure, focus on responsibilities and follow guidelines strictly. Here I was surrounded by people collaborating, improving together, *joie de vivre*, joint creativity and flexibility. This environment had the same effect on me as water has on the Rose of Jericho. A plant that grows in the desert and survives several years without water and soil. It is often dry and grey but if you put it in water, it unfolds within a few hours and turns fresh and green again. Precisely what was happening to me.

Returning to Germany, to my house, car, bank account, safe job and career I felt something was wrong. Very wrong. In this environment I was in severe danger to dry out again. Something had shifted. I wanted to live differently, with more creativity, openness and collaboration. I had to break free, find a new habitat. Another admin-job wouldn't do. I always dreamt of living abroad, exploring other cultures. This thought opened a new door that felt entirely right. I did not want to just travel; I wanted to find roots somewhere else, be part of a different world where I could bloom.

Nine months later, I am working at the United Nations' office at Mexico City. I immerse myself in a new culture, new team and community. Working and living with people from different backgrounds enriched my thinking, allowed me to grow. I now share my experiences and knowledge on this subject. I believe together we achieve things so much bigger than each of us individually. It is good to be strong, independent and responsible as long as I am also open to others and their input. During my time in Mexico, I re-trained myself to react differently to challenges. Rather than disappearing into myself and engaging my independent mode, I sought out other people's input, truly listening to understand their needs.

Supporting individuals, teams and companies in collaborating and co-creating are my current mission. Together with my sister, we have connected over 2000 solopreneurs to explore the power of co-creativity through online seminars and group training. For 16 years, I've been coaching leaders and global teams in a variety of companies, inspiring hard-working individuals to enjoy the flow, ease and success of collaboration. I love hearing people say to each other, "It's great working with you," and truly meaning it — especially when I was called in because the situation was the opposite. Making people talk to each other creates trust and understanding, focusing them from ME to WE does magic. I am living what I was always looking for and allow others to benefit from that.

As leaders we have to walk our talk to create a collaborative environment. I always have at least one success partner – someone I talk with regularly. We set goals together and support each other us with ideas and feedback. I am part of professional networks, creative mastermind groups and collaborate in many projects. I am mentoring and helping others to connect. This keeps me up to date, prevents me from getting stuck in limiting thinking and challenges me to grow continuously. The power of collaboration and co-creation not only allowed me to achieve big things, like writing a book, working on three continents and speaking internationally – it also waters my soul that dares to be part of a bigger WE.

My desire is to help you to appreciate your individuality, be open for others and achieve results that are so much bigger than you. We are all connected and you are a part of a bigger community. Reach out, share and receive. Working with others while being yourself creates flow, ease and success.

IGNITE ACTION STEPS

If you would like to start a collaboration, take time to prepare.
• WHY do you want to do it? It is good to be aware of your drivers.
• HOW does it have to be – to make you feel comfortable? Know your limits.
• WHAT should be the outcome for you, for the other person and the greater good?

You can also invite your collaboration partner to reflect on these questions and then exchange your thoughts. Together you can build an excellent base for your collaboration and also clarify whether you are the right partners. The new WE is built by strong individuals with a collaborative mindset wanting to positively impact others.

Ulrike Stahl
Speaker, Author, Coach at The new WE
www.ulrike-stahl.com

ALINA CHRISTINA BUTEICA

"We are here to crack open from our shells and in doing so – expand!"

I invite you to ask along with me, "What if we are not here to settle for the ordinary? What if we are ALL extraordinary?" That is what I am continuously realizing, as I have taken the chilling plunge into what proved to be for me, much like in ancient myths, my own heroine's journey. It is my hope you wish to step into your own heroic status.

THE GEM OF YOUR GREATEST CHANGE IS YOU

What if… what if we're not here to be comfortable? What if the things we feel scared and exhilarated by, at the same time, hold our greatest key to growth?

Nervousness. Mind chatter. Yet a great sense of aliveness as well. Not knowing what to expect, not knowing what my bed will look like that night, nor if it would be easy to create meaningful connections like the ones I was leaving behind.

The flight date finally arrived. That flight that had taken me weeks to decide whether I'd board or not. The flight that my loved ones were in disbelief I was boarding. The flight that held promise to new life.

I don't know what first comes in front of your eyes when you think new life, but for me here, in this context, "new" meant completely unfamiliar. Completely different than where I had been raised and all other places I had lived in before. As the flight was taking off, I told myself: "That's it, there's no going back now." I gently allowed myself to lean back and my heavy eyelids to rest.

It was June 2015 and that flight carried me straight into the unknown, busy and bustling streets of the largest metropolis of Sub-Saharan Africa. A city of 21 million souls.

A month before, I was staring in grand surprise and excitement at the email that was about to change my life; to drop me straight into the abyss of a crossroads decision. To plunge or not to plunge? That was the question. The email was masterfully titled "Ready?" and it was from the CEO of the fastest growing tech company in Africa.

I was on the cusp of turning 30 that year and had gone back to Europe, to my home country Romania, after having spent one year in Africa working with another large multinational company, in various locations, as a corporate trainer. Yet during that whole year, I had not spent more than one month in each country, from Ghana and Benin to Burundi and Kenya, from Congo Brazzaville to Madagascar. I'd always been on the go, having a glimpse into the soul of each place but with no permanent attachment.

The challenge this time, was different. I would have to be based in Lagos, Nigeria and spend pretty much my whole time there, with the exception of the 20 contractual days yearly leave. I was a little bit in disbelief, since it was an open-ended contract. In order to bring my level of adrenaline down, I decided to tell myself that I also had a significant leverage on when I'd want to leave and could pull the plug at any time. That relaxed my mental state and allowed me to focus on the mission ahead of me, which was nothing short of a career leap and beautiful personal challenge: building an academy of trainings for the largest tech company of the continent.

There's something that happens inside of me whenever I get a challenge in my life of this magnitude. I can only compare this to what the great explorers of the past centuries possibly felt whenever they set foot on a new piece of land, after endless days and excruciating months at sea. The sea is also, in a sense, the sea of all our fears. It is a dying of the old and stepping into the new. A new version of us may emerge as a result of stretching outside our comfort zone.

Lagos, Nigeria. It resonated vividly in my ears. On the one hand, I was beaming with excitement and honoured. On the other hand, I knew close to nothing about the country I'd be going to, except for the news channel reports, which did not always portray it in the most generous light. From accounts of the Boko Haram insurgents in the North, to the recently contained Ebola epidemic in West Africa, there were... let's just say, quite a few things to be considered when making such a trip.

I had travelled to 10 other countries in Africa before, but not Nigeria. Not the 'human powerhouse' of Africa, not the country that *The Economist* predicts to be the 3rd most populous in the world by 2050.

I had no clue what to expect, nor had any friends there, prior to relocating. Back home, my family and friends were wondering if that was truly the step I wanted to take when I was touching my 30s. Yet I was never one to conform to the norm, at least not from the moment I hit my early 20s onwards. My life choices had always been puzzling to most people, *even to me*. Any time I move to a new country, my mom loves telling me the story of her dream she had the night I was born. After a tough, 18-hour labor, her body succumbed into a deep, restorative sleep. All of a sudden, she saw herself in a train station, anxiously searching for me on a train. She knew I was leaving. That's what she mostly remembers; the feeling of having to trust and let go. Whenever I hear this story, I get chills because deep down I know that her instincts and her insight were right. My mother spends more time saying 'Goodbye' rather than 'Hello'. She still smiles.

I always had this deep yearning and longing inside of me for 'more'. More expansion, more depth of feeling and living... more passion, more exploration. I'm what you call an explorer at heart. A curious, ever-wandering explorer enamored with life. Which is why I didn't fit the societal landscape when it comes to a young woman in her 30s. I was still unsettled, still searching for more. Then again, who says when we should settle? And where does this idea of 'settling' come from after all?

So there I was, moving to Nigeria. Getting acquainted to the city of Africa 'that never sleeps'. Nigerians affectionately call their Lagos the same as New York, as they believe the insomnia quality of its constantly-packed streets and crammed markets reaches a whole new dimension here. How does Lagos stay awake 24/7? Well, through its *keke's,* its *danfos* (buses unlike any other bus you've seen in your life, that take on double or triple the passengers than the actual number of seats), its constant honking, the roaring sounds of the open markets, the scorching heat, the peppery (aka hot) food, the loud voices, the Victoria Island skyscraper-buildings, the shanty town of Makoko floating village, the aliveness in the faces of the children and open curiosity of the people. I was told that Lagos is a place you either love or hate instantly.

Yet in my case, Lagos grew on me. I gradually fell in love. Some people fall in love with simplicity. I fell in love with contrasts and perplexities. The character of most Nigerians I met were determined to make it big and were convinced life has more to offer than the current conditions. There is a bold defiance, a pride of claiming what you deserve, from which I myself learnt. You see it everywhere, from the oil-rich havens, to the emerging social and environment-driven start-up scene, from the digital tech hubs to the fisherman shanty neighborhoods and makeshift markets, that sell anything you could ever imagine. Lagos nestled me. Lagos nurtured me. Lagos showed me all that I could be and… so much more. Lagos showed me the vibrant contrasts of human life. Lagos taught me to love life, in all its expressions.

One and a half months into arriving there, I was again at a crossroads. Distance had unfortunately laid its deadly mark on my relationship. I had been completely swept away by my handsome Spaniard partner, who had also relocated to Africa with his job - to Rwanda more specifically - around the same time as me. We were each other's pillars of support. He was working with an emerging social-impact fund, while I was in Africa's tech scene, in learning & development. He was my greatest supporter in taking the leap of faith into Nigeria and made me feel like a "lioness" that could achieve anything. His words of wisdom and encouragement were the tune ringing in my ears every time I had even the slightest doubt. He loved to see me grow and wouldn't allow me to compromise anything for my career. All of this only made me love him even more. Yet distance is one of the toughest judges in a relationship. We both gradually started getting engrossed in our work and our new lives.

I'll never forget the 1st of August, 2015. A Sunday morning, five days before my birthday and my partner was supposed to arrive in Lagos. Despite the growing insecurity I was feeling deep in my heart, I was longing to see him. To BE with him. To get a shot of tenderness and affection in a sometimes harsh environment. Things had been challenging at work too, with me solely having to build from scratch all curricula and logistically cover, and run, the whole chain of roll-outs of trainings.

And then the news came. Last minute, my partner called. He had cancelled his plans. I was listening in dismay and started shivering, chills going up and down all my body. What I had feared most for the past few months was materializing with the speed of a ruthless lightning bolt pulverising my heart into ashes. He let me know that he was not going to be able to make it, to Nigeria, 'nor to make it further in our relationship'. I remember so vividly the void that opened in me after the call. And the excruciating contraction in my heart. I found myself in the fetal position, staring into the void for probably an hour, wanting to be swallowed by it and disappear. Because nothing could be worse than that pain. I had only one moment of a sudden glimpse – almost as if my soul was desperately reaching a hand to catch me from the free fall – when I heard from within, "But what if there is a reason behind this? What if there is so much more awaiting you?" It only lasted for a couple of seconds. And then a fresh blast of pain blew over my heart, sinking it even deeper off the cliff of dismay. Over the next few days, I had so many moments of crumpling to the ground every night when I would reach home. I'd also have sudden bursts of tears in front of my laptop at work, which I was desperately trying to hide, as it was an open-space office. Waves of anger and crying remained my overall state, not knowing how to manage it, nor for how long it would last. I started questioning myself, questioning my decision and found myself contemplating leaving, asking myself, "What am I doing so far away from home? Why, WHY am I truly here?"

Again at a crossroads, yet different. It cracked me open, into a gazillion broken-mirror pieces. Yet it also showed me, much like in a mirror, that our deepest wounds hold the gems of our greatest change.

Gradually, I started plunging more and more into self work through emotional releases, journaling, meditation and mindset and energy management readings and online courses after work. I was hungry for knowledge and healing. It took me a bit over six months to start seeing the first results. In parallel, I started expanding my circle of friends in Lagos. I began to be curious about the whole universe I was in.

This time I was determined not to yield to the wound. I was no longer kneeling, but carrying my wound like a torch that would light my pathway into the unknown, my pathway into a new me, that was just emerging. Even though I would still have nights when I allowed myself to feel the grief and the longing, every morning I would rise up and start all over again. My work became my medicine. And I also opened myself up – in a larger-than-life way, with a hunger and thirst I had absolutely no idea I was holding inside – to the country I was living in. On an impulse, I signed up with an NGO that was organizing weekend trips across the country. Started discovering the ancient traditions of West Africa and their pre-Christian cultures, from the ancient Oyo kingdom to the ancient kingdom of Benin. There I was, in the middle of SO many ancient kingdoms I previously had no clue existed.

In the middle of a world that the news reports so often fail to depict. The explorer in me started literally lighting up again. From the inside out, I came alive, living my pain but I was no longer "be-ing" my pain. I felt proud of my scars. Felt the warrior woman inside of me ignite. Felt a new part of me being born. And maybe not surprisingly, all the ancient cultures I was getting acquainted with through my weekend trips, had warrior goddesses in their mythology, from legendary Oya to Mawu. Their transformative stories transformed me.

My shift in energy impacted my results at work as well. I started following more of what was "lighting" me up. I knew I wanted to inspire people to step into their best selves, so I suggested to the leadership of the company that we start building from the grassroots complete tracks of management programs, for junior all the way up to senior managers across all our locations in Africa. The flame turned into a fire and my dream eventually came true: I was given the freedom to build these programs all from scratch – 18 courses covering all aspects of personal and team development. Before I knew it, I was being flown from Abidjan to Capetown, from Nairobi to Cairo, from Casablanca to Accra to roll out the programs. I managed to cover the complete cycle, with astounding feedback from all participants of all nationalities. The maximum score across all training surveys was allocated to the facilitator herself, words that provided deep nourishment to my heart and purpose. My wound had ignited my greatest gem: the gift of inspiring people to discover their best selves. To not settle. To not take things for granted. On the contrary. To reach out for all they can be and more, as there are truly no boundaries other than our own mental and societal constructs around what is possible.

That's when I realized: there's nothing inherently wrong with wanting more, with stepping out of the norm. There's nothing inherently wrong with plunging into the unknown. There's nothing wrong with following the silent whispers of your heart saying "Jump! You will be held. Just trust and jump!" There's nothing wrong with taking the road less travelled. You and only you are the only one determining what lights up your heart. Your family may have a story of what you should do. Your teachers and mentors may have another story of what you should do. Your lovers and partners may have their own crafted story of you. Society may have its own take, its own lenses on you. Yet at the end of the day, the only story that matters my love, is yours. You are the Editor-in-Chief of your own life.

Write a story worth remembering, sing the song that your heart is yearning to hear!

Looking back now on my almost four years in Nigeria, they helped awaken new aspects in myself as a woman that I had little knowledge of before, from strength and determination to a heart-centered wisdom. I am deeply grateful for everything that "Mamma Africa" has ignited in me. I am a wiser, more grounded woman today than I have ever been before. I stand tall in my truth and know that I can, as all women walking this Earth, birth anything from projects to meaningful connections to whole new worlds! My hope is to give back to this blessed land, through the authentic leadership programs I will next be bringing to fruition.

IGNITE ACTION STEPS

• Do this envisioning exercise for 21 days, to start aligning your life to your deepest desires. You can add an extra day for each day you skipped, no worries.

• Breathe in and out deeply, at least 10 times, relaxing every single muscle and tissue in your body.

• Close your eyes, stay centered in your heart and allow it to soften up and expand, with every breath. Travel with your thoughts and your feelings. Imagine you in three years from now, in love and filled up with joy about all aspects of your life, from your career to your relationships to your family life, to your solo time and spiritual life. Dream freely, no restrictions. What would you be doing? Where would you be? Who would you be spending time with? What would be some of your most nourishing activities?

• Allow yourself, for at least 5 - 7 minutes, to FEEL into every aspect of that life. If you sense your mind is coming in and asking "But how is that even possible?", then thank your mind for wanting to keep you safe, but gently go back to your heart and into feeling how that life looks for you. Allow yourself to sense the liberation, the glow, the happiness, the aliveness. It is time the heart (who knows our deepest desires) and the mind (who has been conditioned over centuries into fear) come back in sync, come back in alignment with life.

• At the end of every week, on Sunday, after you have done the above envisioning exercise → write down only one small, practical step you can take starting from the next week, into getting closer to your vision. Make sure you act on that step in the following week.

• You can re-do the 21-days of envisioning your highest desires any time throughout the year when you feel you would benefit from a boost in motivation.

Alina Cristina Buteica
Authentic Leadership & Inner Change Coach
growthhacks.info

NITASHA SARIN

"Remove your masks. Step into truth.
There is power in vulnerability and imperfection."

It is my hope and intention to inspire you to fall into freedom – that by sharing my personal story, you will find strength in removing your own masks. You will breathe and balance into your own divine feminine leadership by embracing the power of vulnerability and imperfection to fully thrive, feel empowered and alive.

REDEFINING SUCCESS: COOL GIRL MUST DIE

Everybody Loves Me and I Love Everybody! From three years old to age eight, those were my favorite words to sing and dance in front of any group of strangers who'd crossed my path. While I was waiting for my mom to finish the weekly grocery shopping – or wherever else she dragged me after school – this was my anthem and the world was going to know it. I was that happy-go-lucky child full of life, light and love. Yet, this chapter in my story almost never came to be.

You see, I am a recovering… PERFECTIONIST. So much so, that at 40 years old, I hit extreme rock bottom. In hindsight, as a high-performing creative 'Leader', I spent most of my years out of balance – pushing away my intuitive feminine energy and reaching for the next mask to get me through any pain, discomfort or dis-ease. This survival tactic turned into disease, as my masculine energy severely suffocated my feminine each time she'd try to surface. I ignored balance. The result? Severe burnout followed by anxiety and depression – I lost my emotional freedom, physical, spiritual, mental and financial freedom – as well as my 'identity', all stripped away – gone. I felt naked. In fear of being exposed, I was no longer singing that song – what I forgot over the years, was Me. I forgot to sing: "I Love ME." I wore masks instead.

Mask #1: Acceptance / Smiling Mask: Brown Cow Nine years old at public speaking finals and I was so excited to get to the front of the class to speak about my Big Brother, when a kid yelled "Brown Cow!" Although I grew up in a predominantly white anglo-saxon community, one of three ethnic minorities in my school, I was never made to feel different – ever. I was utterly confused. But, I had a choice – break down in tears or place a smiling mask on my face and prove the show must go on. I raced to the bathroom afterwards and studied my face in the mirror. I never knew I was different. My dreams of growing up to be Madonna were shattered.

When I reached home, my father noticed my bright light had been diminished. I recounted the day and got a long Nelson Mandela type explanation. My father was firm in his advice, "Forgive." Confused, I took his lesson of forgiveness, but also internalized not feeling my truth towards that child.

Mask #2: Beauty Mask – Skin Disease The mask of smiles remained on as I floated into adolescence. Top of my class in academics, on the athletic council, sporting a bright demeanour and mask of flawlessness, I appeared happy. Always adorned in the perfect outfit, hair and makeup, nobody knew I had a rare skin disease. Terrified of exposure, I quit competitive swimming to hide my boils and scabs of pain.

At 14 years old, while getting ready for soccer, I heard arguing. Mom silent in tears, then Dad, "You are such an emotional bundle. Stop crying." Although I was 'daddy's little girl', his best buddy – I sympathized with mom and defended her. He praised me for being strong and courageous yet at the same time said, "I am not sure many men will love that." I heard: 'Vulnerability is weak. Emotional tears are frowned upon. Masculine energy is approved, recognized, revered.' What a mixed message.

I created a story around the danger of being vulnerable, never crying in front of any man until I was past 30. I believe my skin rebelled at me for not allowing myself to feel. I put on the strong mask, finished high school a year early, held three jobs to fund myself through university to prove something, while missing out on my truest source of power.

Mask #3: Superwoman Mask – Dad Dies suddenly I went through university wearing a mask the entire time. Instead of asking for support, in fear of seeming vulnerable and weak, I tried to hide it. I didn't understand what was happening, but I needed to pretend everything was fine – like Superwoman. The mask I was wearing started to become second nature. So did feeling out of alignment.

At 23 years old, life took a twisted turn as my dad died suddenly. I temporarily filled the void and dated a man who immediately shut down and ran as soon as I had any unique, independent or creatively ambitious ideas. My mask-like porcelain exterior kept me resilient yet my feminine self craved to express, cry and feel alive. I allowed myself to sing and dance again for a short moment, while my masculine was busy getting ready to take over the world! I wrote a business plan to build a Wellness Centre and Medical Dermatology Spa to help high performing perfectionists deal with severe skin ailments and other stress related diseases. I poured my soul into that business and led the team with empathy, passion purpose and practicality. I worked 7 days a week, 14 hour days, but I didn't feel successful and in control.

Mask #4: Bankruptcy Money Mask   Five years later, I was on a successful business high. I had worked long, strong and hard to get my team autonomous enough to the point where I could spend my summers in Europe and was about to expand to two new locations. Relationship status was "semi-single" with my arm's length Mask of Intimacy in tow. I had an on and off again 'relationship thing' that worked for me. I wasn't required to communicate fully, staying in my safety zone of self-provider and protector.

Then the global economic crisis hit - everywhere. Seeing everyone around me as well as my biggest competitors go bankrupt, I denied it. I kept giving it my blood, sweat and tears, pushed the support of my partner away and held on to the very last life preserver, until the ship had no choice but to sink and pull me down with it. I was forced to declare financial bankruptcy. The mask of shame was immediately created, and I held on to that painful moment in silence for years, with knots in my back and ulcers in my stomach. Speaking in front of a group of Entrepreneurs about Flow… then I finally admitted my funk, removed the money mask and started to own my personal money consciousness, financial fitness and redefining my worth with wealth.

Somehow, I was able to redefine my relationship with failure as a learning experience to move forward to the next exciting opportunity that awaited. I retreated to a place where nobody knew me. Central America, a place where I could safely remove my masks, and drop the need to stay strong in my masculine. I spent four months volunteering, stepping into my feminine, teaching, building a school and playing with children. I began to feel and filter through what had happened. I allowed myself to just be real and balanced and free, but again – only temporarily. I still didn't give myself permission to fully fall into what felt right in my heart – because in my mind, it still wasn't enough.

When I returned from my 'retreat', life made another miraculous change. I was recruited to go to Italy to create possibility-minded seminars for children. I foresaw problems of unworthiness starting with the children. I worked hard at setting up a children's program, which taught kids how to have a beautiful relationship with self, through free expression.

You'd think I'd 'cut and revise' of my own childhood story, right along with them. But I didn't learn the lessons, nor end the cycle. I repeated it again. Different country, same story. Different work opportunities, same cycle. My default every time I doubted myself was to slip back into my masculine to prove something to the world. I was self-sabotaging and didn't see it until I went to Monaco.

Mask #5: Monaco – Lifestyle, Credentials, Perfection Mask   Monaco, a beautiful grandiose place with yachts, Lamborghinis, Mediterranean Sea, mountains, to get away from any of my past hurt. I thought the only way I am going to fit in is to make my mark. I joined the old boys club and got my Executive MBA. If I didn't have the mister on my name, I was going to be accepted in any room with that degree.

The truth is, it wasn't the most welcoming of places (for us mere mortals). In comparison to my life in Italy, where my Feminine Power soared and my skin color was revered as a unique Goddess from the South or even Princess Jasmine, as the children named me – here in Monaco, was the first time I felt any sort of 'color discrimination' since the 'Brown Cow' moment. The result? I did what I always did – I reverted back to my survival mode pattern behaviour of placing on the smiling mask, tapping hard into my masculine do-er energy, and did everything in my power to be perfect, fit in and check off all the boxes of society's idea of success.

I chose the path of the overachieving perfectionist – waking every day at 5 AM, running 10 km every day, doing my full-time Executive MBA while at the same time running my corporate consulting and coaching practice. I was teaching yoga on the beach five times a week to university students (helping THEM balance their lives). When I was asked to create a new Executive Wellness division for one of the most affluent luxury hotels in Monaco, I jumped at it. I believed I still had the energy capacity left to take on this feat, so how could I say NO?

What I didn't realize was, I was overextending. I, like my clients sitting on their yachts, was wearing a false mask of success. I felt I was bringing balance to those around me who lost sight of true passion and purpose while focusing solely on power and profitability. Subconsciously, I was playing somewhat of a similar game. I was caught in 'the false spiral of success' – Without realizing it, I too wouldn't go deeper than the surface. I was teaching yoga and meditation and coaching the world's richest on mindset mastery – surely I was doing A-ok! Or was I?

One day I recall teaching yoga to a few of my closest MBA colleagues, two beautiful, supremely intelligent and powerful women from Sweden and Morocco. Both, I felt, were 'balanced' in their feminine energies. That day we got real with each other – remove the mask feedback game, about strengths and weaknesses. When it came to my turn – both Caroline and Samira unanimously and lovingly told me they admire me for my strength and all I have to give. But, (a BIG BUT, AHA MOMENT)... all they wished is, for me to just 'Love Myself'.

What were they talking about? Of course I loved myself! From Italy to Monaco, living on the Mediterranean sea to coaching balance to clients on yachts and exquisite villas, incredible projects and my third university degree. To weekends in vineyards in the South of France, I was living my best life! The Riviera Life! Couldn't they see? I was confused. By default, I placed on my perfectionist mask, smiled, accepted externally and rushed off to my next appointment, (while denying it internally – they don't know what they're talking about). I love myself dammit! Just look at the life I've designed!

Over the next few weeks, I felt sparks of my feminine and masculine energies competing with each other. Staying skin deep – not slowing down and reflecting. Striving to achieve peak productivity. Intuitively my body kept on telling me I needed to live deeper, be in a different energetic environment, do more impact projects in alignment with my heart. But my mind took over and shoved my feminine intuition down – I kept plowing full force! Until the day – I was forced to stop.

It was a beautiful crisp January morning – 8 AM. I was leaving Italy for my one hour commute back into Monaco. All I had to do was drive my one hour joyride on my little Vespa along the coast, get to my apartment to gather my belongings, do two client sessions, teach a lunchtime yoga class and be in my exam room for 1 PM. In my perfect world this would happen, with zero room for error. Even if I felt rushed, I pushed the feeling aside telling myself I'm fortunate for this morning view – look what I've accomplished! Everything is under control.

With that thought in mind, I entered the round-a-bout that would bring me home. Heart beating fast with adrenaline, but smiling as I was precisely on time. Everything was under control… Until it wasn't. BAM! I was struck.

Just like that, within a flash my 'perfect' life got twisted and turned upside down – literally. I may have been precisely to the minute on time, but apparently the guy behind me wasn't and was in a rush to get to his destination. I was hit hard. In seconds, I went flying through the air, not like Superwoman, but as a ragdoll and landed splat in the middle of the road on the right side of my body. My motorbike separated from me for a moment and also took flight, rejoining me as it landed on top of the left side of my body.

Silence. Screams. Sirens. Before understanding anything – I was rushed to the Royal Princess Grace Hospital of Monaco. I woke with the news that I was struck by a car – the driver did a fast and furious hit and run. I had sustained multiple injuries; broken ankle, ribs and clavicle, some internal bleeding but luckily my organs were safe. They asked me to call my family and partner – at which point I hid my phone. There was no way, I was going to burden anybody or let them see me in my imperfect state. Especially not my partner – we had worked to get to this point after our previous pain and loss, and while clearly we were holding on to something that was already broken, I didn't want him to see me like this – supremely imperfect and vulnerable because surely he'd leave me. Being imperfect was wrong and vulnerability was weak, wasn't it? It made logical sense to stay silent.

I was a high performing leader and I wore that title with a sense of Ego disguised as Pride. So instead of slowing down, I wanted to pretend like nothing happened. My mother flew over. The university asked me to stop and pick it up the following year. Out of the question. The Executive Wellness project suggested I delay the proposal date – never. While bedridden, unable to walk for six months, I had them live-stream the classes to me. I'd wake up extra early to ensure I could get it all accomplished to perfection – with a smile on my face, of course I THOUGHT I could.

The day I graduated and gained my third University degree stamp of approval, my body decided to shut down.There it was again. Performance over. 'Love Yourself'. Smiling, as though I made the choice, I moved back to Canada to take care of my aging mom. I felt the superficial lifestyle I was surrounded by was no longer serving me.

I started rebranding my business and created Empowered360 Experiences. Inspired by my observations that neither the richest and wealthiest people in the world with all their material possessions were happy. With the pressure of comparison to keep up with the Jones's or today's Kardashians, we were all wearing masks of our own. We were wrongly defining our own self-worth by society's definition of success – white picket fences, numerous cars, 2.5 kids, C-suite titles, number of speaking engagements, number of countries visited… the list goes on and on.

I write this today warning you with big bright neon flashing lights that BURNOUT IS DAMN REAL. We need to redefine success as more than a dysfunctional drive for perfection. Our identities are not built by societies rendition of successes or accolades. To serve others is noble, but not if we're depleting ourselves in the process. We as women, do not need to always reach for the masculine energy mask to survive, DO and produce. We must allow ourselves to remove the masks, or not reach for them at all. We must naturally fall into our divine feminine flow by rewriting the stories, powerfully making vulnerability and imperfection our biggest allies. We must slow down and just BE. Our truth and ultimate success will shine when we are in alignment with our truest passion and purpose and balance that with power and profitability. That will lead to optimal wellbeing, epic leadership and the ultimate freedom to create and give forward.

IGNITE ACTION STEPS

Love yourself. You are enough.

Make a commitment to love yourself in one way every day. Focus on health, healing and self-support. Reclaim your strength by embracing the powerful realizations that you are amazing just as you are and step into the universal knowing, however you show up, you are truly, deeply and wonderfully enough.

Write this on a piece of paper. Pin it to your fridge, post it on your wall or carry it in your handbag. Read it every day. I NOW LOVE MY IMPERFECT SELF. FULLY. LIGHTS-DARKS, UPS-DOWNS, UPSIDE-DOWN AND SIDEWAYS. I AM ENOUGH.

Say only kind words to yourself. Be your own greatest cheerleader.

Repeat after me: "Not everybody Loves Me. (I'm ok with that.) I will keep on exuding Love, so long as I Love Me. No matter what."

Nitasha Sarin; MSc, MBA
Executive Leadership & Corporate Wellness Coach
www.linkedin.com/in/nitashasarin

Allyne Henesey

"Your soul knows what you truly need. Be still and listen."

My story is about the gifts I received from my broken heart. How I embraced my purpose, my dharma and fulfilled a sacred contract with myself. It is my intention that my story will inspire you to activate a renewed sense of passion and purpose by following your soul's calling.

From Drama to Dharma

We've all had those moments at 4 AM when our deepest fears descend upon us like a dark cloud. Grappling with our inner thoughts, we worry about losing something, or someone, dear to us. Most of the time we're resilient and bounce back fairly quickly. Sometimes, however, the circumstances cut deep into our bones with a pain so acute it's beyond our rational minds to comprehend. This is the pain of mythic proportion where we don't know how we're going to survive the emptiness that we feel. This is what happened to me. I lost faith in myself and God. It was the Dark Night of the Soul.

This encounter took me to the crossroads of 'woe' and 'wisdom'. Here in my darkness lay unprecedented opportunities to heal past wounds and align to my higher purpose. It was the time to call back fragmented parts of my soul that were lost through neglect and ignorance. I had to free myself from my limited beliefs and false perceptions about who I am. My heroine's journey took courage and persistence – and tissues, lots and lots of tissues, to wipe away the tears and blow the 'stinking thinking' out of my head!

I've traversed these badlands twice. Each time, I've learned something new by going deeper into the depths of my psyche. I didn't always want to go deeper, but I had to get a handle on the self-inflicted suffering caused by my own distorted thinking. My first crisis happened when I was 28 years old. I became pregnant and realized I would be raising a son on my own, without his father's emotional or financial support. I had to deal with massive fears, and manifested minor health issues as a result. "How are we going to survive?" I wondered, "Why did he abandon us? Is something wrong with me? God, where are you?" That crisis unfolded into a beautiful blessing as my heart filled with unconditional love for my little boy.

I learned valuable lessons. First, and most importantly, being a parent has been my most rewarding job. I also learned I'm strong and resilient and resourceful. I learned that you can't get love from a man whose heart is full of fear; nor money from a man who doesn't have a job. When my second crisis hit, two decades later, I knew there was only one way out. I had to walk, wade and crawl through the muck in order to free myself from my limiting beliefs and false perceptions about who I am and how I show up in the world.

Everything came to a boiling point in 2011 with my mother's death. After being diagnosed with late-stage breast cancer, she passed away at age 84. Cradled in my arms while she was in bed, my last words to her were "I got you, mom. I got you." I was grateful for that moment. The only thing is, we had been changing the sheets, and I didn't realize she was dying at that moment. I was troubled for awhile, beating myself up for not being fully aware and present as she was passing and that I could have done more, should have done more. It's the typical shame and blame game we play with ourselves. Much later, my sister helped me realize that mom likely chose that exact moment when she was embraced in my arms to let go. That revelation however, took quite some time for me to process. I would have moved more quickly through the grief had a series of unfortunate events not occurred soon after.

Within days of my mother's death, a romantic relationship ended that included losing not only my boyfriend (let's call him "Zeus" for the sake of my story), but also his two preteen daughters whom I adored. My dear son, and only child, was getting ready to go to university. My cat died. Then my dog died. I was living a country-western song.

If I had had a truck, I'm sure that would have died, too!

Feeling devastated and overwhelmed by grief, I found myself front and center on a battlefield with my worst opponent – myself. The wolf sitting on my left shoulder wanted to be fed with sadness and anger. The wolf on my right shoulder did her best to interject constructive strategies and encouragement. But I kept feeding the wolf on the left.

As the song goes, *"I cried me a river"* with gut-wrenching sobs that took me to my knees. Whenever I was alone, I sobbed, which was fairly often; it lasted about two years. Two long years. Looking back, it's hard to conceive it took me that long to let go of the sorrow, but every one of those tears held a divine code that helped me release my greatest fears of abandonment, of being alone till the end of time. Picture the goddess Persephone, kidnapped into the underworld by Hades, separated from her mother and all that grows good on the upper earth. I related to the inconsolable Persephone, and like her, I ate the forbidden seed of regret, keeping me locked in the underground for an extended time until a deal could be negotiated between Hades and his brother, Zeus. Zeus was the ruling god of the Greeks and my Zeus was ruling me.

Soon after we buried my mother, I found myself begging God for some closure with my "Zeus". I missed him and the girls, even though the red warning flags appeared when he decided to go camping rather than attend my mother's funeral. Numb and hurt at the same time, I wasn't in my right mind and tried to hang onto something familiar. I was in the throes of a dark night, a spiritual crisis of faith and it hurt like bloody hell.

One particular day is etched clearly in memory. I was upset and sought comfort in the woods behind my house. Leaning into the great oak tree, nestled by the tranquil French Creek, I said a tearful prayer asking for resolution. Just then, my mobile rings. It's Zeus.

God always answers prayers. I just don't always like the outcome.

I answered the phone, expecting soft words to end our time together. Instead, he blurts out the fateful words popularized by the book by the same title, "I'm just not into you." Then he said something about the fun times we shared and asks if he can still call me and be friends. My body and mind are reeling. A ridiculous image comes to mind, not altogether surprising as I've taken classes in wielding the medieval broadsword, I envisioned the two of us on a battlefield. "What?! I don't think so," I say, as if waking from an alternative reality and feeling his sword strike me down. I fall to my knees, hugging the steadfast tree as if to regain strength. Pierced by yet another gripping blow. I return home to pen my wound into a poem.

Behind You
The battle cry comes too late
As the blade burns through my flesh.

I turn to fight back,
But my opponent is in flight,
Leaving me feeling unworthy.
As I tend to my wound, I see it's deep.
I can only hope it will heal with time.
Yet the scar will remain, along with the others,
A reminder of the warrior's brief presence in my life.

Words have impact. Sometimes we mess up and say something really stupid because we don't have compassion or empathy for what the other person is experiencing. For my dejected lover... Zeus, it was both. Perhaps those skills are occupational hazards for a military man who has succumbed to the emotional ravages of his own dark nights. Without making excuses for his lack of tenderness, I believed his intention was good; he wanted to be honest.

Still, my rational thinking was not helping my heart feel better. My inner child, now an orphan with my mother's passing, was deeply wounded. My heart expanded exponentially with agony. Women, especially sensitive and empathetic types like myself, have historically been the containers for men's emotions. We are the cup; men are the sword. Maybe I took that task on unconsciously, like an old code programmed deep into my cellular structure.

Around this time, I attended a Celtic Women's concert. Their song, A Woman's Heart, describes the universal affliction I was feeling. It's the suffering felt by women worldwide, past and present, for the wrongs caused against the collective human heart. Perhaps I even took on the wounds of Zeus himself, the man and the myth.

The next few years involved "friendly" conversations with Zeus and a few visits with his daughters. We never got back together, but I did foolishly answer his calls. I was trying to hold onto the past as if it would make everything in my life alright again.

As I continued exploring the lessons around our entanglement, I eventually told him to stop calling. I woke up the next morning to find a flat tire, defaced license plate and my name spray-painted on the sidewalk behind the house, spelled incorrectly. It had Zeus' signature all over it. He wanted me in his life on his terms, but I wasn't playing anymore. I was angered by his actions, yet smart enough not to fuel his warrior energy and declare war. His call to wish me a Happy Valentine's Day two weeks later went unanswered. The writing might not have been on a wall, but it was written on my sidewalk in gold spray paint.

My journey into becoming more empowered meant I needed to work through my feelings of rejection and abandonment. From outward appearances, the hurt was caused by him, but truly, I'm the one who had abandoned myself. I ignored my inner wisdom for far too long. My heart knew this to be true. My ego however, had a stronghold on my mind. I decided to make a powerful intention to create congruence between my head and my heart. I wanted to feel light again — to laugh and dance and feel whole.

Grief led me back to wholeness by providing an opportunity for growth with a spotlight on my badly damaged self-esteem. I had to do something constructive; I spent far too much time singing the same sad song. "What's wrong with me? Seriously, God, why is this happening TO me?" I journaled and prayed. I went to kickboxing classes and developed a killer right hook, propelled by my anger. I took exotic dance, salsa and swing classes to rediscover my feminine energy. I studied relationship theory and hired a coach. And then I did something that would truly ignite my life.

I enrolled in seminary to delve more deeply into the study of world religions and spirituality. This wasn't some 'out of the blue' action that showed up like a whim. I had the desire to become a minister for a few decades. Now it was time to fulfill my soul's contract, the unspoken agreement I had with myself. As Socrates said, "The unexamined life is not worth living." It was time to examine mine more deeply.

My defining wake-up call had arrived. These callings provide an opportunity to more fully awaken into our true purpose for living, our dharma. Each person is coded with their unique purpose before birth and that purpose is revealed through our life experiences and relationships. Soul friends, family and lovers often inspire us and help us feel connected and centered. Some appear as adversaries that disrupt our patterns. Some have an extended stay in our lives while others have an expiration date (like Zeus). We evolve through positivity AND emotional pain but, like a classical piece of music, it's the crescendo that fully warrants our attention.

I packed up my troubled heart and tissues and traveled by train to New York City for the first weekend intensive at One Spirit Learning Alliance. My diverse classmates came from various spiritual and religious traditions from all over the world.

The day opened with a song that cast light into my broken heart. The words spoke directly to my sins – meaning the mistakes and shortcomings that I've made. The song called I am Here, Lord, was written by the Jesuit priest Dan Shutte. In this sacred space with eighty new friends, we sang these words:

Here am I, Lord. Is it I, Lord?
I have heard you calling in the night.

We shared why we decided to become interfaith ministers. Some, like me, showed up with wounded hearts with the philosophical mindset of "heal thyself." Intuitively, we knew we had to do our inner work to be of greater service to others. The next two years were meaningful academically and spiritually. We studied world religions, philosophies and practiced an array of spiritual traditions and rituals. Through mentorship with deans and a willingness to be vulnerable, my heart healed. It was a time of soul integration... melding knowledge with wisdom to re-ignite my dharma to help spiritually curious individuals create greater connection and expression in their own lives.

I even took on a new name, a rebranding that brought me great joy. As is common in many spiritual traditions, a new name is chosen to mark the passage from one transitional stage to another. Claiming a new identity felt powerful and energizing and helped me validate who I am, why I'm here, and how I serve. One of my classmates, on learning about my name change, sent me a beautiful Jewish blessing that resonated deeply with my spirit:

"In life, you discover that people are called by three names: One is the name your parents call you; one is the name others call you, and one is the name you acquire for yourself. The best one is the one you acquire for yourself." (*Tanchuma, Vayak'heil 1*)

That helped me to embrace 'Allyne' and led to a rebirth, where, with the support of a loving community, I collected the fragmented pieces of my soul. I took a path, unique to me which helped me reclaim my divine feminine energy. I invite you to think about your dharma, your purpose for being here. Dare to ask yourself the most important questions a person can ponder: Who am I? Why am I here? What's next? Develop your ability to appreciate those who teach you the big soul lessons. Practice forgiveness. When you have trouble forgiving others, pray for the strength to find it. It lightens the heaviness you feel in your heart. This is what I did to move through my grief.

I also examined the vows I made with myself and others. It's a powerful practice with big impact. While sitting on the beach in Puerto Rico a fews years back, I decided to journal about the unspoken promises I made to Zeus. Listening to the rhythm of the ocean, I filled up the pages quickly as my thoughts poured into my notebook. When I felt complete, I glanced at my arms. To my surprise, tiny white feathers, a symbol of peace, were strewn all over my left arm! This miraculous coincidence was a confirmation that God was with me. It was an angelic applause for my efforts.

A year later, I penned brand new vows for my ordination ceremony:

> *I vow to live life as a great adventure with a heightened sense of awareness, appreciation and authentic love.*
> *I vow to be a light in this world, **fully ignited**, to dance with compassion, connection and clarity.*
> *I vow to allow the Creative force of God to expand in my life exponentially, to listen to divine wisdom and act accordingly.*

Now as a minister and soulcologist; an architect of the soul, I help curious people find answers to their biggest questions in life: who am I, what's my purpose and what's next? By helping people uncover their soul contracts, one lives more mindfully. The world needs us to let go of limited thinking in order to become better people and thrive. My work supports this journey on a deep level, with laughter and levity.

Now it's your turn. I invite you to create your own vows to support you in living your fullest life. Learn from the lessons and grow into your best self. I honor and support you.

Ignite Action Steps

Create Your Vows

Vows are promises we make with ourselves and others, spoken or unspoken. There are vows of love, poverty, celibacy; vows to protect, or vows to be loyal – no matter the situation. Vows support our sacred contracts. They can also disempower us if used unwisely or beyond the expiration date of our contract. Consider the promises you have made with a partner, family member or friend. Get a journal and start writing whatever comes to mind. Give yourself permission to break and/or create vows that support your dreams and nurture your soul

Allyne Henesey
Soulcologist (Spiritual Counselor and Coach)
The Soulcology Center / www.allynehenesey.com

ANDREA CAIRELLA

"A woman who honors her time, reclaims her power."

In my journey to be whole, live in integrity and be in alignment with myself, I had to consistently make time to nurture my heart, spirit, body and mind. In the sharing of my story, I want for you to trust yourself more and develop an inner wisdom to make intuitive decisions. This is easiest when we are open to receiving support and letting go of what no longer serves us. This also happens when we continually build in time to "be" and "enjoy" rather than "overdoing" it.

HARMONIZING AMBITION AND FLOW

At a very young age, my heart and soul were already yearning to be fully self-expressed, uninhibited and free. My mother and sister often recall how even at the wee age of fifteen months I was already wiggling my hips and shoulders to whatever music was playing on the radio.

Today, I tap my toes and move my hips in the kitchen with my own daughter, Mia. As we dance to the rhythm of upbeat musica latina. I am reminded of the importance of moving our bodies and and exposing ourselves to positive energy. In choosing to surround ourselves with high-vibrational people, places, situations and feelings our hearts and spirits can fully come alive.

If the title of my chapter *Harmonizing Ambition and Flow* caught your attention, your essence and spirit are likely filled with passion, ambition and drive. As well as a deep desire to add more grace, ease and flow in the personal and professional arenas of your life. Often times, as we are striving towards our goals and desires, we can constrict and become rigid in our bodies and minds. This patterned response unfortunately prevents the flow and ease from entering into your nervous system.

For instance, when you activate your sympathetic nervous system (e.g., the gas pedal) without utilizing the parasympathetic nervous system (e.g., the brakes) on a regular basis you can become overly-activated. This results in an accumulation of tension, anxiety and pressure in the body. Since the body is adaptive, if you choose to ignore the subtle signs of emotional and physical stress, your nervous system will continue to generously overwork itself even to its own demise. Neglecting time for periodic quiet reflection and postponing physical activity for yet another day, may seem innocent at first. However, when the habit of over "doing" it repeatedly takes precedence over "being" and "enjoying", it can lead to physical and mental health symptoms. The antidote is to wisely use your energy units in a conscious, intentional, pleasurable and impactful way, so you can create long-term vitality, inner peace and joy.

Another common tendency is to activate the sympathetic and parasympathetic nervous system simultaneously. This is the result of having a strong desire to take inspired action while also feeling fearful or unsure at the same time. It can feel as if you are stuck in the mud or attempting to go sixty miles an hour with your hand brake on. The frustration of taking one step forward and one step back can lead to over-excitability with no accessible outlet or a perpetual procrastination pattern and a weakened self-esteem. In order to break this cycle, it is important to disengage from the fears and insecurities of the mind and connect with the wisdom and intuition of the heart. Making decisions and taking action from this powerful place facilitates more ease and flow in work, love and life.

In my own life, there have been periods where I relied on my tenacity to move the needle forward in my professional career, instead of providing myself the intimate time and space to listen to the wise messages coming from my higher self. When we are disconnected from our intuition or ignore the whispers trying to get our attention, we can feel out of alignment, frustrated, anxious and stuck.

That happened to me after giving birth to my little girl Mia. I was feeling out of alignment spiritually, physically and emotionally. Simultaneously, I was navigating my new role as a mom, maintaining a loving relationship with my husband and running a successful psychotherapy practice. It was not an easy feat. Squeezing in a self-care routine between breastfeeding intervals, meal preparations, diaper changes and a full work-schedule made me no longer want to keep up with the unsustainable facade of being superwoman. However, choosing to slow down the pace didn't seem like a realistic option either.

I remember looking down at my watch striking 7:45 AM and realizing I only had 15 minutes to detach from my breast pump, clean up and drive 10 minutes down the road for my first client of the day. Imagine a woman seeing two clients back to back followed by a dash back home to pump again, feed her baby and grab a snack before rushing out the door to see another two clients before lunchtime. After three months of this unsustainable pace, I was left feeling exhausted and burned out on busy.

You don't need to be a mother to relate to this go-go-go storyline. In my case, perhaps in your life as well, there's an incessant feeling inside questioning the fast-paced rhythm. Have you grown accustomed to your pace? Is the method in which you work on projects still complimenting your current lifestyle and desires? My search to find clarity and answers began.

Forced to get intimate with the fertile void of stillness in the fourth trimester of motherhood, I began to evaluate my life priorities. I could no longer sustain all the things I did pre-motherhood. I looked at the need to shed tendencies no longer in alignment. I had to be more patient and be in the unknown questions of what to do next. At first, my mind and ego felt restless and unsettled. However, as I refocused on the present moment, the constriction in my heart and throat started to dissipate. My breath steadied and slowed. Over the course of several months, I stayed open and receptive to guidance and intuitive suggestions which serendipitously presented themselves to me.

I was feeling burned out on busy. Operating at maximum speed, running around in various directions and checking off the tasks on my never-ending to-do list. I had graduated to the point of numbing-out, eyes glazed over from the mounting internal and external pressures which existed in my world.

This pattern of perfectionism, people pleasing and workaholism on one extreme and procrastination and disconnection on the other hand were unhealthy coping mechanisms that didn't serve me. These habits were driven because I had received positive results from operating at that level. But more importantly I had learned in my childhood that working hard is a vital and imperative quality to succeed. In order to be seen, recognized and valued, I needed to prove my worth.

For Type A achievers like me, there are several internal and external motives that contribute to the destructive cycle of perfectionism and procrastination. Perfectionism is a strategy to prevent feelings of shame and unworthiness as a result of performing below your personal standards or the expectations of others. Procrastination is a habitual delay of starting or finishing a task that seems risky in nature despite the negative consequences that ensue from avoidance. Each of these habits attempts to protect your ego from feelings of inadequacy. That was me.

Like many working mothers trying to do it all, I was in the initial stages of fine-tuning my messaging for my online business. I recall spending several hours every week filming and perfecting my educational videos. I'd create a script and rehearse, then set up the equipment and film each segment several times. Next, I'd select the versions to use for the final cut, email the editing notes to my editor and review for final approval. This entire process would take me a grueling one to three hours per five minute video. It was painstaking. Rather than enjoying the pleasurable, free-flow process, I was more obsessed with implementing technical marketing strategies. It was driving me crazy.

After four concerted attempts to record my three-minute speaker proposal for the 2017 California Women's Conference using that stifling strategy, I had "zip, zero, zlitch." Each time I tried to improve the previous version, the next take became more constrictive, choppy and contrived. With my arms surrendering in the air, followed by my hands attempting an emergency landing on my head, I exclaimed in an exasperated tone, "There must be an easier way."

Closing my eyes, I covered them with the palms of my hands. I prayed softly and humbly, "God, Source, Universe, I let go. Please lead the way". I allowed the words to flow from me easily and effortlessly so that my heart and soul could speak the truth and deliver the message these women needed to hear from my video. "I am open and ready," I told myself and surrendered to letting go of the way I had been forcing it to be.

After a few moments, a wave of peace poured over me and a rooted groundedness developed on the soles of my feet. I took a few deep breaths to deepen my connection with the sensations I was feeling in my body. When I opened my eyes, a cloud of whiteness and brightness surrounded the upper half of my body. I took another deep inhalation and exhalation, knowing I was ready to speak authentically from my heart – even if it felt vulnerable, imperfect and raw. In one take, the message came through in just under three minutes. At 9 PM wearing no makeup, my hair frazzled from a full day of activity and the lack of video lighting, I uploaded the file without hesitation and hit "send." The following week I received an email saying,

"Congratulations! You have been selected as one of the top 20 candidates to compete in the finals of the California Women's Conference 2017 Speak Off Competition!"

In awe of this miraculous process, I increased my trust in flow, set my inner guidance system to lead the way and asked the collective consciousness of the Universe to open up the doors for me. In the stillness, something miraculous happened. I began to hear the whispers of my heart and soul both nudging me forward subtly in the right direction. Happily, I was one of the top three candidates to share my message on the main stage before a group of purpose-driven and conscious-centered leaders. I know in my heart and soul I didn't get there alone. This experience taught me that relying solely on strategy, hard work and perfection was stifling my access to this joyful and wise co-creative process. In order to inspire and more effectively connect with my audience, I began trusting my heart to know what to say – my soul to lead the way.

During this time, my body was urging me to get physically active in order to receive clear guidance, true wisdom and direction. I attended an Elevate Your Energy class at my gym, which is not your typical exercise class. The uplifting high-vibe music inspired me to intuitively start to lift my feet, clap my hands and sway my hips without any prompting from the instructor. Upon each exhalation the instructor encouraged us to exclaim a guttural "Ha" with the intention of releasing all the pent-up tension and energy stored in our precious bodies. Through a combination of high-vibe repetitive cardio movements, empowering music and intentional affirmations from the instructor, all the old energy began melting away from my shoulders, face and legs. I felt reinvigorated, fabulous and free.

Twenty minutes into my first class, a continual positive flow of energy danced throughout my veins. A tidal wave of creativity followed viscerally liting up my spirit. And inspirational downloads in the form of stories, images, phrases and ideas filled my heart and expanded my mind. I realized this was similar to the intuitive insights I receive when working with my clients. In this case there was an internal nudging to get these ideas down on paper to share it with the masses instead of simply one-on-one. My desire for more women to tap into their true authentic power prompted me into action.

Instead of relying on the old way: *push, strive, perfect,* as my only tools to achieve success, I began trusting the creative process to lead the way. I remained receptive and attentive to the ideas and wisdom moving through me. What I realized throughout this graceful process is the amount of productive ease and joy I experienced.

As a busy entrepreneur, creative, wife and mother of a fifteen-month-old, I was initially struggling to find the currency of time to dedicate to writing and preparing speeches. Initially I decided to take one week off of work at the end of each month to write my book but I found that this didn't allow me to stay in a natural and creative workflow, so I changed my strategy.

Since my dedicated childcare coverage was only available Tuesday through Thursday, I decided to use the resource of the childcare services at my gym on Mondays, Fridays and Saturdays, two hours at a time, to creatively carve out the needed time to write.

Over the course of nine months, in those two-hour time-slots, I would commit to working out for thirty minutes and then manually writing the book for one and a half hours in the women's locker room. Imagine several women wearing robes and towels periodically blow-drying their hair as I diligently wrote in the far corner of an area dedicated to makeup application. Curious observers would often say, "You look really focused" or ask, "What are you writing?" Filled with inspiration, passion and flow, I shared I was writing a book called *No Longer Burned Out On Busy: A Woman's Guide to Harmonizing Ambition and Flow*. The typical response that followed was a breath... and a sigh..., "Oh, I need to read that."

Throughout the writing process, I committed to the practice of harmonizing ambition and flow in my own life. This allowed me to pursue my passion to share while not sacrificing my well-being in the process. Just so you are not under any false pretenses, harmonizing ambition and flow is not a one-and-done mastery course. Your work-life balance journey is an ongoing practice and skill set you will develop and cultivate over time. As you grow your practices, strategies will evolve with you according to the circumstances you are navigating at the time.

Imagine how connecting with the sacred stillness and fostering an intimate relationship with your heart and soul could bring more magic and beauty into your life song. The power of the pause between the music notes is just as significant as the notes themselves. Allowing grace and flow to support you as a leader, helps light you up. You are capable of making an impact and positive difference in the world, without burning yourself out in the process.

IGNITE ACTION STEPS

DISCLAIMER FOR AMBITIOUS WOMEN: Depending on what responsibilities, life events or challenges you are facing in your life, your range is going to fluctuate so don't "should" all over yourself if life gets a little crazy. You will still have moments when things go awry, life doesn't go according to plan and your inner critic won't leave you alone. If you are unable to channel your inner Dali Lama 24/7, don't lose heart. Here are some action steps to help keep you on track.

Step 1: Identify and let go of patterns which no longer serve you: You can identify your ineffective behavioral patterns using a stream of consciousness journaling method. This is simply brain dumping your thoughts on a piece of paper. Next, you surrender and open yourself up to assistance and support of the highest light and love. You then exclaim aloud, *"Please help me remove _____, which is no longer serving me. I am open and receptive to guidance, direction and support."*

Step 2: Connect with your heart and soul: You can connect with your heart and soul through your breath in just 2 minutes. Begin by touching your heart and breathing in from the pads of your feet up into your heart space for 30 seconds. Become grateful for the beating of your heart. Next, focus on two memories in which you feel grateful. Take several slow and steady breaths to allow the love and joy to flow into your heart for 30 seconds per memory. For the last 30 seconds breathe in gratitude for a serendipitous moment in which you felt awe and inspired. Notice yourself shift out of ego and into your heart and soul.

Step 3: Developing Your Intuition and Deepening Self-Trust: You can develop your intuition by remaining receptive to support and guidance from your inner wisdom, nature, spirit, source, etc. Build in time daily to "be" through meditation, stream of consciousness journaling, physical movement, chanting, heart centered connection and sourcing energy practices. It is also important to build in time to "enjoy" through play, pleasure and joyful activities. You can visit www.AndreaCairella.com for free training videos and audio recordings on how to develop your intuition and create more flow in work, love and life.

Andrea Cairella
Leadership Consultant, Andrea Cairella International
AndreaCairella.com

JOANNA MERCADO PETERS

"Princess Warrior: YOU have magic inside of you… You just need to remember to pay attention and let your magic shine!"

I am sharing my story to inspire you to connect with your magnificence and let it light your path and the path of the ones around you! Tapping into your own magic will allow you to create the life of your dreams.

FROM "NOT BEING ENOUGH" TO BEING AN EXTRAORDINARY LEADER

The only thing I was able to think was, "Please don't cry, please don't let him see you cry," as the room full of people kept staring at me. My hands balled into fists feeling my fingernails almost cutting into the palms of my hands. How did I get here?

I fought with the belief that I was not enough since I was seven or eight years old. I remember coming home from school with my report-card, excited and proud to show it to my dad. Based on my teacher's feedback, I was doing a great job.

I can still hear my dad's voice looking over the report, handing it back to me saying, "This is your job, the only thing you have to do is study and get good grades." What I heard instead was, "This is not a big deal. It's not enough for me to be proud of you."

At school the next day, I saw one of my friends playing with a Hot Wheels car his dad gave him to reward his efforts and grades. My friend Annie savouring in recall, how huge and delicious the ice cream cone was that her dad bought her the night before, also to celebrate her good grades. I felt pain in my chest, "Why didn't my dad buy me a treat? Why was my dad not proud of me? I needed to try harder, so my hero (my father) would be proud of me like my friends' parents were proud of them."

I did. I tried so hard and finally the next report card came. I went home and the minutes could not go fast enough. I stared at the clock waiting for the hand to reach 5:00 when my dad would arrive from work. When I heard him coming, I ran to my backpack and pulled out my report card, confident that this time the grades were what he was expecting. He looked over the report and without any positive emotions, returned the card to me saying the same excruciatingly painful words I feared the most. "This is your job, the only thing you have to do is study and get good grades."

Little did I know back then, that I was already getting the highest grades possible. Without that knowledge, I kept trying harder and harder, looking for his recognition and positive reinforcement. When that never came, I assumed I was 'not good enough'. No matter how much I tried, I was never 'enough' for my dad, I was not able to make my hero proud of me. That was a feeling that had been with me the majority of my life.

Moving forward almost 20 years, I was living a life full of accomplishments. I was on the right path, working for a Fortune 500 company, getting promotions and opportunities everywhere.

It was the beginning of 2009, when my boss shared that the VP of Operations for Latin America was going to visit our plant at the end of May. We had to prepare a facility tour for him and each of us was to prepare a presentation of our projects.

I still remember how excited I was; I worked for hours and hours on my product review presentation. I would leave work thinking it over, rehearsing the presentation in my head as I traveled across town to my house. There, I would keep working on the print copies I brought home with me. I was obsessed with flushing out every possible error and targeting perfection. I wanted with all my heart to have an intelligent overview, to make a good impression and show him my potential. I was unconsciously trying to get that 'I am proud of you' I searched my entire childhood for, from another male authority figure.

The day finally arrived, I was ready, my presentation was done. That morning I wore my most girly outfit. I put on makeup, a very feminine perfume and safety-approved jewelry as the final touch.

I remember waiting for everybody else to present and thinking he was a tough manager. His face unreadable. Nothing much more than a slight frown, even when other managers smiled or interacted with the other presenters. When it was finally my turn, the last presentation of the day, my heart beating fast, I stood, walked to the front of the room and gave my review the best possible way I could.

He did not even let me finish when he lost his temper and started ridiculing my presentation and criticizing me. He went on and on. I still remember him at the head of the room smacking his fist on the boardroom table, saying: "This is the most mediocre presentation I ever saw in my life."

My hands balled in fists; my fingernails cut into my palms. As I tried to breathe deeply, calling upon my best effort to not cry in front of him, I felt the heat in my face rising. The thought of my face turning bright red scared me even more. Suspecting he and everybody else would notice how affected I was with his reaction – was devastating.

All the feelings of 'I am not enough' were rushing through my mind, questioning if I was even a decent professional and if I would ever have a chance to grow my career. I remember thinking, that once again I tried my best. I gave 500% of me and that was not only 'not enough' but now was also a 'mediocre presentation'. I was crushed.

My boss at the back of the room behind him, was trying to calm me down as best as he could with hand signals, as he knew how frustrated I was. One thing you don't know about me yet, is that I cry when I am really sad AND when I am really angry or frustrated. That day I was both: because 1.) I was reliving that memory of never being enough, no matter how much I tried and 2.) I knew my presentation was not perfect; but I also knew it was not that horrible.

The meeting lasted another 15 minutes but I felt like it was 20 hours. I am proud to say 'I did not cry' in front of him and as soon as he dismissed us, I ran into my boss' office for a bit of privacy and leaned over his desk and sobbed. My boss and a couple of coworkers rushed into the office and calmed me down. My boss then explained what he should have explained ahead of time: this VP of a multinational company was well known for hating women. He believed that women belong in either the kitchen or the laundry room.

As I listened to my boss and tried to soothe myself. I started feeling disappointed as well as angry. I was hurting inside. I was upset with the 'Let's hate woman' guy and also deeply disappointed that neither my boss nor any other leader in the room – spoke up. They all were so afraid and worried about their own careers, that none of them had the courage to do what was right – stand up and stop the verbal abuse.

The following weeks passed fast. I remember waking up to my 5:30 alarm and desiring to roll over and cover myself with my blankets. I was ready to do or give whatever it took to not go back to work. I was so scared and hurt. I felt insecure and vulnerable. I felt like a failure. I still remember myself walking throughout the factory when I made one of the most critical decisions that impacted my life going forward: I was not willing to give others the power to decide if I was enough or not anymore. I started my journey of changing my beliefs and accepting that I AM enough. As I searched for help, I read, listened and watched every book available in the self-help and self-improvement sections of my mom's personal library and also bookstores. Each new concept, each new exercise, each new word helped me to build my self-esteem.

My confidence and capacity to believe in myself grew stronger quickly. I made many changes as a person and one in particular impacted my career: I decided, one way to 'be enough' for myself while working – was to be an extraordinary leader. This way I would ensure that I will never do something like that to anyone I worked with. Also, I told myself that I would inspire others to become better leaders themselves in the hopes that they will never do it either.

My journey to discover what it meant to be an extraordinary leader began by learning the right skills to grow myself while also learning how to help others. Once again, I found comfort in the infinite ocean of knowledge that we have at our fingertips. I studied, read and researched as many leadership books, cases and interviews I was able to find. That increased my rational intelligence about leadership. My emotional intelligence decided to follow my heart. One thing I had clear deep inside of me, was that an extraordinary leader focuses on developing others and letting her team glow and shine.

A few years later I found one of the most effective tools on my quest. I was attending a training and was blown away with the presentation of John Stoner (President: Biller Solutions) on his 'Leadership Philosophy'. As John presented the final product, I realized it was everything I was looking for and it made all the sense in the world. After that presentation, I started working on 'my leadership philosophy', developing and creating my own framework – the 'how' to get there.

Over the ensuing months, I crafted the kind of leader I wanted to be. I was fortunate enough to have the influence of remarkable leaders in my career, leaders that showed me the real meaning of caring and developing. I also was blessed to have several poor managers that kindly taught me the things I wanted to avoid in my leadership style. Yes, you heard me right, I am grateful for each and every single one of them. (I go a little deeper into how the dots always connect backwards in my chapter titled: *Finding Myself In A New World* in the book *Ignite Your Life for Women*.)

It took me several drafts to hone my personal philosophy on leadership into a decent version. One that contained all the things I learned and admired from others, along with the things I felt in my heart were important for me as a woman. When it was finally ready, I clicked 'print'. I remember staring at the pages in my hand, feeling fear about sharing it with others. "What if it was not good enough? What if they did not like it? What if I failed to be that role model and I was exposed and recognized as a fraud?" The 'what-ifs' haunted me, to a point that I put my *Leadership Philosophy* back in a drawer, hiding it from the world. It took me several weeks more, to remember my conviction to 'never ever let others decide if I was enough'.

One morning at work, I decided to read my leadership philosophy again, this time out loud, while listening to my inner voice. That voice was *yelling that I was 'enough'* and my creation was strong proof of that. I felt proud. In my heart I knew that those words represented the leader I wanted to be and were a clear reflection of an exceptional one. At that moment, after having the printed copy in my drawer for weeks, I signed it with a bright-pink unicorn pen and gave it to the members of my team.

When I share my Leadership Philosophy, I always follow the same steps I did that first time. I hand them the one-page-manifesto which I have personally signed at the bottom, explaining that this is the kind of leader I want to be. I reinforce how much I need and appreciate honest and sincere feedback to help me to be that kind of individual. Lastly, I give them my authorization and set an 'open door' invitation to call me out, if I ever drift away from my commitment. I am aware that during times of high levels of stress, I may start moving in a direction that is not aligned with my leadership vision and I want to know I have people around me that feel comfortable to call me out and help me to get back on track.

I still remember how great it felt to hear their feedback, the warmth in my heart and the joy when I heard word by word their thoughts. Their reaction was beyond what I ever expected. They were grateful and touched by this manifesto and my honest vulnerability to express who I was and who I want to become. They encouraged me to keep sharing and gave me some valuable feedback.

Since that day, the outcome and results have been beyond magnificent. Sharing my *Leadership Philosophy*, first and most importantly, keeps me accountable and true to my daily efforts to be an extraordinary leader. It also creates clear expectations and boundaries in regard to how I work and what is non-negotiable in my leadership vision. I have printed and framed my *Leadership Philosophy* in my office as a daily reminder that I am committed to work continuously to become an extraordinary leader and also as a soft whisper that reminds me I AM ENOUGH; that I have everything inside of me to get wherever I want to go. Looking at that printed page, I am able to see and remember my journey and reinforce the wonderful path I am on.

One of the most magical outcomes of this journey is knowing I am inspiring others to write their own leadership philosophies and move to take action. I have been sharing my story and my Leadership Philosophy for five years now and touched hundreds of people directly. I've been invited to give workshops sharing the framework on how to build your Leadership Philosophy and how to use it to create your unique brand in companies like PepsiCo and universities like Purdue.

I have had the opportunity to travel around the world sharing my knowledge, coaching teams and leaders to become better versions of themselves. I was part of the team that built a facility in China from the ground up. I was transferred to the United States where I met my soulmate. I am living the life of my dreams and a big part of that is because I know the kind of leader I strive to be every day.

What I have learned in the past five years is that childhood beliefs can chase us through our life in an unconscious way. It is almost as if the biggest and ugliest monster in our closets stays there and lives with us for the rest of our lives. Every night, the monster will get out and remind us that it is still there, scaring us, making us fall asleep in tears, feeling unsafe and fearful. That monster is our childhood beliefs. We need to do the work to clear those beliefs and set us free to shine our own light. We need to plan an adventure into the closet with a flashlight, cape and anti-monster spray. Face the monster, destroy it and make it vanish from our closet and our life forever.

I have also learned that there is not one magical recipe to becoming an extraordinary leader – it is not a magical recipe to eliminate poor beliefs. It is a matter of tuning inwards, listening to your heart and combining that with the external lessons you learn throughout your life. Part of being an extraordinary leader is being authentic and faithful to who 'you really are'. You decide the ingredients of your recipe for life and have the tools to create your own masterpiece.

IGNITE ACTION STEPS

You can create your own Leadership Philosophy as well. Here are some steps you can take to start your journey to becoming an extraordinary leader right now:

- Define who you are. (Try to not use qualifications or titles, instead use the traits that define you as a person. For example, funny, smart, caring…)
- Create a list remembering the things that make you happy: what really makes your heart fill with joy and warmth. (My list includes helping others, traveling, making others smile…)
- List your values and your current priorities.
- Research and find the common traits in the leaders that inspire you throughout your life.
- Combine all the above into your first Leadership Philosophy draft.
- Share your Leadership Philosophy with others: your team, your boss, your peers, your spouse, your children. (I share mine with every person I work directly or indirectly with.)
- Ask for feedback and have an 'open door' approach to welcome opportunities for improvement and callouts when you are not walking your talk.

The wonderful thing about this leadership tool is that it can be used and applied to any scenario. You can create and apply this philosophy at work, at home, with your friends, with your spouse or as a volunteer. Any activities where you interact with others are great opportunities to practice, to become the extraordinary leader you already are inside.

I want to say THANK YOU, to some of the wonderful leaders that directly touched my life: my parents José and María, Cesar Silva, Jeff Newman, Tim Donnelly, Alfredo Gamboa and Eric Edmeades – for planting and watering the seed in my heart of servant leadership and inspiring me to be extraordinary.

Joanna Mercado Peters
HPCO (Happiness and Purpose Chief Officer) of Namasarte, Leadership,
Strategy and Corporate Mindfulness. Yoga (Mat & Aerial) and Reiki
practitioner. Namasarte LLC, Joanna Mercado Speaks
www.joannamercado.com

Dr. Judy Gianni

"Look to your history to point to the clues leading
to your life mission."

By sharing my life-path and evolution, it guided me to fully express my-self as a healer and entrepreneur. I hope you, the reader, may see clues in your own timeline and history. Those clues might point you towards the fullest, most authentic expression in your life's work. If you can find your passion and calling, you can find true satisfaction.

The Evolution

"Mom, I have a sore throat… again!" I'd share. Off we went to the doctor for another round of antibiotics doled out for every sniffle, fever or earache. Multiple times a year throughout my whole childhood, this was the pattern. At puberty, acne attacked with a vengeance and off to the dermatologist I went for even more antibiotics and that continued from sixth grade through all of high school.

I was misdiagnosed with strep at 14, when actually suffering from a viral infection (mononucleosis). Doctors prescribed three courses of antibiotics over a six week period. It was the '60s and my mom smoked incessantly in the house so my respiratory system didn't have a chance. By the time I was 18, I had chronic yeast issues, my digestive system was a wreck from nearly obliterated gut flora from the incessant antibiotics, I was riddled with debilitating headaches, I had arthritis in my hip and reactive airway disease. Walking into a room with smokers, my lungs would seize up. I couldn't breathe and I'd cough in spasms nearly turning blue. I was so prone to hypoglycemia; if a meal was skipped or delayed, I would slur my words and bump into walls. I also suffered from debilitating PMS. Between unstable hormones and fluctuating blood sugar levels, I was often on an emotional rollercoaster that to me felt completely real, when in fact, I was being betrayed by my own physiology.

During my senior year of high school, my boyfriend's mother, who referred to herself as a 'health nut', saw how I suffered and offered to loan me some of her health books.

Adele Davis was the nutritional guru in those days and I read everything she wrote. First, I eliminated all the sugar and then took B complex for my energy and chromium to stabilize my blood sugar. Adele Davis supported consuming lots of dairy (ie. cow's milk products) so I drank milk (which I always hated), ate yogurt and cheese. Some things were improving, though I was still struggling.

I started college sickly, spending most of my time in my dorm room trying to recover. A miserable case of bronchitis lasted several months. I now know this was my 'rock bottom'. Things were about to change dramatically. Love and Serve, a small health food café at my college espoused the value of eating healthy vegan food, yoga and meditation. Thrilled to work there, doing food prep, I mixed up vats of homemade tahini salad dressing. I mentioned my lung issues to my coworker. Russ asked me if I was eating dairy and told me to stop immediately. Within 10 days I could breathe with ease. I began to thrive with this healthy lifestyle and spiritual growth. All my lingering health concerns disappeared.

I called my mother, excited to share how simply eliminating dairy products made my respiratory issues disappear. She said, "That's interesting. We had to switch your infant formula when you were allergic to dairy!" (That would have been useful to know!).

No surprise I leaned into natural healing. I read my first book on juicing at nine! My paternal Italian grandmother had a 1946 copy of Fruits and Vegetable Juices by Dr. Norman Walker. I read it cover to cover. "This guy thinks carrot juice can cure everything!" He piqued my curiosity and I wanted more. My grandmother made me celery juice and taught me about herbs in the wild.

The next year, I read You Are What You Eat. My dad also grew interested in reading books on vitamins and nutrition. Inspired by reading Confessions of a Sneaky Organic Cook, in the early 70's, he started sprouting. My sisters turned their noses up at the wee vitamin-packed alfalfa and bean sprouts. I loved them. I was daddy's girl. The youngest of three, this became our thing and I was happy to grow this shared interest.

As a teenager, I'd beg my dad to take me to health food stores. I could stare endlessly at vitamins and minerals and odd-looking dried berries and herbs. The summer of my 18th year, while reading Back to Eden, a complete compendium of herbs and their uses, I committed to memory the common and Latin names of over 200 herbs and their medicinal properties, while my friends were only interested in boys and parties!

My mother's approach to daily living differed so radically from my father's and I could observe the contrast readily. Raised as a city girl, in Bridgeport, Connecticut, she put her faith in modern medicine. She drank, smoked, never exercised, didn't have the best dietary habits and was overweight. My maternal grandmother showed love by plying us with candy; she had a dresser drawer full of every candy imaginable. If we were 'good', we were granted a visit to the drawer, our eyes wide open scanning the collection as we chose our treat.

My dad, born at home, to two Italian immigrant parents, worked the family farm in Fairfield, Connecticut with massive gardens, chickens and a cow. He had a love for nature and a respect for the natural cadence of life. That side of the family enjoyed tremendous longevity, most living to their late 90's to 100+.

In high school, I became quite interested in psychology, meditation, personal growth and yoga. I discovered a real knack for listening to others. For a career, I wanted to help people with personal and emotional issues AND address their physical health. I would say, "If I am treating a patient for psychological reasons and their issue stemmed from something physical, I would be doing a big disservice to just approach it from a counseling standpoint." Pretty insightful for 17, but it reflected the budding integrative perspective that serves me today.

The summer after I graduated high school, a weekend seminar was given on herbs, vitamins and color therapy by a representative of a small naturopathic school in the Midwest. I was the youngest in a class of about a dozen people. I decided then and there I wanted to become a naturopathic physician.

My second year of college, I moved to Tucson, Arizona to attend university there. I started out in the nutrition program but I was completely disillusioned by their rigid approach. Why were we talking about the four food groups and meat cuts and the RDA?! I switched to pre-med studies.

My side job was doing colon hydrotherapy sessions in a natural healing clinic. I watched people turn their health around using the principles of detoxification and cleansing.

Married at 22, I had two children in quick succession but found myself divorced at 26. It was his clinic, so I was out of a job. At our clinic, we used to sell the herbal supplements of a well-known national company, purchased from an older gentleman. We always told him, "If you ever want to sell your business, come to us first." Shortly after our divorce, he came to my ex-husband with an offer for sale. As I was a single mom with two young children to provide for, my ex-husband directed him to me,(he wasn't big on the child support thing). But the parent company, was also not so keen on me.

As I spoke to the national sales director, he explained to me they no longer used small distributors. I begged him for a chance. He asked about my business experience. Though not very impressive to him, he relented due to my sheer enthusiasm. Borrowing $8000 from my father to purchase the initial products, I opened my company, Desert Mountain Herbals. Most of the local health food stores were buying their herbs from a big distribution company out of Phoenix.

To grow my business, I started a monthly newsletter called Desert Mountain News. I learned to set up the graphics and wrote all the articles on herbal healing and included healthy recipes. I provided my accounts a stack of newsletters also promising to inventory their shelves and train their employees about herbs. I soon started picking up accounts in multiple smaller southwest towns. As my business grew, I hired a full-time packer and shipper and a receptionist for the phones. As a single mom, I'd often put my toddler in a child's hiking backpack and head out to take my orders. I was a novelty!

I was relentless on the phone calling my accounts and telling them of the latest specials, extricating orders out of them knowing full well they could just as easily (or more easily) order from my competitor. But I just kept on showing up, interacting with the employees, making relationships with the managers and my business grew. The parent company started flying me to different cities to lecture on herbs. The hours were long and it was satisfying but my heart was longing to go to naturopathic school so I could live out my dream. I just was not sure how I was going to make this happen.

The 'way' appeared when after four years of tremendous growth for Desert Mountain Herbals, executives from the herbal company approached me. They said they were tired of hearing their major distributor complaining about "the little distributor with the baby strapped to her hip" and told them, "If it bothers you so much, why don't you just offer to buy her out?" The very next week, they sent their vice-president to Tucson to negotiate with me.

Realizing I was dealing with the big leagues, I had to position my humble company to appear more impressive. I rented a chic glass table for my previously nearly empty conference room, some artwork and plants and hired my 16-year-old babysitter to dress up and sit behind a desk to be our welcoming receptionist! An hour into the meeting, we shook hands on the sale of my business. I was able to pay my father back his initial investment and I had the funds to attend naturopathic school. Part of my agreement with the parent company was to become their sales rep for two years, but after over a decade of deferring my calling, I started to doubt I would ever achieve my dream. I had two small children. I had remarried and he had children, too. The move to Seattle to attend school seemed almost insurmountable at the time. The expensive legal and custody logistics with my children's dad threatened to snuff the whole dream out in a flash, but my drive was bigger than that. After one year as a sales representative , I couldn't put it off anymore. I left Arizona and headed to Washington to attend Bastyr University.

Whenever additional expenses came up, I utilized my creativity to avoid student loans. I noticed immediately the colon hydrotherapy equipment in our school clinic was very antiquated. So I contacted a manufacturing company and told them that they needed to donate a piece of their equipment and support the naturopathic profession. They told me they had tried many times before only to face roadblocks. I offered to negotiate for them and all I asked in return was a machine for half price. They agreed and I started a small part-time colon hydrotherapy practice.

For book expenses, I hatched another plan. I noticed many of the students did not know about the high quality herbs I had sold in the past. In the cadaver lab, students were exposed to really strong toxic smells of formaldehyde causing headaches, blurry vision and burning eyes. I told the herbal company that I would like them to supply the students with samples of high quality milk thistle to protect them from chemical insult. I became the first student representative getting a monthly check. When my last school bill was due, I sold my colon hydrotherapy practice to a local Seattle doctor and this made my final tuition payment.

School was the hardest work and biggest goal I ever achieved in my life. It was grueling and challenging on every level but I loved it. Despite giving birth to my third child three days short of commencement, I graduated. Studying for the medical board exams with a brand new infant and a sleep deprived brain, I still managed to ace my exams. I returned to Arizona to practice as a naturopathic physician.

Other opportunities and synchronicities continued to shape my career. In the early 2000s, while about to board a plane for a conference, the airline's computer system went down and they announced it was going to be open seating. As I entered the plane, walking slowly behind the line of people, every window and aisle seat was filling up, leaving the often unwanted middle seats behind. I looked up to my left and sitting in a window seat was a familiar face. It was the most famous alternative medicine practitioner, Dr. Andrew Weil, or a very close twin! Andrew Weil is the founder of the Program in Integrative Medicine at the University of Arizona, the author of many books on alternative medicine and internationally known for his contributions in natural and integrative medicine. I nervously waited for everyone to find their seats and luckily fate and the normal disdain for middle seats allowed me to nab the seat next to him. I still wasn't 100% sure it was him. He had the characteristic bald head, salt and pepper beard, but when I peeked at the medical journal he was reading, I knew! I exclaimed to him "Ah, you're busted! I know who you are!" and introduced myself. We talked non-stop about natural medicine the whole flight. He then told me that his team was looking for a naturopathic doctor to participate in weekly case conferences in order to mentor and teach the fellows in his program, training medical doctors in both natural and alternative medicine. If I was interested, I could start right away. Done!

I worked as the naturopathic preceptor of the Program in Integrative Medicine at the University of Arizona for the next three years, going over patient cases with a whole team of natural medicine providers including a homeopath, an osteopath, an acupuncturist, a pharmacist, an energy healer, a stress management psychologist and often rotating guest doctors and healers that would fly in to experience this unique, pivotal way of approaching patient cases. I continue to this day to allow doctors from this and other programs to observe in my office and occasionally still teach for this program.

I had another huge opportunity to work collaboratively with a team, when in 2010, I was asked to work part time at Sierra Tucson, a well known high-end inpatient treatment center for addictions, mood disorders, chronic pain, trauma and eating disorders. Here, I worked as part of the integrative medicine team to assist patients in their recovery. I had a wonderful opportunity to apply what I had learned about the mind-body connection, being able to relate to it personally from the time when I was sick as a teenager and my biochemistry was creating instability for my own mood and well-being.

I believe every challenge I have faced, every struggle, every painful lesson and every triumphant breakthrough in my life makes me a better doctor. I never forgot what it felt like to be so vulnerable when I was sick.

I learned to work collaboratively with conventional medical doctors and due to the supportive laws in Arizona, I'm able to practice integratively. If someone needs an antibiotic, I can prescribe one, but I always like to first choose a natural healing and body, mind and spirit approach.

In retrospect, I can see the beauty of how all my past experiences, good and bad all led to where I am today: A naturopathic physician, who uses diet, herbs, vitamins, cleansing and detoxification alongside with emotional counseling and coaching and incorporating personal growth and spirituality. My deep empathy came out of my own struggles with my health issues and I can convey my faith in people's ability to heal.

IGNITE ACTION STEPS

Enjoy the process and try these very powerful but simple steps.

• Find your passion, bring your unique qualities and you to your life's work. Your personal history holds the clues to these questions.

• Journaling can be one of the most powerful tools in having a breakthrough and gain clarity on your direction in life. Take time each morning on asking yourself questions and giving yourself time to dig deep for answers.

• Start by asking: "What captivated me?" "What brought me joy or made me stop?" Validate yourself: "I have a knack for this!" Write down your qualities, interests and talents even if they seem divergent.

• Then ask yourself: "How can I weave these qualities and points of joy into my work expression?" "Can this bring me to a new career path?"

• Write down your personal story as a journey. Look for the common themes. It will give you clues where your genius and passion lies.

Dr. Judy Gianni, Naturopathic Physician
www.naturemedica.net

JUDY LYNN SUTTON

"Our circumstances do not define who we are. They are a stepping stone to get to where we are meant to be."

I hope that my story touches those who really need to hear it, someone who may have had their own health scare or is living with someone who has had health issues. Maybe you are stuck and need that extra push to do what YOU really want. No matter what we are going through, remember that however dark it feels, tomorrow is a brand new day. Hold on to that and keep going. Don't give up on the things you want out of this life. If I can do it, I know that you can too!

JOURNEY TO LIVING MY BEST LIFE

I have your typical story: girl meets boy at a bar, girl dates boy for a couple years enjoying social drinks with friends in their early 20's. They get married, girl puts her glass away when she is pregnant with their first child. They have their second daughter a few years later. They live happily ever after – or do they...?

I was working in the childcare profession prior to meeting my husband and continued into our marriage until I had our first daughter. Then, I had a home childcare program and did that for six years before packing up and moving across the country for my husband's job. At the time my daughters were three and six and because all my family was near us, I honestly thought about staying, "He can move, but I'll stay here." I asked myself, "Could I do that? How would the girls see their Dad? Oh, I couldn't do that," I told myself, but I really wanted to. Instead, I was the good wife and packed up the family, sold the house and left everyone we ever knew, to move to a small town in western Canada, where I didn't know a single person. I was terrified and sobbed uncontrollably as we drove away from our eastern Canada home in northwestern Ontario. I really didn't want to go.

There was already some distance between my husband and I. Maybe the move and taking on this new adventure would bring us closer together – or maybe it wouldn't...

This can be such a challenge for any family and ours was no exception. It was extremely hard to adjust. We went from having friends and family visiting all the time, to silence, with just the four of us. I can remember the service guy coming to set up our internet and the girls insisted on showing him their rooms! They had no one else to share it with. Thankfully, he had young children himself and thought it was very sweet.

Our first Christmas, I never felt so alone in my life; I sobbed those big ugly crocodile tears as all I wanted was to be close to those who loved us. All I did was grieve. The girls took it in stride but I know they missed everyone also.

Over the next few years, I felt my husband and I drifting further apart. We had different priorities. Mine were focused on the girls and figuring out where I fit into this new little town, and he kept to himself, doing little with the family.

It's funny, as we watched friends and family separate and go through difficult times, we would always discuss, "If that were us, we would never do X Y Z...?" So why is it that that's what seemed to happen anyway?

For our 17th Anniversary, I set up a photographer to take family photos. I felt as if it would be the last opportunity for a family momento and I wanted a treasured keepsake for my daughters. Things were beginning to slide, we were no longer doing things together and our life felt divided. By this time my husband was already sleeping every night in the basement and we were more like roommates than husband and wife. When I look back now, six years later, I cherish those photos but I do wish that what was depicted in them: a happy family, was real.

I had a stranger living in my home and I was walking on eggshells.

It wasn't something that happened. Over time, it slowly snowballed to the point of no return.

My mom flew out and I picked her up at the airport. She stayed with us and I felt a sense of relief. She slept in my room with me, since my husband was downstairs on the sofa-bed. The shocking part was, as the days went by, he still didn't know we had a houseguest. The saddest part was, that meant my daughters hadn't seen him either, as he just simply didn't come upstairs. It was days before he came up to get something from the kitchen and saw that my mother was there. My mom was blown away that it took him that long to present himself and honestly, so was I. Unaware of the discord, my girls were excited, "Grandma's here, Grandma's here," but I felt they should have been saying that three days ago.

We were living separate lives under the same roof and it put a strain on everyone: myself, my daughters and I'm sure on him as well. No one knew the truth of what was going on. My mom's visit made it real that things were not normal between us. Yet, there was nothing I wanted to do. I didn't want *to fix the marriage*. I knew he was not going to change. I would have to do all the work and it would just keep crumbling. The hardest part was not having a partner to share what was happening in my life. I didn't have the support I needed, when I needed it.

Another two years of in-house separation, I found myself talking to the doctor. He gave me consent forms for surgery and told me to go to the hospital, that day, for tumour tracking blood tests. "Wait? What? I don't understand what's happening right now?"

The doctor had to apologize. "I'm so sorry. You didn't know? You have ovarian cancer. We need to do surgery as soon as possible."

I was stunned, in shock and from that moment, I honestly didn't hear another word he said. I didn't cry. I just stared at him as he explained surgery would be faster than setting up a biopsy and waiting on the results. From what he saw in my ultrasound, it needed to come out fast. I went to the city hospital, was put on the surgery cancellation call-list and phoned my parents and just cried. I was an hour and a half away from my small hometown, alone and there was a snowstorm brewing. After the bloodwork, I went to the mall and had some retail therapy that I couldn't afford but I needed a distraction. After a few hours and more tears, I started the long lonely drive home. I didn't call my husband because I didn't think he would even care. I knew there was nothing he would do that would comfort me. Nothing heartfelt had come from him for years.

At home I pretended as if nothing was wrong. I didn't want to worry my daughters who were 16 and 13 at the time. I shared my news with a few close friends over coffee but that was it. I was terrified. At night, I would just cry myself to sleep. No one heard me as I didn't have my husband, the man I had spent two decades with, next to me to hold me and tell me everything would be ok.

After a gruelling surgery, I woke in the recovery room with the doctor telling me it was much worse than he anticipated and he had to take everything, including my stomach lining to ensure nothing had spread. He started talking about the possibility of radiation. I tried to focus on exactly what he was telling me. I had gone into surgery expecting them to keep one ovary. Now I'm finding out everything, like everything, is gone! I was pretty drugged up over the next few days, which were a blur. I was expected to go home by the weekend and I still couldn't even sit up!

On day three after surgery, I was continuing to deteriorate and my blood levels were not coming up. The doctor ordered three bags of blood for a transfusion. I cannot tell you how strange it is to watch someone else's blood go into your veins. It's not warm as you might imagine but actually feels freezing cold. I should have started to perk up but I only felt worse. In the morning the doctor came to check on me and my blood levels were still dropping! What was wrong? He ordered a Cat Scan (CT). A nurse arrived in my room with a wheelchair to take me down. I stared at the chair from my prone position in bed. It seemed impossible to even think about getting into it. I was still on oxygen with a leg-compression machine keeping the blood flowing through my body. I wasn't able to sit, let alone stand. The nurse took one look at me and said, "Change of plans." They took me down in the bed. I felt small, scared and extremely vulnerable, especially when I saw the machine they had to roll me onto, in order to hoist me into the CT machine.

Later that day the doctor, results in hand, informed me I was bleeding internally and they needed to stop it right away. The next day, I went to the operating room for the second time. I was even more terrified with so many "What ifs" going through my head. Mostly I was upset as I didn't get to see my daughters before I went under. My husband was staying home with them and I feared 'what if' I didn't live to see them again.

They stopped the bleeding and I began a long recovery. After almost two weeks in the hospital I was finally able to go home but only if I had 24/7 assistance. My mom flew across the country to care for me while I recovered. My husband was not going to miss any work or step up to look after me.

As I healed, I knew my marriage at that point was over. I was at the lowest point in my life, so I started counselling. I went for over a month without shedding a single tear. My counsellor finally said to me, "You walk in my door everyday dressed professionally, with hair and makeup done and you look like you are on top of the world. I want to hear from the woman behind the mask, as it's the only way for you to heal." I heard what she was saying to me. I really wanted to just tell her everything but I couldn't get myself to speak. I wanted to share the truth, something no one really knows except those very close to me, even to this day.

I was just as bad at hiding from the world as he was. I was trying to protect him and I guess, all of us. Yet, here I was feeling ashamed and it isn't even my issue, I wasn't the one hiding in the bathroom with a bottle. I wasn't the one stashing bottles in the garage. I wasn't the one concealing bottles in the drawers, or ceiling tiles. My girls were very aware of what was happening and they rarely went downstairs because of it. I spent more time telling them how much he loved them, than he did and I still do today. It's not their fault, it's not my fault... yet we hold a lot of shame.

From those sessions, I finally had a breakthrough; I can remember clearly as she sat across from me when she said, "Pretend there is a helicopter hovering over your house and you're looking down at the woman who lives in there. What do you see?"

I immediately broke down.

"What am I teaching my daughters? What am I doing to myself?" My home-life was so uncomfortable for everyone, especially my girls. They were watching the way I was treated and I know they didn't like it. They were old enough to make their own decisions. Actions truly do speak louder than words. Each day that passed, I felt they lost more respect for the man they should love unconditionally.

At the time, I wasn't working. I didn't have my own money nor my own vehicle. I had nothing. I learned very quickly that everything was in his name and not mine. Close friends were telling me to get out and I was very aware of the emotional abuse I received. I'm smart, in fact, I know I am smart but like so many women before me and many after me, I continued to stay. I felt like I was hitting rock bottom and my whole world was out of my control.

I can't tell you how many times I went to the grocery store with my daughters to grab a few things. I always tried to keep it under $10 so it wasn't declined, as he was always transferring money out of our joint account without my knowledge. I kept asking myself, "What is happening? What am I going to do? This is getting worse."

The thoughts of that observer in the helicopter flying over my house made me cringe. "This is so wrong, I deserve better... " I already made a decision to not DIE... now I need to make the decision to LIVE. I knew I had to do something big. I wouldn't have any financial support. I knew it was me against the world.

I truly believe that the Universe sends you what you need, when you need it and when you ask. First, I had to clear and make space in my mind. The emotional baggage had to go. I made a decision to check *those bags at the door* (all the hurt, anger and circumstances that I had been through). I sent those bags off and threw away the little slip of paper I was given to claim them back. I no longer want them; all that emotional upheaval does not define who I am as a person, nor can it weigh me down. I decided to move upward for myself and my girls.

I discovered that a Childcare Centre I worked at in the past was closing and the current owner was selling all of the equipment and with current registrations. I knew at that moment that I had to do whatever it took to get it, as I always dreamed of owning my own centre. I approached some local agencies for support in making a business plan and securing financing. My offer was accepted!!! It was Dec 21, 2015, exactly eight months from the day of my surgery. I felt reborn!

Opening a childcare centre takes more than just a business plan and financing. I had to write up procedures and policy including parent handbooks and ensure I was meeting all of the regulations required, especially since I still had to get approved for a childcare license so I could actually open my doors. I had to have it all submitted by Dec 26th.

Christmas was very different that year. Normally my husband would make a great Christmas Eve meal. Instead, he purchased some buns and lunch meat. When the girls realized what was for dinner, they were crushed... devastated, upset and angry actually, as this was the one time they wanted us to sit down as a family and break bread. Their Dad wasn't even planning on coming upstairs, so one look at their faces and I told them to grab their coats. "We will go somewhere, just the three of us." Being in a small town on the holidays can be hard to find something open but we finally did and we made the most of it. It was our first official Christmas as just the three of us.

Christmas day, the girls and I went to the Centre, to paint and organize, which was a much needed distraction and gave us something to focus on rather than what was happening inside our home. We spent the next week living and breathing at the Centre getting everything ready.

This was the turning point for me. I was completely in control of my own destiny; it was scary but I knew I had no other options. I had to make this work! Inspections were passed and the doors officially opened January 4, 2016, with 38 children registered!!

In a few short years, I was a successful business woman with two locations and 115 children, a two year waitlist to attend my Centres. I completely turned my life around. My daughters were a huge motivator and all the countless hours and sacrifices were worth it in the end. I have to thank the woman I once was as everything I went through inspired me to stand up. She gave me strength and the desire to do more for myself, my family and also for others. I now give back to my community and make a difference in the lives of children and families every single day. There is something about helping others that has made my life so much more meaningful

I have learned no matter what the roadblock, go after your dreams, follow your gut and most importantly pursue your heart. If I can do all of this, you can too. There is so much more to the world then what may reside between your four walls and it just might be your time to kick them down and see where this life can take you.

IGNITE ACTION STEPS

The Universe will give you what you need and manifest what is in your thoughts. Anything is possible, despite what your circumstances may be. Make the decision to LIVE your best life. Do whatever it takes to make your dream a reality and do not let your current situation define you or where you are meant to be.

You got this! Here are a few tips of things I learned along the way:

- **Write it down:** What do you really want? No matter how big or small, what is it?
- **Make a plan:** What are the steps you need to do to get there?
- **Allow yourself to cry:** Seriously – it's actually a release and sometimes you just need to let those tears out so you can push forward to the next step.
- **Leave your baggage at the door:** I could have let all the circumstances crush me but instead, I used them to step up and move forward.

Judy Lynn Sutton
Founder & CEO, The Whole Child Early Learning Centre Ltd

KARI CHIAPPETTA

"Live your life by desire, not by default. Always be the driver in your life, as opposed to the passenger."

My hope is that aspects of my story resonate with you so that you feel inspired and motivated to create the life you want. Realize that you can create the destiny you desire. Find what drives you, what you are passionate about and run towards it – never looking back.

THE GOOD STUFF IN LIFE HAPPENS IN THE CHAOS OF THE UNEXPECTED

Mother, Mom, Ma, Momma. All versions of a word that make my heart sing.

When I was a child and people asked me what I wanted to be when I grew up, my immediate response was always "a mother". Don't get me wrong, I graduated from college and have always worked in my chosen field, but I knew from an early age that my dream of being a 'mom' was bigger than any other career aspiration I had.

I start with this part of my story because, being a mom has driven me to make decisions that have drastically changed the course of my life in amazing ways and directions I never could have imagined. My life has been full of surprises, unexpected detours and wonderful winding roads. Through much self-reflection and sometimes angst at the unknown, I have learned that most of the good stuff in life happens in the chaos of the unexpected!

When I think of the journey I have been on to become the woman I am today, I certainly had no idea where I was going but I can absolutely tell you I am exactly where I am meant to be, doing exactly what I am meant to be doing.

After I graduated from college, I would often get hired to build a program in the community, make it strong and then walk away knowing the work would continue on without me.

Over the years, I had a variety of jobs that were all very exciting and taught me so much about working with community groups and collaboration. When I look back on those years of having worked different contract jobs, I see now that every one of those positions was honing my skills and preparing me for the journey I am currently on.

My journey as CEO of my own life and follower of my passions and dreams didn't begin with my current consulting company. It began in 1999 when my oldest son was just six months old. I couldn't bear the thought of returning to work but knew that I needed to contribute financially to our family income. Two days before I was due to return to work full-time, I called my mother crying, telling her she needed to teach me how to make perogies so I could sell them in order to make enough money to be able to stay home with my son. This began a 5-year, 40/dozen a week perogy-making venture that allowed me to make enough money to balance our household budget. To stay home and be that 'mom' to our sons I so wanted to be. The added bonus was that my mother became my kitchen sidekick, so I got to spend copious amounts of time with her peeling potatoes, grating cheese, filling and pinching perogies!

This venture served its purpose and allowed me to be home with our boys during my first five years of motherhood. It served its purpose... but it didn't fulfill me. I began dreading the tedium of perogy-making. I knew I needed to find something more stimulating and fulfilling.

With the unconditional support of my husband, I found part-time work in my field. I enjoyed working and seemed to have found a beautiful balance between motherhood and career. I was working in a job I absolutely loved at a local organization running a peer mentoring program in local-area high schools. This gave me an opportunity to meet and work with amazing young people in our community. The hours were part-time and flexible, which worked in my world because my boys were still young.

This was a contract job and, like what often happens with contract jobs that are government funded, a new government was elected and the funding for my position was cut, quite unexpectedly.

I mourned the loss heavily. I cried A LOT and felt utterly lost. I was 33 years old and didn't have a clue where to direct my next step. I was tired of not knowing if I would have a job at the end of a contract or at the change of government. I knew I couldn't bring myself to apply for another temporary job. I still believed my fate was at the mercy of investors and employers. Something needed to change.

I allowed myself the time I needed to grieve the loss of a job I loved. After a few weeks of wallowing and feeling sorry for myself, I decided it was time to take control of my life. I am a list-person and always feel better when I can put information into manageable, sequential pieces so I sat down and made a list of all the things I loved about the work I do, as well as my strengths.

Over the course of a few weeks, I read and reread this list many times and a new realization was born. I wanted to be the CEO of my life! I wanted to follow my passion and work in a job that fulfilled me and used the many skills I had garnered from years of contract work.

After much soul-searching and many conversations with my husband, I came to the conclusion that I could be in charge of my destiny and could create the job I wanted. With that realization, Kari Chiappetta Consulting was born.

The thought of taking the risk of starting my own company absolutely terrified me. I would wake up in the night in a cold sweat, wondering if I was making the right decision. I am not a huge risk-taker by nature, and this was an enormous risk. I had never dreamed of becoming my own boss, of being in control of the work I do and managing finances and contracts. I had a steep learning curve but knew deep in my heart that the risk would be worth it.

Once I decided to start a company, I got down to brass tacks and researched where I could obtain business advice and assistance in how to begin. I enrolled in a self-employment benefit program where they taught me how to write a business plan, how to manage finances and generally how to be a business owner.

Aside from wanting to do work that I was passionate about, it was very important for me to be able to work from home and work flexible hours so that I could be there for my children when they left for school every morning and arrived home at the end of the day. The first few years of owning my own company were very much guided by work I could do that would fit into my 'mommy-schedule'. My boys and my husband were my biggest cheerleaders. They supported me every step of the way, often stuffing name tags or delegate bags before a big event.

A few years into my self-employment journey, our boys were teenagers and much more self-sufficient and no longer needing me in quite the same way. Without realizing it, I began to take on huge amounts of work. I was saying 'yes' to all work that came my way to the detriment of my family life. I was working 15 to 17 hours/day, 6 or 7 days a week and often felt overwhelmed and like there were just not enough hours in the day to get the work done. I loved the work I was doing and used that love as an excuse for taking on way too much work. I had always equated being insanely busy and being needed and wanted as the epitome of success… until I crashed.

I was exhausted and not being kind to myself, my husband or our sons. I had put myself and my family last. I had always prided myself on structure and routine and my ability to balance life and work. At this time in my life, I was sleeping just a few hours a night, I had put on 50 pounds. My joints and body hurt all the time. I was snapping at the people who loved me and seemed to be angry much of the time. I was generally not a nice person to be around. My sister and close friends had tried to tell me I needed to make changes, but I didn't want to hear it. In my head I could do it all, be super-mom, be a successful businesswoman and be a wonderful wife.

I vividly remember my husband sitting me down and telling me something had to change because what I was doing was no longer working for me or for us as a family. His loving and gentle way of showing me how much I had changed and how it was negatively impacting our family opened my eyes. This conversation became my turning point. My husband, who had always been my biggest supporter and cheerleader, was telling me I needed to make changes. It hurt to hear him say how our relationship and my relationship with our sons was suffering.

He could tell I wasn't happy and lovingly said, "If you can't figure out how to work through this on your own, maybe you should see someone who can help you." Until that moment, I hadn't considered the option of seeing a counsellor.

This conversation led me down yet another terrifying but amazing path of self-discovery that resulted in a remarkable shift in the way I work. The conversation with my husband, that may seem inconsequential to others, set me on a path that changed my life. That gave me power. That reignited my flames of passion and put me back in the driver's seat of my life.

With the help of an amazing counsellor, I realized that much of my need to always say 'yes' stemmed from FEAR. Fear of disappointing others, fear that I am not good enough, fear of failure, fear of being perceived as unsuccessful. This was a huge weight that I didn't know I had been carrying for many years. It was fear driving me to work insane hours, to say 'yes' to every contract that came my way, to say 'no' to spending time with my family because I had work to do.

Once I realized fear was driving me, I began the terrifying process of working through this. The process was heavy yet freeing at the same time. I felt heavy and guilt ridden because of the choices I had made. When I realized I was choosing work over family and had lost sight of what was important to me, I was devastated. I knew that I needed to shift my whole thought process around work and priorities, but I didn't know where to start. I had been lost in the quagmire of work for so long, I felt powerless to get out.

With the help of my counsellor, I worked through an exercise to look at myself and the priority I was placing on different areas of my life. I pictured my life with me sitting at the head of a large boardroom table. I named all of the parts of me and had them all sit around the table with me. These parts were the CEO of my company, the wife, the mother, the friend, the sister, the daughter, the creative one, the cheerleader, the athlete. The act of naming all of the parts of me was difficult. I had never thought of the different roles I played in my life as "parts of me" but just as one whole.

I put them around the table based on the priority, importance and time I was giving them in my life. This exercise may seem easy on paper, but it was excruciatingly hard for me. Especially when I realized that the CEO was literally sitting on my lap with the mother and wife part of me at the other end of the table. I had always said family was the most important thing in my life, but now I was asking myself, "How had that most central part of my life become so far down on my list?" I had to fight to keep guilt from taking over. I knew I needed to reorganize the 'parts of me at my table' to find balance and seat the most important parts of me next to my core.

I decided to demote the CEO part of myself and get her off my lap. The mother, the wife and the cheerleader were all promoted to sit closest to me.

There was a freedom that came with knowing I had the power to reorganize the parts of my life the way I wanted to. Up until that moment, I didn't realize the power was mine. Without even realizing it, I had relegated the most important parts of me to a lesser role in my life. I had been reactive in my life rather than proactive. I had officially become the passenger in my life.

Once I reorganized, I needed to find a way to keep the CEO at the other end of the table and off my lap and to set parameters around the work that

I would choose to add to my day. I knew I could no longer say 'yes' to everything that came my way.

After much soul searching and self-reflection, I asked myself what was most important to me about the work I was doing. I set parameters that now guide what I say 'yes' and 'no' to.

The first parameter on my list is the work I take on needs to help create strong, vibrant communities. It needs to help make the world a better place to live in.

The second parameter that guides the work I take is that it needs to feed my spirit. This looks different to everyone but to me, feeding my spirit means it needs to inspire me. It needs to teach me. It needs to facilitate growth in the people I work with. It needs to open minds to a new way of seeing or doing things. In short, I need to be passionate about it and it needs to fill my cup.

The third parameter that I use to help me decide if work fits for me, is looking at how it will impact my relationship with myself, my husband and our sons. If I miss too many dinners, don't have the time or energy to go on date-nights with my husband or miss our boys sporting events due to work commitments, it is now an automatic 'no'. I also have made 'myself' a priority. I realized that if I don't create time for me, I have nothing left for my family and my clients. Eating right, ensuring I get enough physical activity and setting parameters around my hours of work, have all helped me to make myself a priority.

Some may say that this list is limiting. I look at the list and see freedom. Freedom to take on work that I am passionate about. Freedom to say 'no' and be ok with that. Freedom in trusting that the work I'm meant to be doing will come my way. Freedom from fear that I am not enough. Freedom in knowing I am strong, I am vibrant, I am exactly who I am meant to be, doing exactly what I am meant to be doing. I have taken control of the wheel and I am no longer a passenger in my life. I am the driver guiding my journey and creating the life I want.

IGNITE ACTION STEPS

Be the driver in your life, not the passenger:

- Decide what your reasons are for saying 'yes'.
- Give yourself permission to say 'NO'.
- Begin to make decisions based on desire as opposed to default.

- Self-reflect using an exercise similar to the boardroom table exercise.
  - Make a list of all of the parts of you or the roles you play in your life.
  - Put your list in order of importance based on your values.
  - Take a hard look at your life: place each part of you at the boardroom table based on the priority, importance and time you are giving them.
  - Once everyone is sitting around the table, take a good look at the placement of all of the parts of you. Are they in line with your values?
  - If the answer is 'no' and you realize you are spending more time, energy and focus on the less important parts of you, remember you have the power to demote parts of you.
  - Set parameters and re-organize your life so your boardroom table reflects your values.

Find what you are passionate about and create the life you want:

- Journal about what your hopes and dreams are.
- Make a list of your strengths and what you are passionate about.
- Think outside the box and don't take no for an answer.
- Decide what you want your life to look like. Write it down. Name it.
- Tell others about your hopes and dreams. Put it out in the universe.

Create your own destiny.
- Set short, medium and long-term goals to help you work toward the life you want.

Kari Chiappetta
Event Planner/Facilitator at Kari Chiappetta Consulting
www.karichiappettaconsulting.ca

SANDRA SMART

"You don't have to have it all figured out before you take that first step. Just take the step."

I'm sharing my story with you in the hope that if you recognize a little bit of me in yourself, you too may have an ignite moment that compels you to take action to become who YOU choose to be (not what anyone else wants you to be) so you can live your very best life.

FREE TO BE ME: KNOWING THE POWER OF ME

It is interesting how life can bite you in the ass when you least expect it. My wakeup call (Ignite moment) was unexpected and showed up in a way that I couldn't have ever imagined. In hindsight, it wasn't surprising. At the time, it was earth shattering. A one syllable word took me down, twice. That word was STRESS.

I was living what I thought was my best life, working for the airline of my dreams, living in the city of my dreams, London (England), in the best role I had ever had. As it turned out, my reality didn't actually align with my dreams. My workdays drifted into my evenings and weekends. I felt like a prisoner with no way out and no idea how I ended up here.

It all started when I was eight years old. I loved geography and dreamed of travelling to far-flung places. The allure of working for an airline was strong and I was encouraged by my dad to write to a few to find out what I needed to do to achieve my goal and work in that industry.

'Achieve my goal.' Achieve, achieve, achieve. It was a mantra of sorts in our house and it underpinned everything I did. Study hard. Get the best marks. Create the best projects. Having 99% on a test wasn't good enough. In discussions with my dad, the point was to discover where that errant one percent went. In hindsight, I know he was well-intentioned BUT it shook my confidence and impacted my self-esteem. Having *'Smart' as my last name didn't help either* and it drove me to work even harder. Failure was not an option. Perfection and the need for it drove everything I did.

This fear of failure and having to be perfect, haunted me for much of my life. Doing the right things. Saying the right things. Being the 'good' girl. Working hard. Pushing myself to unachievable standards. My identity and sense of self-worth was intrinsically tied to all of these aspirations. It's no surprise I ended up being stressed out and having to take medical leave from the job I had always wanted.

The first time stress reared its ugly head, I blamed the company and my managers for all the over-work and being underappreciated. "Didn't they care? Couldn't they see what a good job I was doing? Why didn't they offer the support I needed?" Instead, the work kept piling on. I didn't have the confidence or voice to make it stop. Shockingly, my body put the on brakes. There I was 'happily' working away and one day I just started to cry and couldn't stop. My chest tightened up and I found myself panting like a scared rabbit. It kept happening, at work, at home, at the grocery store or wherever I happened to be. My doctor diagnosed stress and advised me to take a two-week break which definitely helped.

Old habits die hard and it didn't take long for me to get back into over-work mode. It did take longer for stress to take over this time but at least I recognized the arrival of my nemesis. So did the doctor. I was shocked by his solution to my reoccurring issue, "Quit your job." That was it. Blunt and to the point.

I was stunned. I couldn't quit my job. That would mean I 'failed', and failure wasn't an option. "What would people say? What would my dad say? How could I shame myself this way?" It was like my dream was cracking and I felt broken. I agreed to take a month off to give myself time to reflect on my life and what was happening. That space allowed me to come to the realization that it was time to go home to Canada, to my roots. Back to my family and friends so I could recover my health and begin again.

I had no idea what I was going to do but that didn't bother me – I was taking charge of my life. Relief! Freedom! I could breathe again.

After returning home, it took three more years for me to realize that it was me who created the situation I had found myself in. I was the culprit! I set myself up to be stressed. I had to stop blaming everyone else for what happened to me. I had to own it but didn't know how.

My new reality was to figure out what to do next. Find another corporate role? Nope, been there, done that. Retail? Not for me at this point but a possible back-up plan. Then it struck me. "What did I really like doing?" Entertaining and enjoying good food. "What could I do with that?" This was the first time I considered doing something I enjoyed as work. I was going rogue and heading towards the great unknown – I liked it!

My love of food and entertaining led me to culinary school in Toronto. A personal chef career seemed like a good fit. Love grocery shopping? Check. Enjoy having dinner parties? Check. It seemed like a sensible decision. After four months of school and a few months of in-home catering work, I started to wonder if it was for me. Catering is hard work yet that didn't scare me. It was the compensation versus effort equation that was out of balance. Sound familiar? Giving too much and getting too little back. I was beginning to see I had more worth and *was worthy*. It was also the first time in my life I got fired... a small personal cheffing-gig at a cottage in Muskoka. I had 'failed', again! I could hear my father asking, "What did you learn from that?"

It was a sign... another wake up call. What did I want to do next?

I had to earn a living and thought taking temporary jobs seemed a good way to test-drive roles and organizations. My one and only temp-job was in the securities division for a major Canadian bank. While the pay was fair, the job did not challenge me. BUT I did learn about an industry to which I'd never been exposed. There was information, knowledge and contacts that I could file away and use another day.

The interesting thing about that job was that I was asked repeatedly to become a full-time employee because of my work ethic: commitment, flexibility, dedication and general friendliness. I resisted for six months because I didn't want to lose my newfound freedom. I wanted to control the terms of my engagement as much as possible. The most important thing to me was my mental wellness. I still needed to find myself.

By taking control of my highest need, I applied for three weeks off without pay, the company was shocked. They couldn't understand why. I knew exactly why. I was going on an adventure to New Zealand with my sister. THIS became a new habit. I later took several weeks off to work to support friends who needed help with their business.

As it turned out, this opportunity led me down another path. I left that job to return to my affinity with transportation and became self-employed. I loved the freedom that I knew would be mine. I only worked for part of the year and took summers off. Sweet. It also allowed me to work from home and have a flexible schedule, which included some very early mornings and late evenings, but it was my choice. I had broken free from being one of the thousands running for trains, squeezing myself onto station platforms, standing in all kinds of weather and shuffling in and out of office buildings like a worker bee. No more was I going to live my life according to someone else's schedule. I was enjoying my groove and stress was the last thing on my mind.

Then, my world turned upside down. My mum passed away suddenly in 2009 and I became my Dad's housemate. Although declining eyesight meant he wasn't able to drive any longer, he was a fully capable and competent senior. I didn't label myself as his 'caregiver' but as the years went on that's exactly what I became. I held myself responsible for keeping my dad going while he mourned the love of his life. Funny how the child becomes the parent.

A year into this new arrangement, a friend of mine asked how I was doing. I broke down. I was giving all that I had to someone else, and neglecting my needs and dreams, not looking after me. I felt trapped in the role of my father's roommate and my identity was lost. I lost 'me'. I was repeating a pattern from my past and this was another wakeup call. I HAD to make a change. I was ready to reclaim my life.

A random weekend trip to an event in Los Angeles with my sister was the catalyst for change. It was my introduction to the world of personal growth and I learned one fundamental thing that weekend – growth begins by knowing and being true to your authentic self.

Exploring who I was at a deeper level started with taking a simple personality test unlike any I had experienced before. The results didn't tell me who I 'should' be or what I was supposed to' be doing, nor attempt to lead me down a particular career path. Instead, it shared a simple formula – leverage my strengths, don't focus on my weaknesses. That was it. The secret to living my best life was to use and capitalise on my natural strengths and abilities: *visionary, leader, optimist, results oriented* – and design my life around those. My weaknesses: *impatience, high control needs, high expectations* – were acknowledged but held no power over me.

Wow! Talk about an 'aha' moment. I was validated in a way I never thought possible. It explained why I was so driven – making it all so clear. Embracing and using my '*super powers*', made so much sense. Liberty! Freedom!

My strength and confidence started growing. I was making conscious and better decisions. Choices that *suited* who I am versus *changing* who I am to suit the choice. It also meant that's when s#@t happened. I was still in control of my outcome even if it didn't fit with who I naturally was. At such times, I channeled my father and pivoted situations into learning opportunities. I was taking control of my life!

Knowing more about me has added benefits. I now have a better appreciation of others! We all have different gifts and I often imagine the power and magic we could create if our strengths were combined. I imagine a brighter world if we understood each other better, even just a little bit.

When I speak to groups I often say, "I can't imagine a world full of ten or more of me. It would get pretty crowded. I'd likely get on my own nerves and it would be tremendously boring." I feel stimulated and vibrant with others around me who are different. Life is richer when it's filled with variety.

In learning about myself, it helped me find my own voice, which I had lost when I was a little girl. My dad often said, "Little girls were meant to be seen and not heard." My principal in grade school reinforced this, saying, "You talk too much." From that moment on, I shied away from speaking up and sharing what I thought. I was afraid of attention and what people would say if I disagreed with current 'group thinking'. When I was brave enough to speak up, I would blush from head to toe, getting even more attention than I wanted.

My confidence and self-esteem would have been so much stronger earlier in life had I only known myself more. Having said that, I wouldn't change how it all unfolded. I wouldn't have grown and flourished without this journey and couldn't have learned and achieved what I have so far. I have no regrets.

When I think about my professional life, the industries I worked in were very different: airline, equestrian, home building, logistics, coaching and consulting. But my successes were, and continue to be, directly linked to my strengths. When I felt like I had failed, I could understand and appreciate my weaknesses.

Learning and accepting who I am has given me the confidence to be me. To stand firm in my *'me'-ness*. To say what I think but with empathy, caring and compassion. I've learned to be more patient and to listen and hear what people have to say. I'm also a recovering perfectionist which is huge because it's enabled me to be more forgiving and kinder to people because I've forgiven myself. With life as a work in progress, I'm more gentle with myself. I've given Sandra *permission to be human*.

The knowledge and wisdom I've gained was too good to keep to myself and led me to become a consultant with a focus on professional and personal development. If what I had learned helped me to grow and improve my life for the better in my late 40s, I was pretty sure it would benefit others, hopefully at an earlier point in their lives but any time is a good time.

My outlook on life is far different than it was for the little girl seeking to achieve perfection. While always a lifelong learner, I'm now even more curious about people, places and things. I find life so interesting and awe-inspiring. It doesn't take much for me to get excited about something new I've learned or be brought to tears by people coming together and forming authentic connections.

I feel free to see the funny side of life, including giggling at myself. Laughing from deep inside my belly to the point where my body vibrates is truly therapeutic and a feeling I love. It's also a reminder to not take life so seriously. I love being able to share my *true* self with others and I invite you to do the same. Believe it or not, you are so much more than you think you are, and I assure you, others see that in you.

Showing up as the best version of yourself means sharing positive energy with the people around you. When you walk into a room and you can feel there's a negative vibe, be the opposite of that. The greatest compliment I think I've ever received was, "Sandra, you're the most positive and optimistic person I know." That's how I lead now and I encourage you to find your vibe and have fun marching to your own beat.

The path to knowing yourself is a never-ending one, a good one, a hard one, a sometimes frustrating one, but it does make life more wonderful and liberating. It means your life becomes work but it's good work – you just have to be willing to put in the effort. As I said in my power quote, You don't have to have it all figured out before you take that first step. Just take the step and allow the journey to unfold.

IGNITE ACTION STEPS

Taking a simple personality test was one of the best things I've ever done to change the direction of my life. There is a variety to choose from. (See the reference section of this book for suggested URLs.) Use the results as your starting point for self-discovery.

Whether or not you take a personality test, I invite you to take an hour in a quiet place to begin thinking about where you are right now and take a personal inventory. Make sure you have a pen or pencil and paper handy to capture your thoughts. I've found writing in columns helpful.

When you're ready to start, close your eyes for a moment. Take a few deep breaths to get settled. Start thinking about YOU and only you. Now open your eyes and consider...

Are you optimistic, positive and happy?
- Think about why that is and write down as many reasons as possible...

Does that happiness spill over to your work life?
- If it does, write as many reasons why as possible...
- If it doesn't, write as many reasons why as possible...

Do you feel energized by the work you do?
- If you are, write as many reasons why as possible...
- If you aren't, write as many reasons why as possible...

Do you feel you're showing up as your best self at work?
- Think about your strengths and capture as many as you can...
- Are you leveraging your strengths?

Do you feel your work doesn't let your natural gifts and abilities shine through?
- Think about why and capture as many reasons as you can...
- Are your weaknesses playing a starring role?

Random thoughts will continue coming to mind – add them to your 'living' lists. They will serve you well as you begin to plan your journey, highlight the roads to take and those to avoid whenever possible. For the moment, consider what you've written down. Are you surprised? Do your answers align with who you feel you are, with your personality type? If they do not, what action can you take right now to make a shift on your journey to self-discovery? Remember, you don't have to have it all figured out!

Results from the exercise and/or a personality test, will begin creating the energy and momentum you'll need to keep moving forward. The key? – just take the step!

"The good life is using your signature strengths everyday to produce authentic happiness and abundant gratification." - Dr. Martin Seligman, psychologist and the founder of positive psychology.

Sandra Smart
Founder & CEO, MBA, CPC, CAPP
Sandra Smart Consulting & Coaching, www.sandrasmart.com

KIM MCDONNEL

"Be the love you seek. If you want more love,
you need to be more love."

My prayer and intention is that you realize you are the creator of your truth. Your choices can either shape you or break you into the person you were always meant to be. We were designed to be love and radiate peace. My deepest hope is that we join in creating a ripple effect of people leading with love to be the change we wish to see in our world. I wrote this with love for you to create more love in your life.

LEADING WITH LOVE

From a very young age, I sensed people's truth and the pain they tried to hide behind the walls they built for protection. The hate hiding the hurt, the anxiety hiding the fear and the bitterness hiding the betrayal. I had empathy and compassion for even the bee that stung me. I was told I was too sensitive as a child. I sensed energy everywhere. It made life unbearable at times. Feeling everyone's pain and not knowing how to fix it, caused me pain. I felt alone, broken and helpless. I tried for a long time to suppress my own wants and needs in order to avoid conflict. I lost my identity by forcing the peace I was seeking but in doing so, I became the victim I needed to heal.

My life growing up was filled with conflict. My mom was the primary caregiver for my two older sisters and me. When I was six years old, my parents divorced. I made the assumption that it was due to me not being a boy or because my sister and I fought so much. I made it about me. I always blamed myself. Thus, I tried to gain peace by pleasing others. My biggest fear was that somebody wouldn't like me, so I took on whatever role I needed to gain approval. What I didn't realize was how much conflict this behavior was causing inside of me.

As I got older, I tried playing small to shield my light that shined in others' darkness for fear they wouldn't approve of me. I tried hiding my gifts with inauthentic masks of how I wished to be perceived, which didn't match how I felt inside. I learned that every time I opened my heart I got hurt, so I put a wall up against the pain, which prevented me from being the love I was seeking. I numbed my senses with distractions like being everyone's go-to and helper. You know the people-pleaser, the do-gooder who thinks of everything for everyone because she needs to feel needed? Or the daughter who tried to become exactly what her parents wanted her to be? Or the wife who makes sure the house is always spotless in case someone pops over? Or the mother who tries to do everything for her kids? I didn't see my intuitive gifts as good but as a curse. Sensing everyone else's needs and trying to fill them was exhausting! In trying to stop people-pleasing, I felt unloved and unappreciated. I lost my identity of who I was, which made me feel as if I had no purpose. This kept me returning to approval seeking, landing me right back to being what I thought others wanted me to be.

I was living a lie. The truth is, when you are gifted with eyes to see, a heart to love and hands to heal, you will be guided to know and reveal your amazing gifts to the world. I received many lessons in the form of repeated accidents causing me to slow down and dig deeper. I faced deep grief, betrayal, and overcoming diagnosis of diseases such as fibromyalgia, interstitial cystitis, acute diverticulitis and multiple sclerosis. I dealt with depression, anxiety and resentments; which were the real culprits behind those physical ailments. It was the exact awareness I needed in my life to course-correct – to heal that little girl who was so afraid of all the human flaws she saw in others reflected at her. My ability to sit in my own transparency allowed me to realize I was capable of being hurtful if I didn't choose to lead with love. We are all perfectly imperfect humans with wounds to heal.

My struggles came in the form of dis-ease. I searched for answers in allopathic medicine, holistic, traditional, non-traditional, supplements, pharmaceuticals, genetics, epigenetics and more... Ultimately, I regained my health by using natural medicine, food, nature, essential oils, Mindful Movement energy methods, meditation and digging deep to be the love I was seeking in others.

However, the physical healing was only one part of my transformation back to love.

Three years into my physical healing I was feeling good about creating balance with learning to love myself. I was living a full and healthy life, complete with facing my fear of being seen, by being the lead in a play. Singing and acting in local theatre! I was also guiding others to healing with my Biofeedback and Essential Oil business and offering free Mindful Movements and meditation classes. I thought I had figured it all out till I was presented with a different kind of healing opportunity. Infidelity. It was a betrayal I was not expecting; when I thought everything was going so well. I was blind-sided by it all and it was time for things to change in this area of my life – my marriage.

Because I had successfully figured out that you bring energy into your life to heal, I met this situation with that acknowledgement, immediately diminishing its personal attack. I turned it into an opportunity for growth. Don't think me a saint. Soon after that clarity, came the utter disgust and disappointment and I wanted to beat the crap out of my husband. But our son was home from college; recently graduated and expecting his first child, and our daughter was at a very vulnerable age. So, I put on my big-girl britches and carried the weight of this secret and pursued finding its purpose. I remembered I had verbalized to my naturopath "If this is going to make me leave my husband, I don't want to do it." This was me saying: "I'd rather have rashes and migraines and diseases than admit my marriage was unhealthy. Subconsciously I KNEW that my marriage may be at the root of my dis-ease. But, back then, I knew my husband wouldn't change so I was stuck. If I wanted to avoid divorce and chaos I had to comply, play small, and dim my light and that worked for him until it didn't for me. That was the beginning of the next layer of my healing journey.

When the hammer of infidelity hit me hard over the head and woke me up – I had to face what I had known for some time and chose to ignore. I was in a convenient marriage, so busy doing everything to avoid what I felt growing up. I didn't want to face what was missing – intimacy and communication. Sure, we had sex, we went out to eat, we enjoyed our children's lives, but we weren't deeply connected on a conscious level. In fact, we didn't even share the same interests.

All the changes I made to improve my health had cast a huge spotlight on what my husband needed to work through in himself. My first thought truly was, "It's not my fault. There's nothing I had done or said that caused this." I instantly felt free of the judgment and shame that I had placed on myself. "If I can just be enough and/or do enough, he'll love me." His infidelity gave me the struggle I needed to find my strength. A true experience of finding love and peace in me. There was enough momentum in this sense of newfound self-worth that I was able to do the work most people don't. I kept silent and fought the urge to blame and shame him. Staying after betrayal is grueling. When we change, everyone around us is affected. As much changing as I had already done previously, it was clearly time for some more. By choosing to stay for the sake of my family and my health, I was granted plenty of opportunities to grow.

I first had to acknowledge that I wanted to save my marriage and put that above my need to escape or avoid conflict. I didn't want to repeat my parents' story. I didn't want my children to feel what I felt when my parents divorced and I certainly wasn't willing to be depressed, bitter, and resentful for someone else's choices. I had to be in a state of flow to have the courage to not only forgive my husband but recognize the pain and hurt behind his betrayal. I had to allow myself to elevate above the ego for the sake of myself and my children and be the change. But I couldn't do it alone. My husband had to make a choice also. We spent the next three years growing together in love. My mantra for the first year was "today I stay." I literally had to take one day at a time and use all the tools I had so painfully gained, to be the change I needed. When I was weak in my trust in us, my husband had to be stronger. When he needed a shove back to love, I was able to speak up with no fear or manipulation but with conviction of my truth. He could finally hear me. I had changed and so had he. I spoke in a new voice. A confident, secure, grounding voice that didn't question my intuitive gifts or go silent to avoid conflict. My husband started questioning his assumptions that he was always right. He started participating in our life. We had help along the way in the form of therapies, books and the Universe conspiring to keep us going with the birth of our first grandson, which gave us a common bond of absolute love and joy.

This led to a birth of another kind, my book *You Change, They Change ~ How to Take Control of Your Life by Losing Control Over Others.*

Like most trauma, I went into survival mode in the beginning and felt a surge of resiliency that carried me through the painful process of acceptance of what is, while also manifesting what I knew it could be. Visualizing the light at the end of a dark tunnel complete with my husband, children and grandchildren living a harmonious life full of love and mutual respect kept me going when I wanted to quit. I had to keep looking in that mirror constantly and reframing my old mindset from people pleaser and victim to peacemaker and victorious. Keeping my peace in the forefront of every decision ultimately led to everyone else's peace too. Making decisions that were right for me, I practiced patience with my process to find myself, while shedding the layers I built to protect my heart from hurt. I held space for my husband to do the same. I chose to live in the present and let go of the past, constantly.

When you choose love, everything in you that is not love must die. It is the painful and necessary part of healing. When we meet a problem we didn't create, with ego, blame, shame and disappointment, we create a ripple effect of those energies into the situation and our world. When we decide to see everything in life as an opportunity to let go and lead with love, we infuse that situation with peace and understanding. My husband and I now know ourselves and each other in a way I would have never thought possible. We can have the most indepth and conscious conversations and connections enjoying the presence this time led us to embrace. We are finding the passion!

What I know now is that at our core we all just want to be loved! We want to be seen and understood. We all want to have peace. That's what I couldn't understand as a small child. If we all want the same things – why are we acting the opposite of those things we desire most? The answer I didn't know then but know all too well now, is FEAR! Fear of people knowing how we feel or seeing the darkness inside us robs us of being the love we seek. We let the hurt pile up and we arm ourselves with resentment and anger. We deny our truth to manipulate situations to our advantage to stay in control of not getting hurt eventually leading to dis-ease. Then we try and control how others see us for fear of losing them when they were never really ours to begin with. What I realized by letting go of control, I was receiving exactly the energy needed to heal us both and bring us back to love. When we change, everyone around us changes. By being love I was attracting the love in him. When one of us stopped being love the other had to overcome their need to be right or in judgement and lead the other back to love. My children and grandchildren now have parents and grandparents who are present and purposeful with open hearts to connect from a selfless place creating healing in both them and in the generations to follow. I now have a husband who honors me, adores me, and respects my thoughts and opinions as do I. I am free to be me without fear of not being loved and accepted for who I am.

There were high highs and low lows on this healing journey. I wouldn't change one outburst, breakdown, or conflict because I know in my heart I would not be married to the man I am now if this didn't happen exactly how it did. My children and grandchildren wouldn't have the rewritten generational story for them to pass on to their children. I would not have healed my inner child. I wouldn't have complete trust in a higher power leading my every decision. I love who I am now and honor how I got here. If I hadn't chosen love I would not have received my peace. My heart would not be as big and as strong to love again and receive love. I am grateful for where I am today and where I am going.

That's it! That is my gift to you. In all things choose love. This will give you peace. You will attract love and perpetuate harmony in yourself and in your world creating a ripple effect by being the love you seek.

I know it seems so 'Mother Teresa' for us to achieve but if I'm completely honest, it is the only way to survive and thrive. Science is proving that harboring hate, judgement, fear, guilt and shame can cause stress leading to illness. Guilt dissolves in forgiveness. There is no room in your heart for love and hate to coexist. Hate eats away at us and bleeds out into our society like a deadly disease. However, when two or more gather to spread love, it can end wars. Love can save you from illness. You are your own miracle if you choose to be.

When you sacrifice your need to be right and in judgement and choose love and vulnerability you win. Your spouse wins. Your kids win. Our society wins. The human race is depending on this cure. Will you be the antidote with me?

I am happy to report that my little girl, my inner child, was right! I am manifesting more love in my life and it is affecting everyone I come in contact with. I now can be around their hurt and be a catalyst to transmute their energy to love. I can watch how they shift from confusion of the mind to enlightenment, with a new way to think and be. It is by being – rather than doing – that great things happen. When we change our energy to love, we heal ourselves and touch others we meet. My inner child knew love and peace could win. She just didn't have enough faith to be heard. She grew up and earned her voice to speak in the love-frequency, shifting energy with her breath, healing with her hands and creating with her mind a divine existence full of God's grace.

But guess what? She was made exactly like you! You have the power to heal with your hands, your words and your thoughts. Use my method of leading with love and elevate your world by choosing compassion. My vision is that we all join together in creating a healthier, more peaceful world by leading with love and finding our peace within.

I offer free videos, teaching how to be love in all situations. I am a spiritual counselor and offer one-on-one coaching for all ages in all stages. I am proud to say I've helped parents, couples, children and teens to positively shift from a life of anger and fear and dis-ease to be enlightened with love. I know when you step into your power to love, you will experience more joy in your world.

IGNITE ACTION STEPS

*"When we become the change we seek, we see that change in everything.
When we radiate love and peace, we attract that energy into our world,
creating a ripple effect of positivity for generations to come. When we
lead from a heart of love – we heal ourselves and the world we live in."*

- Bless everything and everyone all day long, infusing the high vibrating energy of blessings as much as you think of to do.
- Choose to deal with negative emotions in private through free writing and journaling, allowing them to be felt, processed and released.
- Keep a gratitude journal of the emotions felt in times of bravery to look at when you need to be uplifted and raise your frequency to love and above.
- Give back to your community with the lessons that led to your gifts. My suggestion to you is to find a cause that aligns with your purpose and give more from your heart.
- Continue to seek self-growth and evolve to love. You can use books like mine, You Change, They Change, and the many avenues of learning our world has brought us through online resources to improve your self-esteem. A lack of self-esteem and self-respect are based in the fear that keeps us from love.
- Focus first on what matters most, which is self-love so you can pour from an overflowing cup of love onto others. See my website for my Mindful Movements videos on grounding and meditations to keep you open to be and receive love.
- Choose a community of others leading with love. Feel free to join my tribe of love-leaders on Facebook called You Change, They Change.
- Acknowledge that leading with love can sometimes mean leaving in love. When you have made the essential changes in you, arriving at peace with who you are, you will have clarity to make the decision that's right for you in any situation: jobs, relationships, locations, friendships, setting boundaries – all with love.

Be blessed on your evolution back to the love and peace you were designed to be.

Kim McDonnel
Author and Spiritual Counselor
www.kimmcdonnel.com

LIZZY KOSTER

"Ignite your light, heal and create magic."

I hope that my story will inspire you to always follow your intuition and heart. Have strength and faith – the Universe will always guide you towards the light.

I AM LIVING BY EXAMPLE

I can't stop the tears but they need to get out. I feel them running down my face. "Why are you crying?" David, my new love, asks me. I know he's confused. I feel him staring at my eyes, while holding me tight at the same time. I hear the words in my head. I would like to speak, as I do understand what's happening inside of me, but I only speak silence. It's 3 AM in the morning; we're both tired, physically and emotionally. He tells me, "You don't have to do so many things for me, I will love you anyway!" My heart melts.

This feeling of being truly loved is new for me and it's definitely overwhelming! To be able to live with an open heart and fully receive love makes me emotional. Unexpectedly, it also triggered an old limiting belief but... is it really old? Most probably it was just dormant. I'm so touched as he reminds me that I don't have to push for his love. He makes me feel beyond ordinary. All my life I'm so used to pushing myself to the limit. I often put too much responsibility on my shoulders to fix the problems of others. I go all out to help and save my loved ones, while losing myself in the process. I am sure the Universe just gave me another sign: that I'm loved and good enough. That the new road I'm going to travel is safe and it's definitely time for my next step. My playing small, is over. I feel the confidence to share my spiritual gift with others.

My name is Lizzy, I'm Dutch and I consider myself a leader (among many other things). My style is I'm living by example. I love the life that I live. I'm the type of woman that does not fit in a box. If you were to ask me for my title, I would have to give you several. If you were to ask me what I do for a living, I would have to answer with what I prefer to do at this moment, as it is constantly changing. I don't like routines. My soul craves variety. I like nature and authenticity. All my life I've been a creator, a connector and a visionary and, for the most part, I have invented my own jobs. When possible, I have worked from home as I don't like the feeling 'going to work'. More than once I have followed my heart and intuition into the unknown with full confidence, like I was guided. If you were to ask me about my most important "ignite" moment, I would have to give you several, as they're all connected.

I never thought I was really special; I'll admit, maybe I felt more than average. I had always felt strong, different but foremost, misunderstood. At the end of my twenties, an intuitive healer told me it would be wiser to stop trying to make others understand me as it was a waste of my energy. I just had to accept that most people were not able to comprehend me as I was an old soul, just like he was. He also told me that more than once, he had to leave love relationships because his partners could not understand him. I clearly remember the moment he told me that being an old soul could, at times, be hard and lonely. At that time, I didn't get the total meaning of his words, as I was still at the beginning of my spiritual journey. Now, almost 25 years later, having lived his words, I totally understand.

Although I always considered myself to be pretty ordinary, my actual life was not. In my early twenties, my much older step-brothers took advantage of my naivety and youth. I reached out to them for emotional support when our 76-year-old father turned ill. In their desire to obtain his inheritance I felt extremely betrayed, a feeling that transformed into anger. When I was 21, they began an endless crusade against me and my mother after his death. I started to build a wall around my heart to protect me from future betrayals by people I loved.

Unwillingly, I took over the role of my father and became my mother's comforter, always trying to convince her, and myself, that everything would be okay. My mother's experience, as a child in a Japanese prisoner of war camp in Indonesia, had left a mark. Trying to transform her fear into a safe outcome was exhausting. The lifelong court cases with my step-brothers, turned my relationship with money into an ambivalent one and I found it difficult to trust people from that time onwards. I bravely carried this heavy load of baggage with me for many years.

But there was more ...

In my early thirties, my ex-husband suffered a brain stroke, one year after we split up. It was shocking, yet I always had an inner feeling that something serious would happen to him. It was the beginning of my intuitive awareness and ability to foresee things. Years later, I had to deal with numerous, nasty court cases initiated by a crazy ex-girlfriend of my daughter's father put an unbearable pressure on our long-lasting relationship of 14 years. That made me see, in almost all of my love relationships, it was mainly me who was rowing the boat. I left little space for my partners to lead, protecting myself from disappointments and losing my female side in the process. I was certain about one thing, life was definitely unfair! I became bitter, cynical, negative, turned into a control freak and oh… I became pretty good at blaming others for my misery.

Looking back, I realized that my father's eight month stay in the locked department of a mental hospital, as an Alzheimer's patient with Parkinson's Disease, had a huge impact on me. As he also suffered from psychosis, it was impossible for my mother, who was 25 years younger, to take care of him at home. She was also still working and we did not have the financial means to hire a private nurse. At that time, I felt as if I was living on a completely different planet from the situation at home. I was studying Communication Science at the University of Amsterdam and making extra money while singing in a band. I was ready to discover the world. Instead, I had to come home on the weekends to see him. It was surreal and I often hoped it was just a bad dream.

But it was real; eight times a month I visited Saint Willibrord Hospital. With my mother sitting next to me, I drove my father's car to the mental hospital. I could feel my energy change as we passed through the gate. We were entering a completely different world; the dark side of our society, the closed world of psychiatry. It was very depressing and I didn't want to be there yet felt I didn't have a choice. As usual, we'd find my father sitting in a chair, staring around, locked up in his body with eyes of despair, doing nothing. We'd visit with him for hours, feed him and have small monologues. I felt uncomfortable and would allow my attention to drift away. I prefered to observe what was going on around me rather than being present. I was intrigued by the other patients and tried, in my mind, to uncover their stories and illnesses by reading their faces and behaviour.

My biggest observation though, was that my father didn't look like my father anymore. He was very fragile, thin, had a bony face and was no longer able to express himself. It was like being with a stranger. I knew my mother still loved him but, did I? I was so angry and disappointed; angry that I had an older father with Alzheimer's disease who was dying. Angry he didn't properly arrange his will and finances, which was already affecting us. Angry because he hadn't had the courage to tell my step-brothers openly what he really wanted done with his estate, so relationships were becoming estranged. The family was feuding over what he was leaving behind. I was disappointed that my mother was not treated with the respect she deserved as my step-brothers were turning against her. I was even more irritated because she didn't want to see it. Maybe my father would have handled his business differently, if he had known that his avoidance and fear would leave me and my mother tangled in court cases with his sons for most of our lives.

Although we never had a close bond, I did try to see him with love. I realised that he would always be my father, so I kept visiting. Only, I was not sitting there as a caring daughter, I was resentful and doubting my love. When we would go to leave, he'd shuffle slowly to the door, appearing puzzled as to why he couldn't come with us. I was left feeling sad and powerless to be leaving him behind.

Seeing those patients of all ages in that institution made me realize that time on this earth is very precious and that life can look very different from one moment to the other. This awareness fueled my first ignite moment when I decided that I would never do anything in my life that I did not like… and that's what I did. After my father died, I finished my studies of Communication Science and decided not to go into a career in the advertising world but instead to continue being the lead singer and one of the energizing co-founders of my band, Jam Square. I chose to make a living doing what I loved most at that time; performing and singing. We believed in our dream and became one of the best party bands in the Netherlands in the 90s.

When the band needed a website, one of the players suggested I make one. I bought "The Dreamweaver Bible", reading it on my holiday and started making my first website at home. After many websites, I founded 'Web Girl', my own web design company.

Web Design supported me for many years. It allowed me to take the boldest and best decision in my life when I was 33. I relocated with my cat and dog to a Greek island, after ending my marriage and singing career. Moving away felt safe, necessary and natural. I label it my second important ignite moment; the start of my spiritual journey. I am sure the seed of my spiritual awakening had already been planted on my first visit to Aegina Island when I was 24. The island's beauty felt familiar; I could be completely myself. It felt like home and continues to even now, after living here for 17 years.

No, I didn't move because I had fallen in love with a Greek guy. I moved because I was looking for a different life, for a different 'me'. Moving away from the Netherlands, helped me to live the life I wanted to live, closer to myself and to nature. I needed to hit rock bottom first to understand that I had no other option than to start my journey within and to free myself from everything that blocked me from moving forward. Rock bottom came almost a decade later, when the relationship with the father of my daughter was at a dead end and the Greek debt-crisis had reached its peak. The daily discussions with my partner about the Greek crisis, led to negativity in our relationship. I felt completely stuck, drained and started to have problems with my health. I was also sure that working behind a computer all day could not be the purpose of my life. Actually, I had no idea at all about the purpose and meaning of my life; was there something more that I was meant to do?

There was no way I could escape anymore, so I began my internal journey to search for meaning and purpose. I had to find my true self and had to go within in order to connect to my soul. I discovered painting, writing, new ways of expressing, nurturing and feeding myself. For the first time, I felt understood and supported when I entered the world of online learning and signed up with a spiritual business coach. The shift in perspective of rewriting my life story, ignited a light I hadn't seen before; my third ignite moment. It was mind blowing when I understood that my life had happened *for* me and not *to* me. I felt complete relief when I realized that life shouldn't be a struggle. It helped me to make different decisions and allowed me to say 'no'. It took a lot of heaviness from my shoulders and my anger was able to transform into acceptance. I learned the importance of forgiveness and love of self. It paved the way for my real spiritual healing journey of transformation and revelation.

I loved being a student again and soaking up wisdom. Natural healing drew my attention. Something clicked when a friend showed me how I could measure energy with a pendulum. It immediately fascinated me and I bought one. I dove into the world of dowsing, practicing and experimenting. I developed a system that helped me to receive answers to my questions. I intuitively felt this was for me and the answers were real. I wanted to know more and, with whom I was communicating.

I already felt there was an energy near me, probably for most of my life, trying to inform me about what was going to happen and to guide me into a safe direction. I always felt ordinary, though I had good ideas, but now I started to feel as something more was going on. While wondering about things and letting possible options pass by in my mind, something amazing happened. One of the two lights above my dining table started flashing. My first thought was the light was broken but I could not deny the obvious connection between my inner thoughts and the flashing. 'Someone' was telling me I could trust myself. I didn't need to meditate to connect with 'Him'. Him? Yes, it felt like a 'Him'. Don't ask me why, I just felt it.

When I started doing sessions with an Irish intuitive therapist, the real magic started unfolding. I had my fourth ignite moment when she made me aware of my 'healing hands' and explained how I could use my energy to help, energize and guide others. She explained I was tapping into an ultimate truth with my pendulum and I could completely trust the answers coming through. Everything fell into place.

I questioned her: "Can you see who is sending me these messages, who is guiding me?" With excitement in her voice she answered: "Yes. I see an old wise man, with Buddha-like energy. Do you have some kind of relation with an old wise deity?" I didn't hesitate long and answered "Agios Nektarios"? As a foreign, non-orthodox woman, I have to admit I was in shock when she actually confirmed that the well-known "Agios Nektarios", the orthodox saint, healer and miracle worker that used to live on Aegina, was my spirit guide. I felt even more amazed when she told me if I allowed it, I could channel his powerful healing energy and people would come to the island to be energized by me!

It took me several weeks and another session to process and understand the full meaning of her words. When I gave it more thought, I realized I had already felt a connection from the first moment I came to live on this island. Countless times I've been at his monastery, drawn to visit his home and the two rooms he used to live in. Just like me he liked nature, hiking, flowers, animals AND he had faced many challenges in his life. I loved to sit down in the old courtyard observing the people that came to visit his Monastery, always wondering why they had travelled from all over the world to be close to his energy. Finally I grasped why so often I had felt different and misunderstood.

For the first time I started to think bigger, realizing there was definitely more to do for me in this life! It made me understand why people wrote me that their life had completely changed after I had sent them icons, holy oil and water from the monastery. I began to understand how I was able to foresee many things.

I've just turned 50 and I feel like I have been reborn. I've accepted who I am, who I was and acknowledged I will always be a work in progress. I've embraced my power and my true soul destiny so that I can energize others. I surrendered myself to love; the most powerful energy that is guiding us all. I trust and have faith and I help others to follow their heart and intuition. I moved my focus towards working with energy and building the foundation for my new project, 'Aegina Healing'.

My new love, David, supports and loves me for who I am. I'm ready for this new phase of my life, ready to inspire, ignite light and create magic in those around me. I support others in finding their path. My style is: I live by example and you can too!

IGNITE ACTION STEPS

I am happy to share with you the key, seven words, that ignited my transformation. "When YOU change, YOUR ENVIRONMENT will change." This wisdom from Deepak Chopra made me understand that my life-long attempts of: trying to change my father, mother, partners etc... had only turned me into a frustrated, angry and sad person. It was a waste of my energy. I had to stop the blame game and to take full responsibility for my own life. No more escaping. I had to start working on myself!

To release myself from the bondage of my past, I used pen and paper to write down everything that had negatively impacted me. I reflected on the situations, the people and all the damaging things I had said to myself. After that, I was encouraged to write down my past, present and future from a different perspective, as all transformation begins when you see your life through new eyes. The reflection and rewriting was, for me, an emotional process but an excellent exercise to heal from the toxicity that had blocked my energy for years and to open myself up to a new future.

Lizzy Koster
Creator, Coach, Connector and Visionary
www.lizzy.energy

Madalina Petrescu

"Break away from the trap of incessant doing-ness by remembering that the bliss is in the being, in the space between all the doing."

If you are feeling stressed trying to balance all your duties in order to serve the world, I would like to invite you – to serve YOU first. Give yourself permission to engage in a healthy practice of self-care which will create a state of inner peace, abundance and self love. Only then can you give to others that which you have overflowing within.

Finding the Bliss in my Chaos

I rush out of the hospital, glancing at my watch, realizing it's dark outside again. 9 PM, shoot! I meant to leave so much earlier but once again ran late with the busy clinical service and a late meeting. Hurrying down the steps, I nearly trip as I dial my husband's mobile. "Darling, are the kids still awake?" I ask but already know the answer. I become aware of that familiar knot in my stomach of deep unease. Our daughters, Elise and Sofia, three and five at the time, were likely already in bed.

My husband pauses, used to this question. "No darling, they are asleep but you can still kiss them when you get home." My heart sinks as I walk to the car. Again... I missed their bedtime. A wave of sadness envelops me.

Sitting down in the car, I feel my back pain acting up again. I don't know what feels more horrible at this point, this unrelenting pain or the dense growing knot in my stomach from once again missing the girls' bedtime. I sigh a breath of unhappiness. For the past year I had been struggling with chronic lower back issues that came out of the blue and progressed to the point I was no longer able to work out. Exercise was my way to de-stress. I went from being a runner to barely being able to walk. I recall all the time and energy spent on doctors' visits and the many tests. Each time being told there is 'no clear physical cause'. Meanwhile the pain persisted. I couldn't help but notice the obvious pattern that the back ache seemed to be brought on by all the stress and pressure I was putting on myself to 'do it all'.

Yes, I admit it. I was quite the perfectionist. Taking on a big plate of responsibilities and achievements that seemed to be getting heavier by the day: a busy cardiology career, director of the Echo Lab, head of advanced Structural Echo Imaging, serving on the Medical Board and Workforce Committee, as well as on the Medical Faculty giving talks. All the while, I was trying to be there for my girls, husband, extended family and friends with whatever time I had left. I spent late evenings at the hospital to be there for my work team and sleepless nights on call. I would work through lunch and sit for long hours shut away in my office on the weekends preparing for talks, sacrificing quality time with my family – leaving not a minute for me.

My life felt as if it was on fast-forward and I was constantly rushing to keep up. No matter how much I did, it was never enough. There was never enough time in the day for all the tasks on my list. That was me, pretty much all the time. I felt teary eyed for all the missed breakfasts with the kids, the bedtime snuggles, the recounting of daily excitement and their school events. All these priceless moments I could not show up to, because I was so busy running to the next work-thing.

It didn't help that I was the 'yes' person; the giver. Somehow the word 'no' didn't make it into my vocabulary. I was trying to be there for everyone — patients, colleagues, family, friends. I wanted to serve and fulfill everyone's needs. There was never any time for *me*.

I had become successful in my job; a leader by virtue of personal sacrifice and hard work. We learned quickly in Cardiology Fellowship Training that the value of a 'hero' is measured by the one who works *the hardest, longest and gives up most of their personal self*. Praise was doled out to the ones who showed up earliest, stayed latest and slept the least. They were the heroes amongst us. I embraced that 'hero' definition to prove that as a woman, I can survive and thrive in this man's world, in this male-dominated career.

I grew up in a family not afraid of hard work and personal sacrifice. My parents escaped Romania's communist regime when I was nine years old. Enraged by their escape, Ceausescu's secret police declined the lawful right of my brother and I to join our parents after they fled to the United States. We had no choice but to remain behind with our grandma. I can still remember the look of distress on her face, as she tearfully explained the unbearable situation. In that moment, hearing that painful truth, I learned to swallow my feelings and 'toughen up' to survive, imprinting in my heart that sacrificing what we love was embedded in the experience of life.

It took two long years until we were joyously reunited with our parents, only to face another hard reality – we barely saw them. Starting over from the bottom, my parents had to work two jobs back-to-back to put food on the table, often not home until after midnight. They required every inch of courage to build a life for our family. We lived in an area of Los Angeles where we'd sometimes hear gunshots at night. I felt terrified and scared. It was just me and my younger brother home alone to comfort each other.

Despite being dirt poor, my parents succeeded at building themselves up. They became my true heros, teaching me that anything is possible through hard work and persistence. However, inherent in that life lesson was also the strong belief that personal sacrifice is *encoded* in the fruits of success. Hard work mattered above all else which is something I took to heart and blindly applied. I didn't know there was any other way to be than to follow this hard way of life. That led to countless accolades, massive achievements, a high-powered career, plus a loving husband and two wonderful kids.

An epiphany came to me that changed my life. You know those intense 'ignite' moments that are so emotionally poignant and powerful that they shake our hearts? We are never the same again!

It happened one day in Hawaii at a medical conference, the last day of presenting medical talks that I put so much work into. As I walked out of the cold, dark conference hall to greet the warm, sunny gardens of the big Island, I remember feeling torpedoed with a whirlwind of thoughts and emotions. The vibrant natural beauty of Hawaii ignited in me a sensation that something was dearly missing in my life – a big deficit. But I couldn't define it. I could only feel the unpleasant gap.

I was making my way on the garden path to join my girls and husband who were eagerly waiting for me by the pool. Here I was in Hawaii and instead of being relaxed, I felt drained. My head felt heavy, in a fog of confusion. My heart felt empty. Externally, I seemed to have it all: rising with my achievements, recognitions, successes and serving everyone who needed me. But internally, there was a mismatch. Instead of fulfilled, I felt depleted and stressed. Instead of energized, I felt exhausted and burned out. My back pain started to tighten up severely, radiating down my legs bringing me to a full stop.

In one split moment, just like that, instead of following the path to greet my family, I impulsively broke into a run toward the beach. Despite the back pain. Running fast, away from what my life had become. From all the incessant thoughts and 'to do' lists, escaping from my stress and unhappiness, the rushing, duties and giving. Arriving at the beach, I took off my shoes and stepped barefoot on the warm sand. The ocean and winds were in concert with my internal state. The waves were rising up forcefully beckoning me forward. The winds blowing powerfully, pulling, drawing, wrenching all that was buried within me, what was wanting to be released. Yet unnamed.

Reaching a remote spot by the ocean, I threw off my bag in the sand and took a few steps forward to the shore. I fell to my knees, letting the water wash over me. Then something happened, before I knew it was going to unfold. Without intention or plan.

In that moment as I felt the ocean run over me, I spontaneously gave myself permission to let go. I surrendered to the waves. A sensation of deep relaxation and lightness swept over me. Freeing me from the familiar mental buzz of incessant worries, thoughts and expectations that tethered me. I was transcending into a space of timelessness and deep aliveness, becoming a portal to love and freedom. In that moment I was feeling as if I had arrived at the place I was running after – oneness. In the bliss of this awakened presence. I became a peaceful living *Being* connected to the beauty of that moment.

Time stood still. I never wanted it to end. When I gazed upon the ocean and nature, I felt struck by the aliveness around me. The water never seemed so clear and blue. The clouds so white and pure. The palm trees so green and lush. It's like I was seeing life with a new set of eyes. Awakened to a deeper way of living.

I realized I had experienced a deep state of consciousness. We know it only when we experience it. The silencing of the mental buzz allowed the inner voice of my heart to speak and I listened. I felt the truth of how I had been living my life trapped in a state of perpetual doing-ness, working and achieving. I was so entrenched in the weeds of endless tasks, inherent in the expectations of my busy career that I had lost touch with the purpose and meaning of life itself. I had fallen prey to the trap that 'if I keep doing more, only then can I feel fulfilled and be happy'. I had forgotten that the bliss and joy of life all along was in the being, in the space between all the doing. I was so busy living in the future rushing to do the next thing that I forgot to be and connect with life in the present moment. The Now, which is the only moment we truly have. *The being as the source of true aliveness.*

I felt the truth that I was so preoccupied with taking care of others that I forgot to take care of myself. Ironic, here I was a cardiologist so busy taking care of others' hearts, that I forgot to take care of my own. I had bought into the illusion that to be a successful leader, I had to be solely 'other-focused'. I had to give, no matter what and sacrifice with little care for myself. In my effort to serve as the selfless martyr, I was running to catch up with all the work 'agreements', endless appointments, the 'yes' obligations.

Isn't true serving defined as the giving of something we must first have within?

I had to ask myself. Can I as a doctor truly heal patients, when I don't first practice personal health in the holistic sense that includes physical, emotional and spiritual wellbeing? Can I truly inspire others when I am in a state of exhaustion and lack? Can I pour into those that need me when I have not filled myself first?

Before we can truly serve others we must responsibly; first and foremost, fill our own hearts to an abundant state. Only from this state of overflowing wholeness can we give to others that which we have created within ourselves. I realized no one can give me permission to serve myself first in this healthy way – except me. By doing so, I can be the change I want to see in the world.

That day as I stood overlooking the ocean, I felt empowered by the magnificent waves. I made a promise to myself: to create a space for self-care that would generate a state of abundance. I reached for my bag and pulled out my journal. I excitedly wrote down what I felt in my heart would manifest this state of abundance and fulfillment, naming it: *Things in Life That Bring Me Joy* that I had put aside and forgotten.

Over the next few months I developed a morning practice which became non-negotiable and top priority. I created boundaries to support my personal practice of self-care. Boundaries that included me having to say 'no', in order to say 'yes!' to me. Upon waking up in the morning, instead of my previous tendency to rush out of bed, check email and start the compulsive worrying about endless tasks, I made a change. This change spawned a pivot-point in the direction of my new life journey.

I committed to a personal policy of '*no electronics*' until I completed my practice of self-care. First, I attended to my spiritual health through meditation to enter a state of presence that generated profound inner peace, energy and abundance. In this state, I expressed gratitude for all the gifts in my life. Next, I attended to my emotional well-being through self-reflection. We are all spiritual beings living in an emotional world. It is our responsibility to feel and process each feeling. Emotions left unprocessed can lead to us projecting them onto others. This greatly compromises our energetic state and our authentic interaction, leading to an inevitable cause of conflict.

Over time, a massive inner transformation unfolded. With each practice, I felt my heart expand with abundance. The more I focused on serving me and making myself whole, the more energized, peaceful and joyful I became. I transcended the cultural myth that self-care is selfish. It was quite the opposite. The more I served myself, the more I became whole and the more I had to give out with love.

I started showing up to the world as the best and highest version of myself. Worry and reactivity diminished. Because I felt internally *filled*, my interactions with patients, colleagues, family and friends changed. People started telling me: "I love your enthusiasm" or asking, "What energy drink are you having? I want some!"

My connection to my family deepened. Relationships at work flourished. I started laughing more; not taking everything so seriously. Giving no longer felt like an effort. Rather there was a sense of ease and joy because I was giving from an overflowing cup. I showed up to work meetings high on my natural energy and was able to lead from the heart, inspiring empathy and connection. When seeing patients, I was able to fully be present with them and care from a compassionate state. I had energy to be silly and play with my girls. Many months into this personal transformation I also became aware of a miracle that had manifested unintentionally. My lower back pain had completely healed. The back pain had been my messenger to get me to *stop* living life in a way that was no longer serving me. To get me to *cease* focusing on external healing alone. Stopping the rushing, the doing – letting me drop into the full depth of my emotional and spiritual essence in order to heal from the inside out.

Life was more meaningful and enjoyable as I became more grounded and present. As I moved into a healthier work/life balance, I felt more fulfilled. I started fully living, playing and leading from an abundant heart. You too can do this. I invite you to give yourself permission to honor and prioritize *yourself* first. To fill your heart to an abundant state and live with PRESENCE and BLISS.

IGNITE ACTION STEPS

Here are some points for a personal self-care practice to start off your day: Commit to waking up 20-60 minutes earlier to honor this sacred self-care practice every day.

Try the practice of no electronics in the morning until you've completed your self care routine. It may help to put your phone on 'airplane mode' the night before. This way you are not greeted by a stream of messages that may tempt you to break your promise.

Start off each day with a practice of meditation to enter the space of presence, which will create a sense of inner peace and harmony. Focusing on your breath is a great way to ground in the present moment. You may find that your mind may become active with incessant thoughts or worries. This is normal. Practice coming back to your breath and watching the thought instead of getting hijacked by it. Become the witness. Keep breathing and smile. Accept what comes up naturally and without judgement.

Reflect and process any feelings you've experienced in the last 24 hours. Journal in free-style without holding back. Consider the circumstances when you felt triggered by a person or an event. Resist the urge to blame and point a finger. What within you is asking to be further understood, processed and healed? Each trigger is a teacher in disguise, holding up a mirror to show us our resistance to inner growth. By leaning in, we have the opportunity to take ownership of our learning and expand our awareness.

Make a list of what brings you joy and commit to doing at least one of those per day. Let your imagination open up freely. Some examples are: a trail-run in the woods, snuggling up with a soulful book, writing poetry, free dancing to your favorite music, or watching the sunset or sunrise...

End the practice with any movement/exercise that you love: walking, dancing, jogging in nature, biking, Zumba, practicing yoga, swimming, etc. Movement is a great way to allow stored stress to be released and to enhance a positive emotional state.

Now you are ready to enter the rest of your day, 'high' on your authentic loving energy. Ready to embrace whatever comes your way from the elated state of your highest and vibrant self; grounded and ever-present. Enjoy!

Madalina Petrescu Agafi
Cardiologist at HeartQ
www.heartq.com

NADIA LA RUSSA

"Ride the Waves and Throw the Lemons!"

Leaders, life is going to pitch lemons your way. There will be times where you are submerged under waves so deep you feel emotionally constricted, unable to breathe. Rise up, ride the waves and pitch the lemons back at life.

THE YEAR OF HELL

The Year of Hell started on June 10, 2017. I exited the Waves of Superior Spa with my friend Lauren, having just spent a glorious day being pampered, laughing and finally feeling the knot in my upper shoulders start to unwind. As a mother of five and the owner of nine small businesses, it was an extremely rare escape from the demanding life I lead. I was happy to have some one-on-one time with my close friend.

Lauren had treated me to a weekend 'escape', a gesture that was an indication of the depth of our friendship. We are the type of friends that can reconnect after time apart as if no time had passed at all. She understands how my brain works and we have a similar sense of humour. It's these types of connections that propel me to continue growing.

We started the two-hour drive towards Thunder Bay, Ontario passing through Grand Marais, Minnesota. My cell phone rang. It was Mike, my ex-husband. My daughters, 15-year-old Andria and 11-year-old Camryn, were with him for the weekend, enjoying their time out at his cottage. For him to be calling me in the middle of a sunny Saturday afternoon, I knew something was wrong.

"Nadia," his panicked voice began, "I'm in the back of an ambulance with Camryn. She was in an accident and she has broken her leg. We are on our way to the hospital and I need you to meet us there."

A wave of nausea overcame me, the glory of the weekend getaway erased in an instant. I was nearly two hours away and my baby girl was in the back of an ambulance. Lauren wasted no time driving and dropped me off at the hospital door.

I entered the room to see Camryn on a stretcher. Mike was there and my new husband Brent and my 10-year-old stepson Logan had joined him. Camryn's left leg was exposed, swollen to twice its usual size. A nurse stepped towards her bed, revealing an xray on a screen. It didn't take a radiologist to see that the left femur had broken clearly in half.

"Hi baby girl," I said quietly to her.

"Mama," she responded, her small face pale and her eyes wide. Her long, brown hair spilled onto her shoulders. "Where am I? Can I have an iced cappuccino please?"

"You're at the hospital," I gently explained. "Your leg is broken. You can't have an iced capp right now, because it looks like you will need surgery."

"Hi Mama!" she answered. "Where are we? Can I have an iced-capp?"

I turned to face Brent, Mike and Logan, confused. "She's been repeating the same few questions a number of times. We aren't really sure why. It could be the narcotics given in the ambulance or it could be a concussion from the accident," her nurse explained.

I asked to see Mike in the hallway. I'm thankful, despite being divorced, Mike and I maintain an incredibly communicative relationship, in particular when it comes to our daughters. He was visibly emotional; his eyes welled up as he told me what happened.

"She was riding a dirt bike. She went to the end of the driveway and didn't stop. She was hit by a truck." At that moment, fury mixed with shock and grief overcame me. The next words out of my mouth, anger towards him, fell on a man who was already covered in his own guilt. I felt Brent's presence beside me, his strong hands on my shoulders. It was this that refocused me to what was important – Camryn. The next day, the skilled orthopaedic surgeon repaired her leg and we embarked down weeks of recovery and an adapted summer for my spunky girl. Thankfully, her cognitive functioning restored perfectly and the only lingering reminder of that event is a long purple scar down the side of her leg.

The end of September marked a time where I was finally breathing easier. I wasn't watching Camryn like a hawk and fussing over her safety. I had started to relax into the fall season and we scheduled a trip away to enjoy the Route 91 Harvest Festival in Las Vegas. Joining us were our friends Alison and Mike, fellow country music lovers.

It was their first time in the city and we spent the days showing them some of our favourite spots, eating good food then heading to the concert grounds to catch the musicians and bands that were performing that evening.

The four of us were excited for the Sunday lineup and we made plans to meet up that afternoon. Sunday at 4 AM, I woke up and could not fall back asleep. I quietly got dressed and found some casino chips in Brent's pocket.

Downstairs, the normally busy casino floor of Mandalay Bay was quiet. I found a seat at a Blackjack table and engaged in light conversation with the dealer. For about an hour, I played cards there, until something quite remarkable happened.

I won every hand for an entire shoe of cards. The dealer came to the end of the deck and dealt me an Ace and a Jack. "Well!" I laughed, "I've never had that happen before!"

"And, I've never seen that happen before!" he responded. I collected my chips and headed for the cashier. I wandered upstairs with $400. By the time I returned to the room, Brent was stirring. I presented the winnings to him triumphantly.

Later that day, the four of us wandered around the concert grounds. I spotted a restaurant called The House of Blues and noticed it had a rooftop patio. "Hey guys! Let's see if we can get seats up there for tonight!" I exclaimed.

We approached the booking desk and were told that there were four seats left, at a price of $100 each.

"Hah! YES! We're going up!" and Brent handed the concierge my morning winnings. The rooftop patio's open railing system gave us a safe but clear view of the happenings below us. We marvelled at the view, enjoyed the private bar, separate restrooms and gave thanks that we weren't in the crowds on the lawn below where we had spent the last two nights. We found a spot on the rooftop bleachers that had space for the four of us and as the music began, we danced the night away with our friends.

The final act, Jason Aldean, started at 9:40 PM. At 10:00 PM, Brent and I gave each other the type of knowing look that exists between married couples. You know the one, the "So, let's start making our way out towards the door so we beat the crowds back to the hotel" that a wife can give her husband and he knows to finish his drink and get moving towards the exit.

That's when we heard the fireworks, background noise at the moment, just part of the show. I turned to Ali, "We are going to make our way back now. See you tomorrow?"

"Ya…," she responded, her face turned away from mine. "Wait – why is everyone running?" The four of us craned to look over the banister at the crowd below. The fireworks started again.

"Is that… shooting?" Ali said. I grabbed her arm and pulled her to the deck. Brent joined us. I held Ali's arm as tight as I could and turned to Brent.

"That doesn't sound like shooting." I said to him. No sooner were the words out of my mouth when the stage went dark, the lights went out, the music went off and all we could hear was screaming. The noise, previously identified as fireworks in my brain, was now the unmistakable sound of the firing of an automatic weapon.

Brent was no longer looking at me. His head was now raised and he was scanning the chaotic crowd. The shooting started again. Ali screamed. We heard bullets ricocheting off the chairs and beams around us. Brent moved his body physically over mine. While continuing to scan the crowd, he verbalized a plan.

"Ok, we are going over that fence. As soon as he stops shooting, we run." It was then that my brain started piecing together the possible scenarios occurring out of my view. What made sense was that there was only one shooter and that he was hidden or not in the crowd. What none of us could tell from our vantage point was where he was shooting from. While I was trying to process that, the shooting stopped. We ran.

We made it behind the bleachers where we had been sitting, when the shooting started up again. We crouched behind the bleachers and watched people running past us. By this time, the fence we had been planning to climb over had been knocked down by the thickening crowd of people trying to make their way out. Brent continued to survey the crowd. Sirens could be heard in the distance. Police cars that had been stationed around the grounds were pulling closer. The shooting stopped. We ran again.

Taking the stairs off the patio, we ran out the back of the concert grounds to a church located about a block away. We took cover behind a brick wall, where several other concert attendees had found refuge behind this solid structure. Everyone was crying. I saw two girls that had been injured by bullets. As I was trying to catch my breath, an ambulance pulled up and the shooting started again. Brent pulled me away and said "We have to keep running. Let's go!"

We ran until we reached the back of the MGM Grand Hotel, where Brent hailed a limo bus. The driver, clearly unaware a shooting was in progress, allowed the four of us in and asked, "Where to?" Somehow we decided on the Venetian, a hotel on the opposite side of the strip, farthest away from the concert grounds. Ambulances, fire trucks and police cars were screaming towards the concert grounds. My step-app on my phone congratulated me on completing a 5km run. I called my mother.

"Mom," I said breathlessly, "I need you to listen. There's been a shooting at the concert. We ran away... we're safe, we're still running. It's likely not hit the news, but it's bad. My phone's about to die. I don't want you to be scared."

Safe in our room at the Venetian, we hugged each other and cried. The news of the shooting was hitting the Twitter world and various news channels were showing footage of the aftermath. Over the next two days, we gathered our things from our original hotel and flew home to our families. For days – it seemed the tears wouldn't stop. Brent hovered around me, never moving more than a few feet away. When we were within reach of each other, he had his hand on me.

Our friends didn't know what to say. It was hard to answer the question "Are you alright?" because physically, we were. Emotionally, we were not. I flipped between intense gratitude and extreme guilt. I knew I should be feeling blessed to be hugging my children, but with each embrace I thought of the mothers who might not be hugging theirs.

A few days after we returned home, the noise of a car bouncing off the curb, found me diving under the kitchen table. This was a signal to me to take recovery seriously and we made it a priority to work through the trauma that we experienced. Through the fall and Thanksgiving, we immersed ourselves in post-traumatic stress therapy, rest and taking the time to learn about what our lives after this event would look like.

As Christmas approached, I began to look forward to the birth of my baby niece or nephew. Our family learned that the baby had a heart condition and would need surgery shortly after birth. I had faith this wouldn't be another wave that was trying to drown me.

I was wrong.

My beautiful niece was born in early March, weighing just over three pounds. I met her the next day, held her hand and kissed her head. The tubes and wires attached to her little body did not hide how beautiful and precious she was. Ten days after her fight began, it ended. Her life, though short, was full and impactful in countless ways.

The year of hell transformed me. It would have been easy for me to retreat into a negative mindset and cut myself off from experiencing joy. I could have allowed my emotional and mental health to suffer, become selfish, angry and damaged my relationships.

From Camryn's injury, I learned life is fragile and precious – spending moments directing blame is pointless. True leaders operate knowing most of us are doing our best at all times. It seems that we tend to judge others on their actions but judge ourselves on our intentions. It's important to seek to understand each other before assuming the worst.

From the shooting, I learned that the daily, trivial arguments within a marriage amount to nothing. When we get married, we vow to love, honour and cherish each other. Wives, I hope you can know now, without going through something like this, that if you have a man that will physically lay his life down to protect yours, he deserves to be honoured until your last breath.

I certainly wasn't the perfect wife and I don't proclaim to be now. But, what I have now is a much clearer view on what actually matters. How I treat people matters. Who did or didn't clean the dishes or went out with friends or left the bathroom a mess or any of that other trivial crap – DOES NOT MATTER.

From my niece's short, sweet life I learned that even a short life can be a complete life and can leave lasting effects on the relationships that remain.

Leaders, life is going to pitch lemons. There will be times where you are submerged under waves so deep you feel emotionally constricted, unable to breathe. Rise up, ride the waves and pitch the lemons back at life. Leadership extends beyond the workplace and permeates our entire lives. I believe that true leaders guide with their behaviour and demeanour in *all* areas of life. Leaders are always being looked up to!

Ignite Action Steps

Action Step #1 – When something happens to you, do you immediately look to place blame? Imagine how it would feel if you were on the other side. Consider how you would feel. When situations arise where you want to blame someone else, instead extend grace. Show empathy and don't let your emotions drive your actions or words. Additional strife aimed towards the offender is pointless but a heartfelt "This must feel horrible for you" or "I understand" – would serve you better.

Action Step #2 – Think of your primary relationship. Are you showing up as the best partner you can possibly be? Are you holding up your part of your vows to love, honour and cherish your spouse? If not, change that immediately. Be the wife you want your daughter to be, or the husband you want your son to be. Be the spouse you can look back on with pride. Soften your tone, greet your spouse with a warm smile when they enter the room and become the person that you'd want to be married to, regardless of how your spouse shows up.

Action Step #3 – The loss of a loved one can rip families apart. When someone dies, especially at a young age, it's important to foster stronger connections instead of creating distance. Use the loss to become stronger and closer to your family. Celebrate together and cherish the memory of the ones you have lost, being open about your pain without judging others and how they are grieving.

I know that there is more trauma ahead of me - more loss, more unexpected situations, more things that will try to derail me. I encourage you to truly experience the joy this life has to offer. If you happen to get handed a lemon, throw it right back.

Nadia La Russa
www.nadialarussa.com

PHYLLIS ROBERTO

"Step Up! Stand Out! Be Seen! In being an advocate for yourself, you are an advocate for others."

Life presents opportunities that create and craft leaders. Sometimes we are thrust into a role by our circumstances. At times, we don't know we are leading; other times we take the lead because it is the right thing to do. Through my story, I hope you realize your lowest moment may be the spark that ignites you to lead. Those times you are tempted to play small, may you choose to shed light down a new path for yourself and those who come after.

TAKE THIS CUP

Close to the end of the 12 hour night-shift, there was just enough time to offload the tanker car that was waiting in the rail dock. As a lab tech, it was my job to transfer the product from the car to the storage tank. This would take a couple of hours... or so I thought. I had no idea it was going to become one of the longest nights of my life.

Maneuvering awkwardly on the tiny metal-grate platform atop the rail car, I struggled with the bulky, woven, stainless-steel, four-inch flex-hose. Training had taught me the unhooking procedure for when things went right. There was no preparation of what to do in the event anything went wrong. Although cumbersome and difficult, the routine was going as usual.

Suddenly I was blasted from beneath my feet. Liquid sprayed everywhere with enough volume and pressure to knock my hard-hat back on my head and blast my eye-protection up onto my forehead. Dripping in chemicals, my face covered and coveralls drenched, my internal voice was screaming, "My eyes, my eyes!"

I knew I had to stop the spray. I bent over and groped until I felt the connection and could close the valve handle; it must have been bumped open by my foot when wrestling with the heavy, obstinate hose. Crawling, I made my way to the ladder and climbed down to the rail dock. I called for help on the radio, then fumbled my way to the emergency eye-wash station – no water! Then to the emergency shower – murky, smelly water came out in a dribble. Panic was setting in.

In a few moments that felt like hours, my supervisor arrived and helped me to the first aid room. It was excruciating to hold my eyes open for the required fifteen minutes, while the first-aid attendant flushed them with water. In the locker room, a female coworker helped me as I struggled to strip off soaked clothing and climb into the employee shower. I frantically scrubbed my body with rough paper-towel where the chemical had soaked through to my skin. Drying off and climbing into street clothes, I was taken to the hospital to see a doctor.

Freezing eye drops, a quick look see and we were done. I couldn't believe it. The doctor had only briefly reviewed the chemical information on the Material Safety Data Sheet (MSDS) pages brought with me. He was willing to send me back to work that very night with little opportunity to sleep and my vision impaired. I was struggling to hold back panic, afraid my eyes would be permanently damaged. There seemed little care for me.

Despite their lack of concern, I was grateful to be taken home where I climbed into bed. How wonderfully warm and cozy that bed felt. I nestled down, flooded with relief to be able to rest and close my burning, swollen eyes. Sleep was welcomed. The grueling night was finally over.

I had barely drifted off when I was awakened to the insistent ringing of the telephone. "New developments." The voice said. "The company wants you to immediately go for a drug and alcohol test." I was incredulous. It was so wrong to be dragged out of bed after such an ordeal with no time to recuperate. The company had bandied back and forth with the union for months on a new policy regarding substance abuse. The implementation was not clear and had never been enforced. *Why choose now?*

The voice said. "The company is adamant; all the arrangements have been made and there is a time limit."

Refusal would mean being suspended indefinitely – the same as if the test was positive. Taking the test meant I would only be suspended until the test results came back negative. It would also ensure I would be paid for lost days. I felt I had no choice.

Reluctantly, after only a couple of hours sleep, eyes still inflamed and sensitive to light, I forced myself up and got dressed. The dayshift foreman and second in command picked me up from home. Realizing I couldn't see well they helped me find my way into the back seat of the car. The click of the child locks reminded me I had no option.

Expecting we would be going to a medical facility, I was confused and alarmed to find myself at a local hotel known for its hourly rates. I knew my face was flushed and swollen, my eyes red and weepy. I looked like I had been beaten up. I lowered my head to hide my face in shame, as the three men, my union representative having met us there, escorted me inside and up the stairs.

The room was foul, smelled of urine, stale beer and cigarettes, the pattern on the ancient carpet indiscernible. Space only for a bed and table, my escorts sat uncomfortably on the bed while I was seated at the small table with the test administrator, another man. Only able to keep my eyes open for a second or so at a time, I needed help filling out the paperwork. There was no privacy. It was awkward to have the test administrator read the questions and record my answers.

Two hours sleep in the last twenty-four, my head ached and my eyes hurt dreadfully. I was outside my body and no longer thinking straight, confused and helpless to do anything on my own behalf. If I didn't go through with this, I wouldn't be allowed back to work until the powers that be said so. I couldn't afford that. Did these men think this was okay? They were the union president and company managers. Why did they not use their authority to say? "STOP! This is wrong."

"Take this cup," I was told. I had an hour to produce the required sample amount. Realizing the bathroom shared a thin wall with the bed where they waited, I felt silly being embarrassed, knowing the four men would overhear the sound of me peeing.

Embarrassment was soon lost in the condition of the bathroom itself. Only new fixtures would remedy the visible years of grunge. Horrified, still I attempted to comply. I had not been allowed anything to drink and the initial effort to pee was meager. Self-pity welled up. "What could I have possibly done to be treated this way?" I bemoaned. Falling tears did not soothe burning eyes or decrease my sense of violation and betrayal. It was unwarranted punishment – but for what?

Finally able to deliver an adequate specimen, I was allowed to leave and be taken back home.

It was days before I could keep my eyes open for any length of time. They had become dry and scratchy while continuing to be swollen and sensitive to light. My skin started to shed the tautness of the first few days, with a prickly, itchy sensation, a bit like a sunburn peeling.

Although the testing was supposed to be a confidential process, work had become a rumor-mill. I was relieved to be home out of the fray. My teenage children told me of being confronted downtown, "I hear it is your mom who was drug-tested." I felt powerless, exposed and vulnerable.

Five days, the results back – negative – as everyone knew they would be.

The union insisted I put in a grievance for the way I had been mistreated by the company. I reluctantly agreed. The drug test fiasco was unfortunate but I had not been 'hurt'. I felt foolish, feeling violated when no one had set out to humiliate or cause me harm. I was tired of hearing about it and done talking about it. I just wanted to get back to work and put it all behind me. I didn't want to be that troublesome worker making an unnecessary fuss. I wanted so badly for it to be nothing. A grievance was a reasonable way to ensure the company changed the way they proceeded in the future.

Within a few weeks of returning to work, I found myself sneaking up the back staircase when reporting to shift and avoiding interactions with other workers. I took my breaks in the furthest corner of the plant, hidden away behind dusty conveyor bins. Sleep was eluding me and nightmares had become frequent. I started smoking, a habit I had given up years before. I had to force myself to open the door to go into work and could not muster the courage to turn around and go home. Night shift was particularity trying. I found myself longing to run out the door, jump in my truck and leave.

Known for being reasonable and even-tempered, I found myself in tears and flaring up unpredictably, at work and at home. My family became concerned about my emotional fragility, over-reactions, mental confusion, forgetfulness and inability to concentrate. After a small incident at work resulted in a tearful, angry outburst with my supervisor, I accepted that I needed help.

I sought help from a professional. Within a few minutes I was sobbing as I told my story. The doctor understood that I did not feel safe. He identified the overwhelming helpless humiliation of the drug test as the cause. I was diagnosed with Post Traumatic Stress Disorder (PTSD). On one hand I felt validated; on the other ashamed that I was not strong enough to handle it.

I was relieved to be given six weeks off work, yet embarrassed to accept stress leave.

I had to deal with numerous phone conversations over the grievance process. The company was determined to ride it to arbitration; they refused to admit there was any wrongdoing on their part. My anxiety rose. There really was no break from any of it.

I received one benefit cheque and then nothing. I phoned Human Resources (HR) and they told me there must have been an error. Still no cheque. I phoned the benefit company. "There will only be one cheque," I was told.

Shocked I said. "There must be a mistake. The doctor prescribed six weeks with a reassessment before returning to work." The cold voice replied "It appears to be an employment issue. More about you not liking your work than a health issue. Just find another job."

I was floored. An employee who looked forward to going to work, took on extra programs, began new initiatives and worked overtime, became an employee who couldn't face the door, emotionally unstable, short-tempered and weeping at the drop of a hat. I was indignant. Who was this person at the other end of the phone to judge me?

Feeling desperate, I would have to go back to work, I started to argue that I was not ready. Both the doctor and the counsellor supported me being off for at least another month. The benefit worker remained unmovable.

"How am I supposed to support my family with no income?" I cried.

She replied "You need to get control of yourself. I do not have to deal with these kind of calls." Control was one thing I did not have. The tears would not stop. A few seconds later the phone line went dead.

The Union reps couldn't get involved with the benefit company – the HR department wouldn't talk to the benefit company on my behalf and the benefit company had turned on me as well. I sobbed and sobbed – what was I to do? For a few long minutes, I wallowed in self-pity.

The benefit worker's cold, calloused 'handling' of my case stirred defiance in me and dried my tears. Money or no money, I would take charge of my own life. Finally, I felt the proverbial golden handcuffs of work-security slip away. With relief, I decided not to go back to any work until I was healthy enough to do so.

I realized I had to go through the arbitration process to ensure the company took heed and changed future procedures. I will admit in the beginning, I was motivated by anger. In the end – it was the 'right thing to do'.

It took six years to put the political and legal battle to rest. Six years was a long time to stay angry and in fight mode for what was right. It did make a difference. It was worth it. There would be no further drug-testing until the procedures included dignity in surroundings and a female attendant when women were involved. Companies throughout the province put substance abuse cases on hold, waiting for legislative changes and the precedent that was set in my case. Companies paid attention to the arbitration ruling and made better policies.

Hearing my case out loud made me realize what a fiasco it had truly been and I was not unreasonable to seek justice. I felt vindicated rather than isolated. After decades of always standing up for others, I finally stood up for myself and what I believed was the greater good. I did learn to be more willing to ask for help and that although there are people who want to give needed support, there is no one more invested in me than myself.

I finally accepted that there is no shame in a diagnosis of mental illness: PTSD. Like any illness, it takes time and treatment to overcome. I also came to realize – if I felt 'less than' with this diagnosis, this had to mean I held negative judgements of others with mental illness. I now have empathy and compassion through personal understanding.

Although I did for a time, return to that job my heart was never again in it. My career changed dramatically. When I shed those handcuffs, I had the freedom to choose who I wanted to work with and for. I spent a year upgrading in industry safety and started my own business – helping small companies develop and implement their safety systems to meet industry standards. I would not have guessed the twists and turns my life took. I look back on this segment of my life and realize how different things would be if I was still locked in. I am grateful to have been set free. Adversity brought out strength, courage and endurance I didn't know I had. I am excited to be in my life right here, right now.

Ignite Action Steps

As a way to lay your past to rest, I invite you to use the following journal prompts.

Reflection: An unsupportive view of the past.
a)   What past events still affect you adversely today?
b)   Is there someone you resent? Is forgiveness needed?
c)   Did you play small and now have regret?

Perception: Reframing the point of view.
- How do lessons from past adverse events serve you today?
- Is it possible that you and others did the best they knew at the time? Are you able to forgive - for your own sake and theirs?
- Where has struggle made you stronger and able to take a stand now?

Transformation: Moving forward.
- Allow this new view to help you see the past with fondness.
- Express gratitude for these experiences that created who you are today.
- Look to the future with anticipation and excitement.

For this complete exercise, go to prairierosewellness.com and download the free PDF.

Phyllis Roberto
Speaker, Author, Strategic Intervention Coach
Prairie Rose Wellness / prairierosewellness.com

Narelle Gorman

"Don't segregate your strength. You were born with breath, use it when you feel weak. Expand your lungs and believe in yourself."

My sharing, the true grassroots of my humble beginnings, is done with the intention of giving you the understanding that no matter where or what you are born with – you have the power within you to dare to be an exception.

The Thrill of a One Way Street

The wind was soft against my hair and the sun felt amazing as it shone down in all its glory. The little blue and white boat that was obviously the fisherman's pride sailed smoothly in the Ageanean. The freedom I was feeling gave me the epiphany that this is what pure joy felt like. I no longer had the pain in my heart or the difficulty to breathe which had been so prevalent for the previous four years. It was undeniable. I believe in myself again. The Greek fisherman and me, a simple girl from the Australian outback, although worlds apart, were at that moment together not only in location but in spirit.

Language wasn't a barrier. We were cruising the sea exuding gratitude. My true smile stretched across my face. Happiness coursed everywhere in my body. I felt free. My warm, tanned skin was salt-crusted. I was in bliss. Only 48 hours prior, I'd put pen to paper closing over $350k in business transactions on a Greek hillside.

After years of taking shallow breaths, I finally was using my lungs to full capacity. It felt amazing. I was once again me and comfortable in my own skin for the first time since my life had unravelled and I almost lost myself. This freedom wasn't from closing any deals or the money. I simply didn't feel lost any longer. I was back in my element.

I hadn't smiled like that in four long years. Years full of days I had barely been able to get out of bed. Days where my morning drive was consumed by practicing how to say a 'sweet hello'. I would contort my life for fear of his reactions. There were days I was terrified to walk into my own business, because he worked there. All signs I was in an abusive relationship. I had what looked like success on the outside, even won 'Small Business Award" of the year. I had five employees, a great house in a beachside suburb, lots of friends but I was dying inside. My whole life had dried up. From the moment I met him to the moment I left him, my life was like a bad movie. I was allowing myself to be controlled by another's emotions.

I spent years being broken by chasing love. I managed to achieve more success than most, yet I was still chasing that elusive feeling of being loved by others who weren't capable of loving me. Keep reading and you'll understand more.

I didn't know at the time, I was going to have an ignite moment. I was curled up in the fetal position devastated. It hurt to breathe. I had lost myself by squandering my life savings in an effort to not be rejected. I stepped out of a six-figure corporate position and someone (him) had just hijacked my business and told me I was no longer welcome there. It was the business I owned. Just three years prior, I had signed the lease and put my heart, soul and bank account into it, not him.

That day I made a promise to myself: if I can get out of this fetal position and climb out of the safety cocoon of my bed, I would do everything I could to empower beautiful, intelligent women. Women who were spiritually, emotionally and possibly financially bankrupt and were either on the verge of losing everything or had lost it all in the name of love. I vowed to let them know they are not alone, not the only ones that let relationships cause them pain or have acted in ways that baffled themselves, let alone family and loved ones. I knew I could save myself by stepping into service to others.

That was it. That was the day. The moment I re-ignited my life once again. You see I'm a leader, a survivor and mostly a believer – a believer in myself, in humanity and in people never giving up, no matter what. I'm also a high-school drop-out. So why are you reading about me? How did I get in this book, when I'm from a little rural town in Outback Australia, a girl that grew up with my Nanna literally heating the water for my bath on a wood stove. I am what people would call the exception, that came from nothing and reached great success.

The truth is, we all have opportunity. How did mine turn into leading sales teams and organizing events reaching million-dollar numbers, worldwide? Tenacity, determination and continuously standing up straight. Height has nothing to do with it as I'm only 5'2". People who get to know me, then meet me in person are always shocked, "You're not 5'10"?

My story is all about perseverance. My Dad was a bookie, taking bets at the racetrack and my Mum was a nurse. They had met after his service in Vietnam. I can only imagine how handsome he was in his Royal Australian Air Force uniform and how he swept my Mum off her feet. Unfortunately, by the time I was one-year-old, they had divorced mostly because dad ran off and became a bookie leaving my Mum on her own. She has been the purest example of strength, love and determination I've ever experienced. It is because of her I have never given up. (Thanks mum.)

I've had so many Ignite moments. Each poignant in shaping who I am. I'm going out on a limb and sharing a few but keeping the facts simple to make my point. You may have to stand up in life multiple times before you can stay standing up straight.

She's your mongrel kid - we don't want her.

The sheets were pure white and cardboard stiff with starch on my bed with a steel frame. I could smell the night air drifting through the open window and hear my Nana, Mother and Grandfather sitting on the verandah drinking. His slurred words still ring in my ears to this day, "She's your Mongrel kid. We don't want her." As I write this, the usual tears don't come to my eyes… but I can guarantee the tears I've shed from hearing my grandfather, who I looked up to, the only man I really knew as a child, telling them he didn't want me around… those tears would fill a small pond.

Here's the keys

Worried about where I am going to live, I bought my very own home at 18. It was western red cedar with a verandah all the way around it. I celebrated with a big housewarming party for my birthday. I was so proud of my 2.5 acres. I mowed it every weekend and planted cactuses around the perimeter to create my own little secure fortress. As a homeowner, no one could tell me I was no longer welcome or to move out.

A few years later I was done mowing the lawn and the novelty of having a mortgage had worn off. All my girlfriends were out buying shoes and I was paying down my loan. It was time for me to spread my wings and go find out what the world had to offer. Selling my property was my first experience of having a substantially nice little nest-egg in the bank. I felt invincible. This security was something I never remember feeling as a kid. It was so foreign, I was happy to pack up and leave, so I bought an open-ended ticket to the United States.

Time to Go back Home

America was a big party and I missed home. It didn't take long for me to settle back into the Australian lifestyle, buy a house and at 23, I was awarded Rookie of the Year… The Company was AV Jennings, the largest residential home-builder in Australia. It was a male-dominated industry and being young and female, I felt like I had arrived. Maybe Dad (who I had reconnected with) might finally be proud of me. In fact, he did tell me he was proud. It wasn't enough for the little girl in me yearning for more fatherly love. Even though I was managing a team of Australian salesmen, I was a woman afraid of rejection. My career was taking off, so it seemed only normal to leave again!?

So, I bought another one-way ticket to travel the world.

I've always felt a thrill at the idea of a One-Way-Street – seeing what will come from driving the wrong way! Now, I know it was more about rejecting the award givers, the company, whoever was recognizing me before they rejected me so I could preserve my independence and not be reliant on anyone or anything.

Aspen is close to heaven.

Was I in Heaven? Why do I have this green hospital gown on? Why do I have an intravenous drip in my arm? The doctor said I had been found passed out in a snowbank with a .39 blood alcohol content which had him asking if I was trying to take my life. Apparently .40 is clinically dead!

All because two months prior, Christmas Day, I sat next to the phone watching, waiting for it to ring. If you have watched a silent phone, you know my pain - especially on Christmas 6000+ miles away from family. No call. A few days later, I opened my door to loud knocking. Two large men in uniform stood there. All I can recall is hearing the word "Interpol". Wow, what had I done now? Although my intuition knew their purpose and my heart sunk.

My father had left me again. The man I had been trying to prove my worth to since childhood, had ceased his mental anguish by ending his own life. I sat grieving and drinking that day on the side of a mountain in February in Aspen, Colorado watching the most regal bird soaring above me. I hoped it was my father. I can still recall how the sky that day was so blue and clear, almost serene, the air brittle and so was I.

Once again it was time to move on, so I bought a one way ticket to California.

What Greencard?

I pulled over slowly in the little black car. My heart was thumping so hard, I knew I was going to cry. The policeman approached. I took a deep breath. What was I going to say? "License and registration," he asked. Geez, I was on my way to a job interview. All I wanted was to live without looking over my shoulder. I'd overstayed my US Visa. Going home would mean Dad was really gone. I didn't have a 'driver's license or insurance. The car wasn't registered either. Now caught, I might be deported. Part of me wanted to pretend I was from Texas to answer his first query, but I honestly said, "I'm Australian." He was taking his wife to Australia and had a million questions which I happily answered. I drove off with a sigh of relief and a warning to have my paperwork with me next time. I couldn't go on living like this.

You better Get a Greencard

I needed a green card, so I married one…(This is a way bigger story than fits here and might be titled "No Longer Anonymous" and might inspire Ignite Your Life for Recovery.)

A Legitimate Job

You should see me shoot pool. I'm somewhat of a shark. According to the guy I was playing against. My response to him, "That's nothing, you should see me in the boardroom." A few days later, that quip led to an interview.

In a fancy office building, I sat nervously waiting. Next, I'm sitting opposite an extremely good-looking man, wearing of all things, a necklace with a gold-shark pendant. He bears a close resemblance to a movie character and introduced himself as the Vice President of Sales. He has shiny shoes, a great smile. I know I like him. What I didn't know at that moment was that I would take over his position a few years later and embark on an amazing career in Sales Leadership.

I didn't know that he would also give me the keys to the freedom I have in my life today. It took courage to confess in his office, "I think I might be an alcoholic." His response? "No Shit" and then he suggested I go to recovery.

He later walked me down the aisle for my second marriage.

One Million is your Quota

That's a crazy number is all I could think. It's a great number but how would we be able to get a result like that? There were 45 people on my team, all hand selected. The big-cheese, CEO was walking around in his power-suit and you could feel the energy in the room. We were the pioneers of website marketing in the medical industry and that particular day we had A BIG GOAL. The lights weren't going off till it happened. I paced the floor and cheered every time a team-member ran to ring the sales bell at the front of the room. With each roll, the energy heightened and conversations buzzed louder. We reached $560k at 2 PM. I used a megaphone, which sounds crazy. "We are here to get the word out. Our marketing services help them help their patients. Let's over deliver in our service to them!!" It was like a scene from Boiler Room, to show you what I'm talking about.

At 7 PM: the tally board clicked $1,040,000. Tired, elated and jumping for joy, my team persevered: single mums, musicians, young college grads, older gray gentlemen. What made them unique was I'd hired them based on the character of the person versus the paper. The thrill that goes with leading a team to success like that is the "buzz" or tingle you feel all over your body. I love being a Leader!!

Canned Rejection Letter!

"You might want to read my resume again" was the Subject line I had written a few months after I stood up and got out of that fetal position I shared with you at the beginning of this story...That was the Ignite moment that has me in this book. I had received, "The thanks, no thanks" rejection response that crushes thousands of people every day. However, I was going to be the exception. I felt in my intuition these people need me and I need them. I had what they were looking for in an Empowerment Consultant and I had nothing to lose, if I just stood up again and kept trying. There was a fire inside of me that wanted to empower others, women and people who had not had the easiest of lives. People like me who knew they had a gift and were ready to share it, not only for their benefit but to benefit others. After my second email, they read my subject line and invited me to start a conversation about why I wrote it. I was honest; I took a big deep breath and explained what I was capable of and that it was time for me to make an impact on the world. That determination won me the position.

As a result of that subject line, I've sat on a Greek hillside, danced in

Jamaica rains, played in Spanish drum circles, hugged women executives that advise on boards of companies that generate more revenue than a small country, I've been to retreats in Bali with Goddesses, facilitated diversity conversations at Google headquarters and watched corporate Bankers cry on Wall Street. Life has blessed me by allowing me to walk the streets of once war-torn Budapest, support orphanages in Mexico and console battered women on skid row. I have been overpaid in experiences, lounging in suites occupied by the President, sailing amongst the playgrounds of mega yachts, giving freedom to alcoholics and addicts worldwide. Most importantly, I have learned the art of living life one breath at a time. Just a small-town girl, I'm a walking-talking example of how to lead yourself to greater experiences, when you wipe off the tears and keep going.

With everything we do, there needs to be a leader that is willing to drive the wrong way or walk into the jungle and cut a fresh path to lead others. Without leaders we would have no one to learn from. We all have a gift – find yours and lead others to step into their strength. The adventure of life is like valleys and mountains we see off in the distance. Many of us continue to climb up and down for the entirety of our lives… I'm looking forward to staying on the plateau that I'm riding now. Come join me.

IGNITE ACTION STEPS

- Remember, "NO" is not about rejection, it's about getting closer to what is a YES.
- Knock on doors a lot – Follow your heart to the door that is yours.
- Pray to a power greater than yourself.
- Remember that you never know what someone else is experiencing.
- Say Hello to people you don't know. At least three of them a day. They might be the one to open the door you've been looking for.
- Listen to your intuition. When something is too hard, it is for a reason.

I like to believe that my grace and dignity has me living a life that flows with ease, that even with the challenging experiences I've had, I've blossomed into a Divine Feminine Leader. (Thank you Susanne Rodriguez – Co-author in: *Ignite Your Life for Women.*)

Narelle Gorman
Global Connector with Selling with Integrity

Rachel Hayek

"Believe you are worth everything you can dream of and more."

My hope is that my words will show you discomfort and uncertainty ultimately lead us to expand ourselves. My wish is that you uncover your incredible worth and abundant strength in your own stories. I want you to know you can reframe your 'now' and your 'future' through the choices you make. One choice can change the course of your life. When life is challenging, trust in your own strength and decide you have the power to reframe your beliefs whenever you choose. Hold space for a positive outcome and immerse yourself in your experiences.

Redefining Leading Self

My body cannot conceive, gestate or give birth.

This has been my reality for almost seven years and it still stings a little. My reproductive system is at a different stage from most women my age.

I take a deep breath.

I've put off writing this story for some time. As I sit here with tears streaming down my cheeks, hands shaking, I wonder and question what has been holding me back from putting pen to paper.

When I dig in, somehow, deep inside, I know why. It's what always holds me back: discomfort and fear of the unknown. Reluctance to step into uncertainty is like being afraid of the dark. Darkness is only scary if we don't go in and explore it. Once we step into it, our eyes, our senses and our perception adjust and begin to understand it. Often in the darkness, there is beauty and in the unknown, there are possibilities.

In my thirties, I didn't know how life would unfold post-fertility and I don't know how it will unfold now. I wipe away my smudged mascara, take in another deep breath, exhale and continue to write.

Through the course of this journey, I created many stories to explain what doctors, surgeons and specialists could not. I constantly had to ask why my body failed me. I've finally landed in a peaceful place where I understand the 'why' is no longer important. It's what I DO with the resulting reality and HOW I choose to show up that really matters.

When this first began to unfold, my thoughts and feelings centered on my lack of worth. I felt like a failure. It felt like I was mourning the death of a dear one. For some reason, I believed others were grieving more than me. Seeing the pity in people's eyes was too much to bear so I'd look away and force myself to bury my pain. In my head, I imagined their pity was sorrow and I made myself believe it was harder on them than on me. It was so difficult to face my own pain and look inward. Instead, I looked outward and focused on them.

People don't know what to say in these situations and in an attempt to provide comfort, they offer things like, "You never know. Miracles can happen and I know someone who gave birth to twins after she was told she couldn't conceive."

Hearing those words made me feel worse, as if I had the added task of explaining why I wasn't a medical anomaly. My body doesn't function in that way and a crucial part of my reproductive system is missing. It was so frustrating to be placated and compared to others. I couldn't hear what they were trying to say even though they were doing their best to be kind. If I could have told people how to support me, it would have been, "I don't have the answers. There aren't any right words except, I love you."

I believe in positive outcomes and we can choose to be optimistic about the challenges we are given. Fantasizing that I could conceive without eggs and functioning ovaries, was running away from reality. I knew that wasn't possible so I pushed my feelings down and it would be some time before I could admit to anyone how I truly felt, including myself.

As a kid, when my friends would talk about how many children they would have when they grew up and what those children would look like, my normally vivid imagination was blank. That indicated maybe I wasn't supposed to have kids. To cope with the inner knowingness that I wasn't destined to be a mother, I told others that I didn't want to have children. As I approached the end of my twenties, I began to forget about this inner awareness and my stance on having children softened to a maybe. But somehow, deep inside, on a subconscious level I knew; not me, not in this lifetime.

By the time I got engaged at age 29, I completely forgot about my intuition and having children had become part of our plan. We would have the first five years of our marriage to ourselves and then we would start a family. In my early 30s, I knew something in my body was off. I had my doctor run a gauntlet of tests and the results showed all was 'normal.' Deep inside I knew something was not right because it 'felt' imbalanced. I was scared and desperately wanted the results to be reassuring but I didn't believe them. I allowed the experts to know my body better than me and I pretended to accept that nothing was medically out of alignment. In truth, I was too scared to keep searching for answers. I never looked for a second opinion.

At age 34, I had the first emergency surgery. The pain was intense and excruciating, even with the maximum dosage of morphine. I didn't know what was happening, but I knew it was connected to the signals my body had been giving me. In those agonizing, moments prior to surgery, waiting for tests to be complete so I could receive treatment, my body continued to experience the severity of the physical pain while my brain ceased to care. I was exhausted and the experience was beginning.

My right ovary had twisted and barely survived. When I endured the same experience for the second time 15 months later, it didn't make it. I was devastated.

With so much damage from all the inflammation and trauma, there was only a very slim chance of ever becoming pregnant. My left ovary was a casualty; it had little functionality and very few eggs. My specialist offered me in vitro fertilization (IVF) as an option and I'd have to act fast.

Deep inside I knew IVF wasn't the path for me. Having a baby in this way did not resonate even though I had acquired the belief that it was my role as a woman to be a mother. Getting pregnant naturally was unlikely but not completely off the table.

Despite my frustration at my body's 'failure to work properly,' I subjected myself to multiple humiliating tests and stood in line, confused, with other scared and sad women in hospital gowns, while doctors and nurses did their job. During that time, my body became a specimen and I hung on to the glimmer of hope that motherhood was in the cards.

I persevered although time was running out. Six months later, what I had always somehow known was now real: I would never have a child of my own. I was so sad and in those moments, although I was surrounded by so much love, I didn't know what to say. I kept my outward sunny disposition shining as much as I could and told myself, everything was fine. I brushed it off as if it was no big deal.

That was my outward attitude. Inside it was tough, because now I could never go back and change my decisions. Listening to myself and knowing what was best for me, I had made the resolution to forego IVF without consulting my husband. I'd made so many of my decisions based on how they impact others, especially when it came to my spouse. I always believed I was compromising. I was sacrificing my power and my voice. No more. I was stepping into my self-worth toward a new path. I considered myself the number one stakeholder in the decisions I was making. I was redefining how I led myself. This new way of making decisions eroded something in my marriage and the relationship began to unravel. I felt guilty about this and over time, I realized that at some point I would have to put myself first. Alongside the guilt, a fire and passion arose inside me. It wasn't about fertility or IVF or motherhood. It was about treating myself as if I mattered.

Shortly after the results came back that I was unable to conceive, my sister learned she was pregnant. My body would never perform the miraculous function of giving birth but I was so relieved that hers would.

As I embarked on my healing journey, I became acutely aware of the 'missing' right ovary. That tiny piece of my body was so significant and I felt the gap it left. A part of me withdrew and I kept silent. I felt like I had a hole where the ovary once was. Though the left ovary was still physically present, it no longer functioned either. From the outside, I still appeared to be a vibrant woman with a big smile while echoes of my fertility floated like ghosts on either side of my womb. It felt so quiet inside that part of my body.

As I adapted to this new reality of childlessness, I sometimes volunteered parts of my truth. I felt awkward with my answers when people often asked the question, "do you have children?" as a conversation starter.

When I said "no, I don't," they'd ask "why not? Don't you want children?"

They never seem to expect me to respond with "I cannot conceive. I'm not fertile."

Keeping something so intense forcefully stuffed inside me caused it to leak out before I could shut my mouth. When asked about children, even from strangers, I would blurt out, "No children. I'm down an ovary."

Some people awkwardly changed the subject while others said, "So then you will adopt, right?"

People's facial expressions showed their discomfort and I learned that many of us, myself included, didn't know how to talk about this. I discovered that I needed to be mindful of how, when and with whom I was sharing my intimate truth. There seems to be this idea that a woman's life and her worth is tied to being a mother.

I continued to grieve privately, behind closed doors. Hot tears flowed freely, yet with each drop, some of my pain evaporated. A part of me felt relief – no diapers, sticky surfaces or sleepless nights. Another part of me felt sorrow for the void that a motherless life would offer. As I continued to question my feminine purpose and my worth, my marriage continued to crumble. If motherhood was no longer on the table, was this relationship what I wanted, or better yet, was it what he wanted? I remember telling him that if my infertility was a deal-breaker, I would give up our marriage for his happiness. I'd already made the big decision to forego IVF and I was neither ready nor did I have the courage to declare, "our relationship isn't what I want anymore." We grew apart over the next few years. Eventually, I got what I had passively asked for. He ended it.

My courage grew as marriage and motherhood faded away. Left with just myself to care for, I boldly stepped into my emotional rebirth. I got to know it, I observed it and my confidence grew. Questioning why all this had happened, I learned I had to forgive myself for compromising so much. Forgiveness became my practice. The whispers of my subconscious rose up and I reconnected with my intuition.

With much support from friends, family, coaches and healers, I began to examine what I 'could' do to bring more joy into my life and to move through this transition with grace. Instead of withdrawing, I plunged in.

Reframing motherhood was another step that helped me to heal and redefined how I led myself. Present at the birth of my first niece, I marveled as I watched her sip in her first breaths. The instinct to love and protect her was all-encompassing. I spent her first night in the hospital, beside her on a reclined chair. My sister and I cried together, celebrating the beautiful new addition to the family and pausing to acknowledge the pain of what I had endured. I began to reclaim motherhood and what it could look like for me, now an aunt and female role model. Self judgement began to dissolve and as I learned how to practice acceptance, the new me was starting to blossom.

We live in a time of change: so many of our social structures and belief systems are shifting and transforming. Historically, women unable to bear children were looked upon unfavourably. There's a bit of that stigma remaining and part of my journey is to help reframe that in a positive way.

I now share my story to empower women. I am inspired to lead them to their own truth and embrace their wholeness. I want every woman to pay attention to her body and trust that she knows what is best for her.

I did not know that the decision to forego IVF would be a catalyst for some big life changes. The experience led me to understand how I wish to lead myself. Though I am not physically fertile, I have given 'birth' to creativity that feeds my soul. Where there was once a feeling of worthlessness and lack of purpose, there are instead ideas and abundant possibilities. Through written word, teaching yoga, learning about plants and nature, coaching more powerfully, speaking more truthfully and creating more with my hands, I am leading my life with a deeper sense of clarity and peace.

I thought I had a hole in my body, where my right ovary once lived. Through our 'holes,' literal and figurative, our opportunity is to lead ourselves inward to the beauty of our completeness and spaciousness. What emerges is our light. Through the big stories, big emotions, hormonal shifts and so much pain, I've been led here to this moment, pen to paper and writing a new chapter. Now when my mind says "you'll never give a partner a child," instead of feeling inadequate, I smile to myself. I know what I need to do. I have so much to give to my human family. Part of what I offer is the confidence that within the wildest challenges, there is light, love, forgiveness and joy.

Underneath all we put on ourselves: the 'shoulds', the guilt, the expectations, plans and pressures, lies our truth. Through faith, trust and hope, I've discovered that I am the author of my own life. Although I am not a mother in the traditional sense, my destiny to embody the qualities of a mother brings me boundless joy. I now see the light others see in me and I see it in you. By surrendering to the journey, I've developed a deep sense of care and love for myself. I offer the same to you. Being better equipped to love others and knowing that when you look into someone's eyes and see love reflected, you are seeing your own beauty. I see the light in you.

IGNITE ACTION STEPS

When facing a painful or difficult challenge, here are some things you can do to practice self-love and to support your connection with your truth: Be patient and give yourself time to process. There are often many layers to what we experience and it takes time to get to the center of what we feel.

- Ask yourself: What am I believing to be true and what is actually true about my situation? Keep asking that question to peel away the layers until you find what lies underneath. You can do this verbally, through self-reflection in silence, or by journaling.

• Get curious about anything that sparks your interest and moves you to feel deeply. Regardless of the emotion, be open to exploring.

• Maintain a sense of awe and wonder for all things and all people. Pause to marvel at the world around you.

• Let others in to how you feel. Share your feelings with those you trust.

• Ask for, and receive, help by starting small. Let someone pick up the tab at dinner, help you carry something heavy or give you a ride home.

• Focus on abundance. Notice all you have versus what you don't have. Make a list if that helps.

• Trust that everything eventually changes. Impermanence is inevitable.

• Get clear on what you want. Try guided visualization, journaling, support through coaches and healers.

• Be open to forgiveness, towards yourself and others. Be diligent and practice often.

Make self-love a habit. Do at least one thing every day just for you that brings you joy. Say "I love you" in front of a mirror even if it feels silly. Practice this until you can do it with ease. Remember that you are a gift and the world needs your light.

Rachel Hayek
Culture Programs Specialist | Self Love Coach, YTT 200
rachelhayek.com

SAMANTHA RIDLEY

*"In the most challenging moments search for stillness
and listen for your inner voice. It knows your path."*

I hope my story inspires you to go back to that one moment in your life you've had difficulty letting go of. Allow me to ignite you with my personal story and the choices I made to listen to my inner voice. I invite you to share your story with another in order to heal from it. Trust in that we are all standing here waiting for you to arrive. We all have it in us – we are all worthy – we just IGNITE at different times.

THE WINNER IS...

Long before the Women's National Basketball Association and Women's Ice Hockey in the Olympics, if you preferred Tonka Trucks over Barbie Dolls, you were labelled a tom-boy. From young, I refused to comb my hair, wear girlish dresses or even bathe if I didn't have to. Every day I heard the words *"brush your hair!"* through my mother's teeth and sometimes, "or *I'll cut it off!*" She threatened to count to three many times where I was concerned, although I never heard past two and three quarters.

Having a mind of my own, I pushed my luck to three that day. Forced to the limit, my mother cut my hair. *Short!* Honestly, it was a win-win for me. No more brushing my hair. No more fighting over it.

Days after the shearing, I went shopping with my mother and as per usual, I wandered off. Climbing up the top bunk of a furniture display, I was talking out loud and playing a game of make believe, like this was my room. Two boys barged in, one pointing, *"Is that a boy or a girl?"* Without even thinking, I landed like a superhero with both hands on my hips and blurted, "I'm a GIRL!". They scattered like mice.

My instinct was to chase after them, but something glued me to the floor. I'd been emotionally hit. I couldn't breathe. I was winded, as if I'd been punched in the stomach by The Incredible Hulk. It was the first time I felt self-conscious and at a loss. Grasping at my hair with both hands, I started yanking desperately. "Please grow, I promise I'll brush it; please grow, I promise I'll wash it; God, if you grow my hair back, I promise I'll never ever disobey my mother again."

It was my first genuine prayer; not the ones you learn in school or in church, or even kneeling at your bedside with your parent. It wasn't a prayer for world peace, to solve world hunger or to save a life. I wanted God to grow my hair back right then and there. I knew it was selfish, but I felt anguish. *"They didn't know I was a girl."* I was embarrassed. It took me a minute to gather myself. I saw my reflection in the car window on the way home. I closed my eyes, took a deep breath and when I reopened them, glanced at my image again and asked myself, "Is this true?" My voice, deep within me answered gently, "Clearly, you're a girl. *You know who you are.*"

At age 14, I locked myself in the bathroom on school-picture day. Still a tomboy, refusing to wear a dress yet, I was dreaming of being on the cover of Elle Magazine – as an International Fashion Model. I know... it's difficult to explain, but I'll try.

I played every sport I was allowed, basketball, volleyball, I even made my brother's baseball team. I inherited my athleticism from both sides. My father's love of sports influenced me the most, making me extremely competitive because, "When you're a Ridley, second sucks!" Post winning a basketball tournament, while inhaling my dinner, I petitioned my parents to watch the Miss Universe Pageant.

I remember beautiful women: Miss England, Miss Malaysia, Miss Canada, Miss USA... Wearing my sweaty uniform, stuffing my mouth full of spaghetti, I thought, "I could do that." I was absolutely mesmerized, their sparkling eyes, brilliant smiles and shimmering dresses. The global diversity of these women was unbelievable. They weren't just beautiful – they were educated, athletic, talented, well poised and many worked and/or supported charitable causes. This awakened inside me, a new calling – my feminine.

I envisioned my very own runway being paved just for me and imagined a jet plane taking off to faraway lands. I was the pilot. The pilot of my own destiny. I enrolled in the local Modelling School. I wish I had a video of my first day to show you, with my jogging sweats, t-shirt and high tops. America's Top Model? Hardly. More like America's Funniest Videos. The other girls were impeccably dressed. They walked up and down the runway spontaneously twirling with puckered lips and attitudes that caught my attention. This was alien to me; I was totally unfamiliar with "strike a pose." Even their topics of conversation were like a foreign language. They discussed top fashion designers, newest trends, best mascara and latest perfume. They were real girls, sugar and spice and everything nice... only they weren't nice to me.

No encouragement was sent my direction, unless there was an audience watching – mostly mothers. I felt so out of place, uncoordinated, awkward and way out of my comfort zone. It's like knowing you're a duck: you talk like a duck, you walk like a duck and you look like a duck, so clearly, YOU are the UGLY duckling.

Contrary to my awkwardness, my mother was a swan. Elegant and graceful, a true beauty even without makeup. She preferred, in her shyness to sit off by herself, away from the others, which was misinterpreted as mystique. This drew these 'Mothers of Dragons' to her like bees to honey. The beautiful woman I most aspired to be like, was my mother. Yet, here I was trying hard to walk like and pose like the other girls. Nothing worked for me, no matter what I did. I studied the mirrors around the room and I just couldn't see me in any of them. Then one day it clicked?! They announced a modelling competition. I didn't understand walking with a book on my head, but I understood what a competition was.

Overnight, I became a full-fledged Girl! I was committed to practicing and my focus became winning. I had a reason to wear dresses, put on makeup and walk in high heels. I practiced up and down the runway like I owned it. I was determined. There was pandemonium when they called my name, "...the new Miss Fashion Model is: Miss Samantha Ridley!" No one was more stunned than I was. The looks I got from the 'coven', priceless! This was MY Kodak moment *(for the Millennials: Instagram Moment)*. With this win, I was assured a place with these girls, right? Things would be better for me. But they were worse. Now, I was enemy number one!

Next came the Modelling Association of Canada, hosted in Toronto. There were numerous categories and of course, the prestigious catwalk. The goal was to attract and sign with one or more agencies from around the world. All my clothes were sponsored. My largest supporters were Irma and her daughter Josie from Irma's Bridal Boutique, in my hometown. I am forever grateful for all they did.

The contestants were not much different than the ones I left back home. They had the same attitude, just more expensive accessories. All the models were wearing black tight dresses, heels, perfect hair and immaculate makeup. They moved like a synchronized swim team and I was the buoy. I wore a matching two-piece: baby pink skirt with three ruffles, a fitted top and white high heels. I stuck out like a wad of bubble gum on a hot tar road. This oddity wasn't new for me. I could feel the pressure building. It got to me. I ran off with tears pooling in my eyes. My mother caught me at the elevator. I pleaded with her on the way back to our room. "Please, I want to go home. I hate it here." She reminded me of how strong I was, how I stood up for myself, went after my dream, "All you need to do is just show up. If you don't go back down there, you will never know how things would've turned out."

Her words resonated with me. I stood up tall, shook my head, looked straight into her eyes, "I hate my hair." Into the washroom we go. I clean off all my makeup. We wet my hair and gel it back off my face. My eyes recognize me in the mirror. I take a deep breath and compose myself.

I chose to go back down there. I walked the catwalk. I *won* their prestigious Runway Award. The judges told my mother they admired my confidence of no makeup. My natural look with my hair slicked back. They said I stood out; I was unique. I had tuned out all the noise and made my way back to that runway, reached inside myself and found the courage and the belief that I was just as worthy as any other girl there. I didn't quit. I got right back out there. I did it. That moment, the one where I showed up… 'chose' to show up. That 'was my winning moment'.

The following year I entered the local Miss Teen Thunder Bay Pageant for the second time with renewed confidence. Each evening started with us walking up to the microphone, stating our name, age and school ending with "I am contestant #52." Laura, my rival from modelling school, did the same ending with "I am contestant #53." We both made the cut to the second night, so we received new contestant numbers as the judges narrowed it down to almost half. "Good evening, my name is Samantha Ridley, I am 17 years old; I attend St. Patrick's High School and I am contestant #52" (it said #28 on my tag). I didn't even realize the error but heard all about it from Laura as I stepped off the stage. I was mortified. Then not two seconds later, I heard her introduction, "Hi, I'm Laura Woodbeck, I'm 17 years old, I go to FWCI; I'm contestant #53" (it said #29 on her tag).

The temptation to give it back to her ten-fold was so strong, I could barely contain myself. I thought of a clever, smartass thing to say and waited for her to walk past me. The moment had arrived and something unexpected happened. I was overcome with compassion. I remembered moments before how horrible I felt making the same error myself – I chose kindness instead. That moment has stayed with me till this day.

When they announced Laura as the first runner up, just before she walked to the front of the stage, she paused. She turned and looked back at me. I always wondered: 'Was that her way of saying 'thank you' to me? Did she know they would call my name next?' I like to think it was a little of both. It was a beautiful moment for me, "The new Miss Teen Thunder Bay, Miss Samantha Ridley!"

I had a wonderful modelling career signing with Metropolitan (New York), Elmer Olsen (Toronto) and Elite (Milan). I travelled the world: Italy, Switzerland, Vienna and of course New York City! I shot for Vogue, walked the runways wearing Coco Chanel, Donna Karan and Gianni Versace. I did it, tomboy and all!

Almost 30 years and 30 pounds later, I drive to my local gym. Completely beside myself, with all my broken promises – I haul my ass in there. Feeling fat and fed up, I walked in with my fake-it-til-you-make-it persona and this tall, buff beautiful firefighter – I mean 'trainer', strolled over and introduced himself. We hit it off instantly and in my head I'm like, 'Oh hell no, this isn't happening, please God don't let him see me in shorts, EVER!' He's charming and I'm fixated on his muscles, I have no idea what the hell he is saying, then I'm like, "Is he hitting on me? Seriously, Ridley. Keep it together. We're here for a personal trainer, not a date. Yah, a date with a hunk that could 'technically' be your son."

I tell him, "I can talk a hind-leg off a mule and back on again. Getting my way is my thing. So, don't give me some young, dumb kid with no backbone to instruct me because I'll eat 'em alive! I need someone with a strong personality – like superheroine strength! I've been avoiding getting back into shape. Get me the best you've got."

"I've got the perfect person for you!" he assures me. Out walks Melissa… buff, not an inch of fat on her perfectly sculpted body, tattoos, clearly meaningful with the Japanese Cherry Blossoms across her shoulder cascading down her side. Trendy black glasses, shiny chestnut hair and a perfect ass (forgive me – but it's true).

For the next eight months, I never said, "no" to anything 'My Meliss' threw at me. But, I never said I did it without complaint. That was the deal. I'd do whatever she asked but not without consequence of my mouth.

There was a constant moan and groan known to the regulars. I could patent T-Shirts with my common slogans: "You're trying to kill me!", "You suck!", "Seriously!", "Are you f#@ing kidding me?!"

My fitness journey was a huge undertaking and is still a work in progress. Eight months, three to four times a week, 'My Meliss' encouraged and pushed me. I lost body fat and gained muscle mass but something else began to build. I got to know her strengths, her struggles with family, friends, relationships, her life story and ambitions. I began to coach and guide her in life. I saw so much potential in this young woman and so much of my younger self in her. I chose to share my life stories, experiences, wins and losses. All in hopes of offering a seasoned perspective to assist her to make better choices earlier than I did. This transfer of energy grew so organically, it ignited in me the desire to teach and guide other women to their best versions of themselves. (My Meliss' has forever permeated my being and I am eternally grateful and honored that she entrusted her soul to mine).

We started to train together outside our regular sessions, travel together where she introduced me to Reem, mentee number two. This led me to reach out to many other girls like Megs, Nicoletta, Steph, Pamyla, Cole and Kinga. I am overwhelmed with gratitude and the level of unconditional love I experience watching these women blossom. The bonds and friendship are contagious and fills my heart. I share in the reward with their wins and have fulfillment I never expected. All I have learned, provides a great opportunity and responsibility to not waste my experience but instead, to pass it on. If it helps even one person, then it helps me. I also get to experience a different outcome, a different path through them. I am their crystal ball and they are mine.

I hope to offer you faith to believe in yourself. Know that people will judge you, but it's what you tell yourself, that internal dialogue that really matters. If you have a dream, believe in it, believe in yourself. This will make your dreams become your reality. You can be whoever you choose to be. Be brave. Be kind. Do the work. You're worth it. Find and let your inside voice lead you. Trust your instincts and you will love who you truly are. You will find acceptance in yourself and therefore be accepted. We are all searching for a way. Be your best example. Be yourself.

Ignite Action Steps

When we don't fit in, it can be painful. You may not know it, but in time you will learn being different has its own beauty.

- **First**, when you feel like you don't fit in, find a quiet spot. Stand or sit. Still yourself. Just breathe. I breathe until I can block out all outside stimuli. Then stay still, wait and listen. Often, you are just telling yourself a story in your head. Ask yourself, "is this story I'm telling myself true?" Practice this exercise and you will come to find, if you quiet yourself long enough and listen, your true inner voice will start speaking from deep within. You will hear that voice tell you what is truly going on. Listen and follow your instincts. Remember to be kind to yourself like you would to a friend in need. Make a decision from that place. Even if it doesn't turn out the way you hoped. From my experience, when I listened to my gut feeling, I found I could live with the outcome because I showed up authentically. It isn't always easy to follow your own voice especially when it's at odds with everyone else in the room. But if you practice this, it will teach you to embrace your own uniqueness.

- **Secondly**, find an accountability partner. Bouncing something off a trusted person is recommended. This can be anyone, a lover, a parent, a sibling, a friend, or even an acquaintance. I have spoken to a stranger on a park bench and received another perspective that gave me clarity. Sometimes just saying the words out loud to yourself or another, whether you get feedback or not, can provide you the answer.

- **Lastly**, practice self-reflection and prayer. Review challenging moments in your life, which may or may not have turned out well. Pray or meditate for a better way it could have been handled. Offer yourself forgiveness. Recognize that you showed up the best you were in that moment. Being able to stand in your own space no matter how painful, reach inside yourself, look for your own voice and it will guide your way. If you fail, start again. Start as many times as you need. No one walks the first time they try. Self-reflection reveals God's grace. Remember where you started. Practice gratitude for your blessings and dare to strive for your dreams.

Your inner voice is the key to unlock and IGNITE your limitless possibilities. I encourage you to share your story with another. When you focus on helping others, the reward is – you end up healing something inside yourself.

Samantha Ridley
CEO of Shipp Shape Media Group
www.shippshapemedia.com

TANYA DONAHUE

"No matter the success or failure of your venture
– it does not define you or your value."

When you have dared to step into the leadership position, the road can be hard. In sharing my own experiences of feeling disappointment and wanting to quit, I show how you can find your strength and reasons to persist – to triumph through the valleys and persevere.

WHERE ORDINARY MEETS CONVICTION

"I do not fear death but how tragic it would be to live a long comfortable life and never lay down all that I am for the one that laid down HIS life for me."

This is my internal force, my meaning and purpose.

I value others immensely. I am deeply disturbed by the injustices that take place in our world. I feel the burden and the pain of those who are vulnerable and exploited. I try to experience it as though it were happening to me or to someone in my family. BUT I don't always respond as though it were happening to my own children because that would be utterly false. If it were my own children suffering, not a moment of any day would I cease praying. I would give everything that I possess and relinquish all that I am, for their freedom.

I am vastly bothered that I don't have this complete abandonment of self in order for others to merely survive, as I believe I should.

I struggle to live in the tension between the wealth of my North American life, with the luxuries that feel normal to me. Paying $6.00 for a coffee, buying a book when there is a fully stocked library a block away, purchasing new clothes when I have an already full closet and enjoying warm, fun vacations; the list is endless. How do I balance this life with the awareness that child labour and human trafficking is happening every single day. These are real people being exploited for greed and selfish gain. How can there ever be a balance I wonder? How do I still have joy in my own life without shutting off to the pain that permeates someone else's?

I was a normal average kid growing up in a middle-class Canadian family in Northern British Columbia. Each week I would watch the hour-long World Vision show hosted by Alex Trebek. Every segment brought the world from afar into my living room. I experienced places unfamiliar to my own and was introduced to the reality of poverty and human suffering. My eleven-year-old self was moved by what I saw and I began to sponsor a child, each month donating $27.00 from my babysitting and dishwashing money.

I was eventually discouraged by my well-meaning family to stop, as they believed the money was not reaching the intended recipient. Things changed for no particular reason and I grew into a teen that didn't much care about anyone or anything other than myself. I met my husband, Scott, at age 16, moved in with him at 17, got engaged at 18 and we married when I was only 19. By the time I was 20 we were living in a new city and I was alone most days with a small baby, while Scott was working away for weeks at a time on a drilling rig.

We bought a new-to-us home and our neighbor invited me to church, "Thanks, but I don't really feel comfortable going without Scott," was my response. Whew, bullet dodged I thought! But she eventually invited me again and this time mentioned that there was free childcare. I still didn't want to go but free childcare was pretty alluring, and I felt bad that she clearly had no one else to join her for the church's 'Bring a friend' day. Unbeknownst to me she was bringing people to the first and second service.

Then it happened, my life changed forever, for real – predictable perhaps but it happened! That day my heart was irreversibly touched through a drama production. Standing alone on stage, hanging from the neck of a woman was a large, flat, cardboard circle painted all black. This black hole represented the void she felt in her life. Next, was her attempt to fill this emptiness: she began grasping into the air and figuratively placing a new job, traveling, buying a car, getting married, starting a family… anything and everything to put purpose and meaning into the black hole. Whoa, this was sounding familiar. She would experience a temporary high but then inevitably she was right back to the place of searching and un-fulfillment. The message was that the only one who could fill this void was Jesus Christ.

This spoke to me in a place of longing I wasn't aware existed. I didn't run to the front and surrender my life to Christ but I was definitely shaken. The answer seemed simple enough and eventually as I returned a few more times I grew to understand all that Christ had sacrificed for me. I made peace with God wholeheartedly and fully embraced His unconditional gift of grace that He so blessedly offered.

It wasn't a happy-clappy version of fake promises and obscure religious rituals. It was breath in my lungs, purposeful and gave life meaning. I learned life is still life. Hard, full of struggle, some self-inflicted and others simply because existence is difficult in this sinful, fallen world. It just is! I discovered Christ laid down His life for me and though He doesn't promise me that things will be easy here on earth, He promises He will never leave me. This grace, this salvation is a free gift. I am not required to feel guilty and/or to prove myself. I am simply accepted as I am and counted worthy because of Jesus.

What happened over the next twenty years is best referred to as an amazing transformation; things that matter to Him began to matter to me. Slowly my values and my desires have become a reflection of His heart for loving and serving others.

This heart change is what brought our family of six to move and live fulltime in Haiti. It was a dream come true, even with four less than ecstatic teenagers. Two of our children were adopted from Haiti as toddlers and I loved the opportunity to move and live in their homeland. We were involved with business development and our purpose and intention were palpable. My primary work in Mirebalais, Haiti was to establish a Café-Spa-Boutique, offering employment to locals and a place of respite for foreign visitors. My work eventually led me to working with 16 artisan partner organizations to supply the boutique with handmade goods for visitors to purchase. When we had to return to Canada, a year and a half later, it was very sad for me. I knew I could carry on my work in Ti Kokoye with the capable Haitian staff but I also knew I needed to continue our work with Artisans. The best way we know to help alleviate poverty and aid people rebuilding their lives after disasters and tragedy, is through job creation.

After much prayer and consideration, we decided to begin Mango + Moose, a socially conscious fashion and lifestyle brand that works with

Artisans in 11 developing nations to curate and design life-changing collections. This is the very endeavour that would bring me to the end of myself and having to face what it meant to truly surrender.

We had done hard things before. We've been married for 21 years and have four children, two of them from international adoptions. We have started and have ran successful businesses. We have walked through the pain of a business that failed. We have traveled and lived abroad, and we even lived in an orphanage. Yet nothing prepared us for what happened with Mango + Moose. We were not naive enough to believe that just because we were doing something 'good' that it would be successful, but we were after all, hopeful.

We put all our collective energy into building Mango + Moose. Combining my deep passion for ending poverty with my love of design and adventure along with Scott's business acumen and whew, we laid a pretty terrific foundation! Two people whose sweet spots are start-ups.

Unfortunately, there is always a middle that follows and as with ALL things there are no guarantees. We had made some pretty large mistakes, some his and some mine. Some out of our control and some we could have avoided if we had known more. We over-invested on inventory and software and did not put nearly enough into marketing. We chose a route for selling that we both struggled with and the cost of the platform was huge and unrelenting in time demands and finances.

If there was ever someone who wasn't going to accept the middle well, it's me! I fight with myself. I constantly have to talk myself into carrying on. I mentally beat myself up, I find everything challenging and get extremely unpleasant to be around. Meanwhile Scott's desk was an arm's length away from mine and we were spending every waking minute of our lives together while Mango + Moose flailed, and our life savings plummeted. Blame was looming and desperately trying to get a foothold.

I knew there would be adversity when we began our business. I knew that stepping out of my comfortable life to stand up for equality and putting HUMANS FIRST, was not only going to require hard work and determination but a lot of strength and faith. I still wasn't prepared for the toll it took on all the areas of my life.

I had actively chosen this path and was now feeling the full weight of my decisions.

It is often said that at the end of your life the worst thing to have is regret for unlived dreams! But what about when you have taken the leap and it isn't working and you regret it. When you feel a total fool for it and have lost all hope. For, me failing meant I was failing all those who work with me and depend on the sales from their Artisan goods. Sleepless nights of worry and stress became regular. Barely a moment passed without me casting judgement on myself. The mental barrage of self-incrimination was endless, "Perhaps all our past successes were really more of a fluke than anything to do with me. Were my motivations wrong? Was this really about me seeking glory for myself?" When I looked in the mirror, my reflection revealed all the hopelessness and disappointment I felt inside. I was hurting.

I ended up buried under my covers feeling so low that I wasn't sure I would be able to crawl out of it. I struggled to remember my WHY. I could have done a million other things, mentally conscribing my list of lost alternative options. Simultaneously reminding myself of how unequipped I am for the route I chose, stupid in-fact and that anyone but me would have been better to do this work. I have never been in sales. Why did I ever think I could sell artisan goods? I am an introvert; how did I ever think I could be the public face for those who desperately need fair and ethical practices and opportunity in business. I hate being in the public. I thrive on privacy.

I cried long and deep, words failed, I raised nothing but tears and a broken heart to my Father God. This was the lowest point, following months of uncertainty, questioning and desperate, seemingly, unanswered prayers.

I can't even remember when the light finally broke in, but it did. My heart was soothed to a place of peace, a place where I could catch my breath and remember that I am loved no matter my circumstances.

I was reminded of my elusive 'Why', my purpose and desire to show others Christ's love was always there. The pressure of life had only buried it for a while. Reminded that suffering and pain are always felt deeply and that I hurt because I care.

My dear friends, we are not the sum of what we have achieved or lost. Whether what we try works or it doesn't and no matter the degree of success or pain it brings, it doesn't change the truth that each of us holds immeasurable value. We do not need to prove our worth to Christ; we are enough because He is Enough.

We were created in His image and He says, "Come to me, all you who are weary and burdened and I will give you rest. Take my yoke upon you and learn from me, for I am gentle and humble in heart and you will find rest for your souls. For my yoke is easy and my burden is light." - Matthew 11:28-30

So, when I think about our world and my place in it, I remember this, I am not the final answer, none of us are.

I am grateful for my small role and I persist in the pursuit of equality, of loving others but this does not define me. I am worthy because He says I am... period.

The end of the story for Mango + Moose is not yet written. We work with those who are vulnerable, those who have been exploited and abused: former child soldiers in Uganda, women rescued from the red light district in Asia, families in Haiti who desperately want to keep their children and not relinquish them to orphanages because they can't feed them. Our partners in Nepal are working in a remote village where there are no girls aged 14-18 years because they have all been trafficked. This is not the end of their story; this does not define who they are.

We are in this together, we continue to whisper to the broken-hearted with each step we take, "We see you. You are not alone. You are not forgotten."

Today we are bombarded with information from across our globe and for the most part, it has had a desensitizing effect on all of us. It wasn't like when World Vision was the only show in town; now we can read or see something every minute, from the far corners of the earth. The effect this has is unnerving. We can be completely moved by what we learn, saddened, even outraged however we have the ability to move on from it very quickly, to keep scrolling and to bounce back without a scrape. We are now suspect of most stories, given the influx of fake news that is vastly distributed online and this adds to our indifference. We ask ourselves, is this really real? It could be but how do we truly know, we don't have the time to investigate every claim.

In addition, the fallacy of all or nothing is also something that permeates our society today. Unless we are able to completely eradicate an issue, we ask what is the point anyway? This mindset nags at us to give up before we even start. But what happens when we don't allow these things to give us permission to quit?

This will look different for each of us and the beauty is this means that all we aspire to can be reached. What stirs your heart, what makes you feel unjust every time you think about it or causes you to be moved towards doing something greater than yourself, start there! That will lead your way.

IGNITE ACTION STEPS

Continue to breathe in and out each and every day, get out of bed, put one foot in front of the other and persist.

A lot of my persistence and motivation comes from the ordinary to-dos of life. I have a family to take care of. I have staff who count on me. Artisan partnerships in 11 countries. Responsibilities each and every day to which I must attend. I also read a lot and I draw inspiration from others who, like me, are simply sojourners here on this earth. I can rest in today knowing that this life is not the end.

Pray. I like to call out to God for mercy, for help, for Him to give me wisdom, favour and the ability to Trust Him. Nothing in my life has or ever will compare to the power of prayer. Romans 8:28 tells us, "...in all things God works for the good of those who love Him, who have been called according to His purpose." He is my helper. I know He loves, even though a circumstance may not look the way I would like; He has not forsaken me; I can go to Him for help and He will answer.

Share and be vulnerable with at least one close and trusted friend or family member. Choose wisely but do this! You need someone to encourage and pray for you!

There's a funny saying, '...about going to the throne *and* not the phone...' while I would agree that prayer and petition trumps all else, we are also a people of community. We need others. Apart from my husband, only one friend did I trust with all – and I mean all that was going on. Because there is a great geographical distance between us, that meant a few tearful *(read that as sobbing)* phone calls on my part that went back and forth over several months. I cannot overstate the value of a friend who listens, cares, encourages (and prays for) you.

Tanya Donahue
CEO + Founder of Mango + Moose
www.mangoandmoose.com

ASHLEY AVINASHI

"Knowing that we are enough, just as we are, is our birthright.
Remembering this along our journey is our gift."

It is my hope in sharing my story, that you will find the keys to transforming your life and legacy through exploring and loving yourself truthfully. It is in reclaiming the open and curious hearts with which we were born that we come to lead and serve through love. My wish is for this story to remind you that you are worthy of taking a chance on following your heart's whispers in this lifetime.

BEYOND THE MASKS: A RETURN TO LOVE

'Keep it together.' 'Be happy.' 'Don't show too much emotion.' 'Just be grateful.'

I had lived several decades absorbing these beliefs from my environment. From growing up in a busy household of twelve, to schooling, competitive sports, community work and the corporate world. I couldn't escape the messaging that spoke loud and clear to my heart – we can conform in order to be fit in, or we can choose not to belong.

Over the years, I became masterful at shutting down, hiding away the parts of me that felt unseen or unwelcome. My sense of self-expression had found a very comfortable, yet deeply rooted pit within me to call home. The heaviness of carrying my buried heart grew over time, though it was, strategically masked under all the layers of a strong exterior shell and my 'good girl' persona. On the outside, my life was seemingly perfect. Many members in our community would often share with my parents that they wished they had a childlike Ashley. Bright, driven, loving and kind. Every parent's dream to hear this from their friends and family. Yet, those compliments became increasingly difficult to receive as I sensed in my heart, even as a child, how many places I had fit myself into that didn't feel quite right for me.

I was the square peg, chiselling off all of my corners to squeeze into that round hole. So determined was the little girl in me to gather the love of those around her, a love that she felt she had to work for. So afraid was that little girl of not being enough for the world that she had forgotten who she was underneath it all. So much that the masks she wore became the only way through which she knew to experience life.

And so, I continued as I knew to, determinedly meeting all the markers. Good education. Check. Financial stability. Check. Marriage. Check. Children. Check. The list of 'successes' went on and on.

Overall, it was working beautifully for me. *Until one day, it wasn't...*

This is where we take a trip down memory lane to understand just how I arrived at the point of not being able to go on as I had. The point of no return where I could not unsee what I had seen. The point at which the pain had grown so intensely that I could see the life-inhibiting cells moving through my body like wildfire if I didn't choose a different way.

You see, I was ripe for 'success' being born into a family where my parents would do absolutely everything they could to create a good life for us, more than they would have had access to in their home countries before coming to Canada. This meant that they would find a way to educate us well and provide us with whatever support they could, often at the expense of themselves and their own comfort. Both were exceptionally hard working and could create something from nothing, being the bright and creative souls that they were. They were the sort of people whose generosity and open heartedness spilled over into every relationship they had. They would take the shirt off their own backs for anyone who appeared less fortunate than them. They had come from humble beginnings and their spirit of simplicity and putting others before them was the foundation on which they rested their hearts.

But these were also the grounds that bred a disconnection with their emotional selves. In my parents' era of navigating the waves of a new culture, with the loss of their home life and surviving scarcity, there was no time to even contemplate what it meant to sit with their own emotions. The simple story is that they had left their families heroically to create a better life for generations to come.

To further exasperate a disengagement from their own needs, our East Indian origin suggests little reason for prioritizing oneself. Traditionally, the culture doesn't give much space to the processing of personal emotions. This is the good and bad of a rich community-based culture, where all of our lives are interwoven into one big, beautiful tapestry where the collective always comes before the individual. My parents felt a security in knowing they were a part of something greater than themselves, yet the enmeshment of the culture also kept them tied to its limitations.

Inevitably, this was the way of life I embraced after countless summers spent in India. This way of seeing life had seeped into every ounce of my being. I recall so many of my earliest years visiting the Hindu temple, which my father had built for our community. Each Sunday, I would willingly join my parents while my younger sister kicked up a fuss over wanting to sleep in more. During our routine visits to the temple, I would be the first to raise my hand at any task. I was the kid who gave up playing with other children in order to serve those around me. *Yep, I was that kid.* The 'good' one. The compliant one. The helper. Not only at the temple but in the community, at home and at school.

Now, despite all of the acknowledgement for my external efforts, a feeling of disconnection had entered my heart. I felt myself drifting from children my age as I became increasingly serious and focused on my academic achievements, athletic performance and community service.

I felt less and less able to have a vulnerable conversation with those closest to me. My heart was crying inside for honest connection. Tormented. As much as I longed for meaningful conversation and space to breathe between all of the doingness, I accepted the notion that I would be guaranteed fulfillment on this path of over-achievement. I wasn't inclined to put aside the momentum I had created for a bright shining future.

I stepped into my higher education and graduated from university on scholarship. I was recruited for a dream position with corporate – a fast track into management. This meant I would be mentored by the organization's CEO and work alongside him at head office. One-hundred-hour work weeks became my norm. I had learned to thrive in busy, fast-paced environments, not only by growing up in a joint-family of 12 members but by always carrying an overflowing plate. I had been an over-achiever, over-doer and over-performer in every aspect of my life. External validation had become my drug of choice. The more validation I got, the more I needed... it was a vicious cycle.

Yet, if I assessed myself honestly, I was empty. Most days, I was running on a reserve of the previous night's dinner of chicken and greens. A meal I'd prepare in a dichotomous haze of strength and loneliness, around midnight in the small apartment I'd been given just 15 minutes from the office. Each and every day, I continued with my familiar way of being – checking the boxes and putting everyone's requests before my own.

I started to contemplate why I was doing what I was doing but found myself continuing to push through my discomfort. After all, I was the resilient, middle child who had taken on a role of 'responsible' one. I had to get it 'right', especially since I had moved away from the family for school and to follow my dreams in the corporate world. I identified with being strong and driven. The logic-driven rules still had a hold on me, unknowingly. *I didn't question my roles and responsibilities until my life starting crumbling.*

Raging waves of humility passed through me as I came to learn that in fact, I was not invincible. My health had deteriorated by this point. I had avoided visits with my parents for some time as they had caught onto my lack of self-care and unprecedented levels of stress. Increasingly restless in my sleep, I was chronically exhausted, impatient and irritable when outside of the workplace. I had no emotional bandwidth to hold space for a relationship, let alone the one with myself. I started losing weight worrying about my future. My skin was growing pale. I was plagued with an unshakable sense of failure.

I was aware of the constant inner battle: speak my needs or serve the desires of the greater collective. In this case, the corporate entity. That said, self-sacrifice seemed to be the norm, not only in my culture but for many women in my life. It was ever so familiar as I'd witnessed my own mother hide away so much of her own desires for the sake of those around her.

With time, I hardly recognized myself, both alone and in connection with others. I had spent decades trying to prove that I had a place in the world. My worthiness was rooted in outside success of likability and love. I hadn't come to know what it meant to truly connect with another without the purpose of seeking love or proving self. I was struggling to find who I was in all of this.

Only later did I realize this is when the burnout started creeping in. There was no sense of freedom from it; I felt like a robot, deeply exhausted, confused and often isolated in my pain. Up to this point, I had done wondrously well at covering it all up, pretending I was just fine. The mask of being strong and keeping it together was all I knew. My heart felt a gaping void that could not be filled as long as I ran on the proverbial hamster wheel.

The deep pangs of my distress were so alive within, that I could not ignore the feelings any longer. The masks I wore weren't working as they once had. Something within was asking, "Get out from behind the wheel. Assess the road ahead."

And then it happened. The light shone down on just what I was ready to see.

I received a phone call from our CEO, just after 8 AM. We had yet another high-level strategy meeting that day. I had gone to bed just five hours prior after finishing my regular routine of working out, inhaling my late-night dinner and then returning to my computer to prepare for the next day. In my absolute mental, physical and emotional fatigue, I had slept in. Already late, that request alone, to run to the office as soon as I was able to, shook the dark abyss within me, like a single guitar chord being struck, interrupting the silence of a vacant auditorium. His words echoed through every cell of my depleted body. I collapsed in tears on the floor. My whole world was shattering. I had become so physically incapable of serving at any level in this state. My intellectual capacity had become so compromised through ongoing sleep-deprivation and stress on my nervous system. Yet, I was living the dream I had so long ago desired for myself. My entire life's energy and focus had brought me to where I was today.

Later that week, several VPs were let go on the very same day, without any notice. The organization was restructuring again. Global headquarters had given immediate orders. This selected group of VPs were escorted out of the office, with hardly a goodbye to those they had built life-changing relationships with.

I could not unsee what I had just experienced. The temporariness of life became so evident in that moment. What was all this for? I saw that I could pour my heart into an organization for decades – all to be dismissed abruptly. I had given up my health and inner peace for the sake of climbing the ladder and serving others more than I could serve myself. My cup was beyond depleted and could not be replenished in the life that had come to be. I knew I had to take a leap into choosing differently for myself.

I mustered up the courage to meet with our CEO, a brilliant and kind-hearted man, with high expectations for those around him. The sadness of what I was about to share swept through me as I slowly moved towards his office door. The tears were streaming down my face. I spoke about my appreciation for the opportunity to be chosen by him personally for the fast-track program and for all the support and resources that had enabled my expedited trajectory into management. There were many others who had hoped to take part in such a program, yet I had been chosen. It had truly been an honour. Though as much as I felt to be a disappointment for terminating my side of the agreement prematurely, I knew I could not continue on this path. My heart was calling in a new way of life that held my needs first, so that I could give from a place of abundant love and joy, rather than from deprivation. He received my decision gracefully, wisely suggesting I follow my heart. Phew! What a relief it felt to be understood and accepted in all of my pain. But why had it taken me hitting such an unbearable threshold to really listen to what was screaming out from within?

With growing awareness, I came to learn that a large part of being stuck in marathon-like energy was my fear of not being loved or acknowledged. This was the only way I knew love to be. It took time to dissolve the beliefs around it. I began contemplating a new way and with that, I came into gratitude for what I saw was the best of both worlds growing up. I learned to exercise my individuality in the Western world and embraced the collective and spiritual essence of my Eastern roots. I realized I had a choice in what I believed and could embody all that felt closely aligned for me.

Through reclaiming the hidden parts of myself, I freed up ample time and energy that had otherwise been consumed by deep guilt, shame and judgement. Sharing in authentic love and connection began with deconstructing the beliefs I was attached to... The idea that we can't choose our own unique path. The misconception that we must be completely enmeshed in the systems around us to feel that we are contributing or valued. The voice in our head that tells us we always need to do it alone or have it all together. The falsehood that we can't meet each other where we are in our authenticity. The illusion that we need to be 'successful' on the outside, to feel enough on the inside. Instead, I learned that we operate as completely different people when we know we are loved just the way we are.

Knowing that we are enough, just as we are, is our birthright.
Remembering this along our journey is our gift.

I invite you to explore your full truth and have someone meet you there with unwavering acceptance. Without the masks. I am here to listen to your story and the universe is here to hold and support you too. There are simply no accidents. When we are willing to dive in and meet ourselves, we can begin to connect the dots that lead us to reclaiming parts of us that we left behind and empower others to do the same.

As leaders, I believe we can only inspire others when we find the courage to remove the masks we used for protection from that which we feared. Only then can we ground in our heart space, where we find the freedom to be ourselves. Where we do away with self-judgement and accept whatever we are moving through. This is where we create allowance for ourselves, to live our deepest, truest purpose and find support in our desire for connection. It is in this willingness that we will find ourselves leading with love.

IGNITE ACTION STEPS

Take time and space for self, daily. Listen to the rumblings within. Journal, allow for the emotions to surface. What may be coming up for you? Where is the pain being held in your body? What are you most excited about right now?

Step out of what is comfortable. Try something new for yourself once a week. Allow yourself to be in it fully and experience whatever may come.

Surround yourself with people who have taken chances on revealing their true selves, without the masks and those who inspire you to step out. Decide to listen to their podcast, attend a local workshop by them. Call or email them and ask to meet for coffee. Contemplate your way of being. Let others inspire you to step out. There are many willing to share their stories and gifts if asked.

Seek assistance where needed – a safe container in which to share and be seen just as you are. It may look like a retreat. It may be an energetic healer who can help identity the misalignment within. It may be a breathwork session. Ensure you have the right support along the way.

Remind yourself daily that the only permanent truth of you is that you are innocent, you are enough as you are and that you are ever evolving. This can be in the way of declaring such affirmations out loud while standing in front of a mirror or in nature. We were born full and whole and though we may forget along the way, we can come back and remind ourselves of our truth – we were all born from love.

Ashley Avinashi
Founder, Raising Humanity
www.raisinghumanity.com

TARANUM KHAN, PH.D. CCS

"Love wholeheartedly and leading will take care of itself.
Lead by example as leadership rests in authenticity"

I am sharing life-incidents that have shaped me, with the hope that you might learn from them. To me, leadership does not rest in age, experience, position or title. Leadership is having compassion, feelings, owning up, apologizing, holding ground, rolling up my sleeves and getting my hands dirty. I believe in learning and growing together, leading with value and authenticity by practicing what I preach.

FROM THE HEART OF A LEADER

I can hear my mother's loud omnipresent voice in my head, "You can do anything you want. Do it by yourself. Do not depend on anybody. Learn everything, so that you never have to say, 'I don't know'. You may not use it all on a daily basis, but who knows when it might come in handy?!" Those who know my mother know she's a hard taskmaster, but her words are true. She's super skilled and a perfectionist. My father, on the other hand, kind, forgiving, loving, all the heartwarming adjectives that you could possibly think. He encourages and gently guides but is never demanding.

Most of our family time was devoted to my mother telling inspiring stories at bedtime. Growing up, my night-time routine was lying down between my parents. My mother would have a book in hand. We would sing together, then she would pull incidents and stories from her knowledge of religion, history, our ancestors and sometimes her own life experiences. My father would softly keep company.

Like my mother and father, I am extremely grateful to all the women and men in my life who stood by me. Nevertheless, I am also thankful to those who acted as sandpaper; rubbing hurt – yet helped me shine. They encouraged me to stand out and own my leadership skills. 'Things happen for a reason' is my belief – though I do not ask for bitter experiences, it was the unpleasant encounters that demanded me to tune into and hone my resilience and strengths.

I suppose my madness for multitasking originates from my mother's guidance. "Don't sit idle with your hands in your lap. Time is precious. Don't waste it!" Annoying right? I'd find her cooking four dishes simultaneously, along with watching TV and knitting all at the same time." She would narrate how she had secretly taught herself to crochet and to embroider. As a young girl, the fear of being ridiculed by her cousins and not wanting to be embarrassed by them, made her work at it until she got it right. After marriage, she picked up ridiculously difficult knitting patterns so that her sister-in-law would not look down on her. I was raised on her adrenaline – and boy was it hard.

Have you ever felt an all-consuming desire to be the best and fight till you win? Looking as far back as I can remember, I have been that person. From an early age, I learned to challenge and love challenges. Asking life to bring it on, ever ready to fight back in defiance. My mother taught this. However, from my father, I discovered that winners are not necessarily leaders. He taught me to lead with love, compassion and understanding. I learned to practice forgiveness, if not, 'live-and-let-live'.

Thankful for my mother, though a consonant directress, she instilled confidence in me to conquer every challenge, while my father nurtured me to face every obstacle with love. My elder son Ayaz uses the phrase, "ass on fire" to describe driven people, but it actually refers to me. I was told and learned, be PERFECT at everything: study, study, study, games, painting, dancing, cooking, gardening, stitching, tailoring… and look good, keep the room tidy, be popular, make good friends, prepare deliciously fancy meals, and become an avid reader. The list goes on – excel, excel, excel…

This reminds me of getting ready to run a half-marathon competing against kids of other staff members at a police-training college of which my father used to be the highest-ranking officer. I came in third. That defeat is the first and most bitter in my memory. I had failed on two levels; first by embarrassing my father's officer-status and second by not being the top winner. It hurt!

Holding back my tears, I stood red-faced to receive the prize. The other two kids stood beside me and to my surprise I was handed the bigger, better gift. It should have been given to the child who had won the first prize. I loved coloring and those sketch pens were great compared to the plain pencil box that I would get for third prize. I had failed to earn them. Wait a minute, what…!!! It was clearly written on the cover, First Prize. Still I thought the individual handing out the prize had made a mistake. So, I went up to the staff member and told them to exchange it. They hushed me and said, "Keep it." First, I was confused, then shocked and dismayed, when the real picture hit me. I was being given the gift to please my father due to his rank. Even at the age of ten, I saw this as corruption and no insult could have been worse. The other kid had been given the pencil box. I could stay quiet, take the colors home and fill up my picture book. I was staring at the prize in my hand when I looked up and saw the kid holding the pencil box with sad eyes. I quietly walked up to him and gave him what was rightfully his.

On my way home I told this incident to my father. I remember his words, "Winning and losing is a part of life. Not every race is to be won, but you are a leader and true leaders always do the right thing." This incident stayed with me and has been foundational in understanding that leadership is not limited to age. I feel that each and every living being should try to be their best self. Some of us do it for selfish reasons, such as to please loved ones or to look good in society, but true "Leaders," as my younger son Mushahid says, "...do it because it is the right thing to do."

My position as a young female officer at the University of Jammu, India, taught me lessons that are guiding my actions to this day. My first supervisor, Dr. Poonam Dhawan set examples that I am proud to follow. In my enthusiasm to make a difference, I was always ready to hit the ground running and she, in her professional wisdom, prepared me for the long-term. She did it through experience-sharing and setting examples. She would be the first one to start moving chairs when a room needed to be reorganised. Without a word, the staff would rush to follow suit. How would you not when you saw the team leader do it? I never forgot her words, "Women have to put in double the work to prove their worth. Taranum, you have the fire to do great things; remember that a fighter might lose, however managers always win. Be a manager and you will always be in charge of the situations you might face."

I understood she was preparing me for experiences she anticipated would challenge me. It did not take long for trouble to find me. While Dr. Dhawan was away, I was in charge of department operations. In her absence, a senior male staff member, known for his amoral behaviour decided to show his true colours. He was disrespectful and rude towards female staff and junior team members. Taking advantage of her absence, he tried to misappropriate resources. He most likely thought an inexperienced 29-year-old female would not question him. Me being me, I did not back down from the bullying. I took the fight head-on. I reported him with a well-documented complaint. As I had proof, the management had no choice but to issue him a warning. However, he had been playing the system and knew his game well, with ties to top management. This episode elicited unwanted attention; I was told, "Do not come with problems, bring solutions, otherwise be prepared to face consequences." Eventually I was transferred. Even though they said, "She is underutilized, we could use her in another department." The message was clear, I must keep myself in check. Did I heed? Not a chance. On the contrary, when another unjust situation happened, I stood up stronger.

I was then working as an administrator at the university for three years and handling the Dean's office. This was a sensitive role which involved high levels of tact in dealing with senior faculty members and supervision of admissions for 34 post-grad departments. Plus, I was assisting on the printing of the academic calendar, curriculum, organising events and conferences. I was also a young mother of two and living a full/busy life.

Things worked well until the new Dean decided to centralise the admission process, which brought undue pressure on office staff. His male personal secretary, having worked this position for over 10 years, was knowledgeable about previous protocol. However, when the Dean began depending on me to get the work organised, he felt ignored. This put a negative spin on the secretary's feelings. To exert control, he tried embittering the office team. I looked past his arrogant behaviour and continued the work. On a day the Dean left early, we were still reviewing, to prepare the admission lists. To keep up with our workload, I asked staff to stay late, which may have triggered the secretary's violent reaction, as he wanted to leave.

He walked towards me threatening. "A 30-year-old woman officer? Unheard of! Who do you think you are? I have more years in service than what you went to school for!" He was yelling at the top of his lungs. "In three years, you think you can run the system. You are just a woman with no experience of how things are done in this office." Two other male staff members watched in shock. I was shaking. In my entire life, no one had ever raised their voice to me.

I stood up and calmly said, "You're right, I'm young. But I do know how to make things work the way they should be done." Visibly upset with bloodshot eyes, he left grumbling. I was angry that he dared talk to me like that. He had no authority over me. Still, I completed my work. When my husband came to pick me up, I broke down crying. I was distraught and felt insulted. Never had a person spoke to me with so much contempt. My husband was livid and wanted to do something. But I told him, "No', this is my workplace. I will handle it."

I filed a complaint. When things were not moving, I approached the Vice Chancellor and after multiple self-representations, an inquiry proved misconduct and found him at fault; he had crossed the line. The committee head asked me, "What action would you like taken against him?" I knew he could be suspended without pay and a record on file against him. I didn't need to think about it. I said, "None." The committee was baffled, "What was the point of holding an inquiry, wasting our time if you do not want any action." To this I said, "I did not lodge a complaint to have him punished. If action is taken against him, his family will suffer more than him. My goal was to make him realise that his behaviour was unacceptable. An example has been set therefore in time to come when his daughter joins as a staff member, no one will disrespect her. A verbal apology is all I ask with the promise that he would never repeat that with anyone." He apologized, though I don't think he had any realization of his transgression. Though time has a way of making people think differently. On my last visit to the university he greeted me with a smile. Though younger in age and experience than the person who wronged me, I made a conscious choice to not personalize the event and set a new standard.

I faced yet another humiliating experience with power. Bullying is another name for the games people play to get their own way. The setting and time were so different! How is it even possible that two people from different parts of the world, cultures, gender, settings and times responded to their insecurities in much the same way.

Eight months under a supervisor, with irrational behavior was like walking on eggshells. Confusing, since our relationship had been respectful in the six years prior to being offered the contract. She was smiling, looking relaxed, "Your contract has ended, sign this termination please." I was not surprised. I signed the paper, still wondering why a manager would behave so poorly?

"Good. Now that this is over, can we come clean? Why is it that you never accepted me as a part of your team? Your resentment has been obvious since day one."

She looked at me, suspicious, "You know this is not negotiable, you just signed the termination!"

I responded, "I'm not negotiating."

I had not forgotten her hostile greeting at the onset of my assignment. Her behaviour shocked me. She had burst out, "I don't know why you're here, you shouldn't have been hired. Why has management given you this role; go back to your other position." To this, I had responded, "I'm not sure what you mean, it's a decision they made. I applied for the position and was accepted. I assure you I will give this role my 100% as I always do." Her reply, "I wasn't a part of your hiring." Once again, a co-worker had unleashed a wrath of unacceptable verbal abuse. In the months that followed, she would not share information and resources, often found fault and blamed me for responsibilities of other staff. I second-guessed myself but ignored her behaviour. Senior management waved it off, "She's hard to please. It will require effort on your part to build trust with her." I worked even harder, but she didn't budge. I raised it with the senior manager again, but they encouraged me to accept she was right. To me, her behaviour was abnormal and raised red flags. I was being bullied, harassed and victimised. Yet the work was enjoyable, therefore I ignored her attitude to avoid conflict. Still it impacted my self-esteem. My husband, Altaf restored my confidence by encouraging me to stay true to myself and reminded that she was not worth my time.

Now that it was over, I deserved to know the truth. She openly blamed me for getting the role as a favour from the management. According to her, I did not have Canadian experience and had thrown big words at her during the interview. To this I responded, "I choose positions only when my heart is in the role." Mocking, she replied "I've been here for more than a decade; my heart is not in this role, but I do it. No one in this organisation can do it better than I. You can work here after I retire." My parting words, "I pity you for working in a role that you do not have passion for. Before I started this position, I knew and respected you as a professional. Unfortunately, now I see you in a different light. Be well!" I didn't file a complaint. You cannot change people who have a closed mind. I informed management about her bullying and irrational behaviour. The onus to keep the organisation free of negativity or to maintain decorum is on them.

I always tell people to choose roles based on passion for the work they do. If you are not following your heart, you will not enjoy it. You may be good at it, but it will lack authenticity. My story shows how decisions in life show up at work. My passion now is working with newcomers transitioning into Canada. I provide them tools, resources and encouragement to be their best selves. People often ask 'why' things happen and get caught in the issues. I, on the contrary, believe that life's challenges are opportunities. If we manage to overcome them while staying authentic, then we get to stand tall and tell the story and inspire. I lead with passion and compassion. A leader is one who nurtures towards enablement and most importantly brings change through reflection and motivation. Lead with love and love to lead.

IGNITE ACTION STEPS

Each one of us has unique leadership qualities; look within, listen to your calling. Genuinely be all you want to be. True leaders reflect passion and commitment in their actions.

Five Steps of the Leadership Ladder: Core skills of my leadership toolbox.

• **Listen, don't just hear:** Listen with all your being, mind, body and soul. Silence speaks as well! Inquire and inspect, then set expectations. It might mean long conversations but assures that you get to the pulse of the matter. Emotional intelligence saves the day. Learn to tune in.

• **Communicate with empathy:** The key ingredient to building positive leadership rests in trusting relationships created through open communication. Don't forget communication is a two-way process. Treat everyone with respect and never make assumptions. Reflect and follow up for success.

• **Look for answers within:** In your quest for leadership, remember that greatness rests in our own being and comes from doing things we enjoy. Be your own competition. Work shouldn't be a burden.

• **Coach and be coachable:** No one is perfect, therefore keep judgement at bay. Empower, encourage and show, in place of telling. Learn from anyone you can and at every possible opportunity. Learning is best taken on as a never-ending process until your very last breath.

• **Be authentic, practice gratitude and appreciation:** Be true to your calling. Riches are not necessarily earned in dollars. Appreciation and knowledge are gifts that multiply when shared, the more you give, the richer you get.

Taranum Khan, Ph.D. CCS, Career Strategy
& Education Optimization Consultant I Author & Speaker
www.etrec.ca

BARBARA SANTEN

"When you make a decision with your intuition, the outcome is always right for you. Always. Fearlessly follow your heart."

My intention in sharing my story is to encourage you to make decisions from the heart. Your heart is your intuition and guidance system, which comes directly from the deep desires you have for your life. These desires guide you to your purpose and are meant to be followed. Fearlessly follow those whispers because they are the only direction you will ever need. They are the gateway to your soul's fulfillment. If you are feeling them, they are attainable for 'no' desire is felt unless it is possible to achieve. Nothing your heart tells you is too outrageous to do.

DESIRES ARE THE WHISPERS OF THE SOUL

When I was six, I asked my mom who 'my' dad was. My friends all had dads and I didn't. I had always accepted my situation of not having a father. I was a kid and too little to think it through. My mom casually answered, "Uncle Bob is your dad." Which was her way of protecting me from knowing he was my father. It was a satisfactory answer to me. I'd known no different my whole life. Uncle Bob was a wonderful man who was fun, a little crazy and over the top and my much older siblings spent every other weekend with him.

My mom not telling me the truth before I had asked, created a mistrust inside myself, which permeated my life, leading to a landslide of poor decisions. I'm sharing this with you as a background to the rest of my life because I believe life doesn't happen to me, I believe life happens 'for' me and this experience shaped me, forever.

Just after I graduated high school, I met the man who would become my first husband. I was only 18. My family was not pleased with our engagement a year later. I was crushed, especially by my mothers' lack of enthusiasm. I wanted her 'for once' to trust me. To believe that I could make a good decision and own my choices. She was fixated on controlling my decisions and I longed for her support. Despite her objection, I married him anyway and believed everything would unfold as it was meant to be. Only, I wish I would have felt encouraged and supported. I remember thinking to myself "TRUST ME MOM! So, I can trust myself!"

This was the beginning of my journey toward having confidence and self-assurance. Looking back, I can see how my experience around 'Uncle Bob' was the first time I felt I wasn't trusted. No one allowed me to know the truth about 'Uncle Bob' being my father. AND no one believed in me at age 19 to make the decision to get married. I hated my family for that.

I became angry and defiant and those feelings pushed me away from what my gut was telling me. I did have trepidation about marriage. My inner voice was whispering, "Is this a good idea?" But I was unable to hear my uneasiness about marrying him because I was so resentful inside. My brain and heart became so full of doubt because of the lack of support from my family, I rebelled. I ended up marrying him to prove that I had the power to make important decisions for myself.

A year later I had my first beautiful daughter, Daphne. Her birth helped me recognize why things happen the way they do. In seeing her, it all became clear. I realized we can't always know the outcomes but need to 'trust' that the journey has a way of unfolding beautifully. My daughter was the amazing product of this seemingly terrible decision. When I looked at her, it quickly became evident, it was all meant to happen because her birth changed all of our lives.

Awakening to this idea, I began to understand that all I ever wanted was to be trusted. I wanted to be allowed to make my own choices and be respected. Inside, I needed to be trusted to forge my own way, regardless of how things unfolded. Even if it turned out to be a mistake. I just wanted support from my family. 'Support!' Was that so much to ask?

That became a very important lesson for me to learn because it helped me begin my journey in supporting others unconditionally. I want them to have what I never had. I want others to feel believed in and trusted. This desire guided me to become a supportive parent, a caring midwife and sympathetic relationship coach in my life today. Becoming a parent created a whole new connection with myself that I had never known before. Out of my commitment to parenting, I grew more committed to myself. My intuition and inner alignment were instantly sharpened. (Motherhood will do that for you).

I became pregnant with our second daughter during the time that we were desperately trying to salvage our rapidly declining relationship. By the time April was born, we were already separated. She and her older sister were my driving force, my reason to do well, stay strong and make a cozy home for the three of us. Which I did!

Despite the marriage ending, she was born easily and smoothly to a loving single mom. The moment of her home birth, supported by midwives, was utterly magical. It impacted me so deeply, I said out loud to the people in the room: (my mom, sister, my children's father and two midwives) – I'm going to be a midwife. And I did. I went on to become a midwife and delivered babies for ten years... But that's another story. This one is about my relationship experiences and listening to my gut.

My next relationship was a 12-year marriage that was mostly uneventful. Deep inside I was trying to awaken. I could feel myself longing for something, but I was too busy with my life to fully listen. I was deep in my work as a midwife, while my husband became an excellent stepdad and helped me raise my daughters with loving support. Our relationship was 'nice' and that was enough at the time. After 12 years he left; he wanted out. I didn't understand but knew from my previous learning, the Universe always has a plan.

I very quickly got myself into another relationship that ended five and a half years later. That 'soul contract' transformed me the most. It was so painful, yet so delicious at the same time. I got a taste of what my heart could feel and became inspired to create this feeling of passion and connection in a healthy way – without any anguish, strife and discord.

That experience ignited in me a desire to search for an answer to my deepest question, "Is it really possible to have it all? To have the passion, the love and the emotional safety in a relationship that I have longed for?"

I realized that my mom had remained single my whole life and never modelled healthy (or even unhealthy) intimacy. The messages I received my entire life were 'relationships are hard, difficult and uncertain'.

My inner voice kept speaking to me and nudging me to believe in something better.

My experiences ignited in me a drive and longing to find authentic answers to my relationship questions. I broke down all the relationship rules I had collected. I started questioning conventional relationship psychology and examined my habits. I embarked on a spiritual path that would eventually lead me to myself – 'home', to the 'inner knowing' that there was more to relationships than pain. To the glorious realization that loving, passionate, healthy intimacy was not only possible but our birthright! I came to understand that I 'truly' can have it all.

This was a message I wanted to share with the world and women who are also struggling with the feeling of 'knowing' there's more but not daring to allow themselves to feel it. Society and family tell us 'relationships are hard' and we blindly believe it. Women who are stuck in unhappy relationships are convincing themselves, "I should stay, because I have so much invested." Women who are single and can't seem to create or maintain the deeply satisfying relationships they long for are telling themselves, "The relationship of my dreams doesn't exist; I give up!"

I was 'not satisfied' by what society was handing me. I felt silenced, with my 'wild ideas' and my dream of a heart-opening, passion-filled, spiritual connection. I rebelled – and searched until I found my own way.

I went through my own birth and rebirth. I have had many painful moments of strife and difficulty. Except, now I see it as 'Growth'. Growth that I needed to have. Ultimately, I realized that all I desire is within me and attainable! I now understand that 'thanks' to all of those challenges I kept evolving. I never gave up. I didn't settle. The struggle served the purpose of driving me to continue searching for my own self-love.

Some people judged me. Many wondered why I was 'having trouble' with men but I didn't see it that way. My journey with my three partners was my growth path. Each relationship gave me a rich evolution that I never could have had otherwise. These experiences were an integral part of shaping who I am today and how I show up with others now.

Therapy had never helped me much by keeping me focused on my past as my problem!

Though the mistrust that happened in childhood caused some pain and hardships, knowing that would not help solve my present challenges. It contributed to my life for sure, but it was 'not' the problem I should be solely focused on. The clear issue was; I was looking at the wrong thing! It was keeping me stuck in an endless loop of pain, rehashing and remembering only my past. I would go to therapy and feel worse, only to return the next week to remember how broken I was and how much I needed the therapist to feel normal – 'except I didn't'!

I became tired of this pattern. There was a part of me that trusted myself to be okay and longed to move forward, 'towards' what I 'wanted'. I finally said, "No more!" and left therapy. I began to see, there was no problem! I had just been conditioned to believe that relationships are hard, so that's how I showed up in all of them!

I soon began to study and earned a Certification in Applied Positive Psychology (CAPP). I attended life coaching courses and relationship coaching training. I read piles of books that resonated with the feeling I was longing for: hope, trust in myself and healing. I was moving forward. Envisioning something better. Living in alignment with a high vibration. I watched videos about relationships, searched articles and slowly but surely, I was getting closer to the answers I was searching for.

That last relationship was a perfect platform for me to learn. Because it helped me awaken to the notion there 'was' more. I learned to listen to my gut. The initial years I overrode a lot of messages from that inner voice. I was going against what I felt because I was attempting to follow the incomplete relationship messages I had received while young. Bravely I started acting on my present instincts instead. I'll admit it was really scary. I knew that it could mean that we might break up. But by then it was worth that risk, because I had learned that the price I'd pay for ignoring that inner voice would never be worth it again. Alignment can be challenging but it's satisfying and feels right when it is honoured. On the other side of that bravery are the gems and the rewards of our life.

I don't claim that acting from your growing inner awareness is painless but it's 'right' and you might not know exactly why your gut is guiding you this way until you can look back much later.

It was the hardest thing I've ever had to do – leave that love. But it was also very clear and obvious the relationship wasn't serving me. (*I had doubts afterwards and even reconnected with him for a while.*) but because I stepped into my Truth from a grounded, centred, 'knowing' place, not an 'angry' or 'feeling hurt' place, I knew it was right for me. I learned to live in the moment and to be guided by that inner voice.

I reconnected with the Teachings of Abraham (by Esther and Jerry Hicks). Who would ultimately help me realign with my guidance system and give me permission to feel good inside (what a concept!). I raised my vibration so that in 'that' place, I could make better decisions. I worked on this for six months by practicing following my gut, which meant doing things that felt 'right' for me and returning to my inner knowing over and over again. Ultimately, in that high vibration, I received the clear, calm message to follow my feelings from within, at all times.

I eventually drew the greatest lesson: That 'me' listening to my intuition is 'always valuable'. It is the voice of my Inner Being, my Higher Self, who is connected to everyone else's 'Higher Selves'. They're all in cahoots, they already know each other, and they've already made magnificent plans.

The messages, plans and paths that are right for you are laid out by your Inner Being. The question is – are you listening to the nudges of your soul? I have learned to live in the moment and to be guided by that inner part of me that deserves to be heard. You too have this guidance system in you. You can tap into it and find your own alignment whenever you need. No one knows what is best for you, except you. You have the answers within, just ask and they are there.

Ignite Action Steps

Learning to tap into your inner guidance is not as difficult as it may seem. It is the first step in re-connecting to yourself, which is the very thing you will need to create a healthy relationship too!

Start small. Follow your gut with non-consequential things like turning right instead of left when travelling somewhere. Choose a lipstick you 'want' to wear. A great way to connect more with your gut feeling is how you order food in a restaurant. Rather than choosing based on price or what you 'should' order for your health, choose a meal that inspires you. Start allowing your intuitive impulses to have their way here and there.

You may wonder how you can know the difference between intuition and fear. Many people find it difficult to discern between the two. However, there are some distinct differences. Fear can be felt physiologically as well as emotionally. It feels like worry and anxiety. Fear is in your head, it makes you ruminate, fixate and grasp for answers. Being afraid makes you feel physically constricted and tight. Your body literally slouches and your breathing is shallow and fast.

Intuition feels soft. It's in the body. Often in the gut. That's why we say 'gut feeling'. It truly lives there. It usually speaks to you softly and early-on in the feeling about something. It is the first instinct or first nudge you feel before thoughts get in the way. There are only a few seconds between the inkling of knowing and your thoughts marching in to sabotage it. Use that short time to act on your impulse. Once you start thinking, your inner voice gets drowned out by logic.

Intuition is feeling, literally in the body. There's a quiet "yes" feeling, an exhaling, a relaxation, a trusting and a knowing. Your body feels open, light and good. There's no constriction, just openness and happiness. To truly hear your intuition, you can start small.

When you wake up in the morning, invite your intuition to tell you what you need for the day… and listen.

When driving to work, follow your intuition on what route to take… make it fun.

At lunch, eat the food that calls to you...enjoy it.

When you see a co-worker and have the impulse to hug them… go for it.

Refrain from asking other people for their opinions and what decisions you should make in your life. Start exploring and trusting what you feel from within. Make it an experience to hear the wisdom from there. We are so quick to reach outward. Sit with your OWN questions. The messages will come.

In relationships, if you feel like there's something off, 'there is'! Hear that. Take care not to get caught up in blaming yourself or others, that doesn't help. Rather notice there is something out of alignment. I can speak from experience; it is when we turn inward we hear the language of the soul. Listen to your gut in all areas of your life. Resist ruminating; you don't have to over think about it or worse yet ask others for their opinion. Just let it be. Fixating on fixing holds you back. Surrender and let the answers rise from within.

Barbara Santen
Dating and Relationship Coach
www.barbarasanten.com/

Trish Mrakawa

"Horses reflect to us who we truly are."

I share my story of my relationship with horses and how they shaped my life as a leader and shifted my perspective on what I thought was possible. It is my wish that through this journey, a new awareness is opened up for you and you find gifts in all of the situations you encounter… and love horses as I do.

Lessons in Leadership From Horses

One flashlight flare meant danger, two flashes meant safety; but I saw three flashes that night from across the pasture and we had never talked about what three flashes meant.

I awoke in the hotel room from that scene that permeated my dream. Or was it a nightmare? Drenched in sweat, my breathing rapid and my heart raced so fast that I almost fell out of bed. What had I agreed to do? Was I out of my mind? I wanted to get on a plane and go back home immediately.

It was the mid-nineties and I was at the annual convention of the National Sport Organization, Equestrian Canada in Ottawa. My best friend, fellow horseman, sidekick and confidant and I were asked to represent our province at the coaching meetings for equestrians. These meetings united coaches from all the Olympic and World Equestrian disciplines: showjumping, three-day eventing, dressage, reining and driving. It also brought together those involved in grassroot development of riders and education of coaches. My friend and I were experts in this area.

It was my first year attending these meetings and my first Global Leadership opportunity. This event brings together leaders from across our vast country who are united by a passion for THE HORSE. I was so excited and grateful to be there. Thinking who will I meet? What will I learn?

You won't believe what we discovered. It's always the first year attendees that get roped into volunteering! Tee Hee!

Volunteering was part of our family dynamics as I watched my mother work as a docent at the local Museum and run events for Engineers' Wives. The weekly bridge club luncheons at my house were a joyful time. When my sister and I began to ride, our mother also volunteered for the Canadian Pony Club locally and on a national level.

My Dad was also active in multiple volunteer positions serving on committees for his coin collecting obsession and professionally for various Engineer and Land Surveyor organizations.

My parents taught me that giving back is just what you do to build community and make a difference in the world. To have an impact for one person, one thousand or millions. It didn't matter. I grew up learning how to step up. That became my mission in life.

But here's the catch... I still walked into that first meeting room with excitement and some trepidation. I scanned the room noticing the strong, proud members of this group. My head held high; the people gathered in a tight knit group – almost for safety. There were people looking over the paperwork to make sure they are fully informed. Then me, the new addition, wondering which was the most neutral place for me to sit while I figured out who was who in the 'herd'. The table was long and rectangular in shape. At each end of the table sat groups of strong, dynamic leaders and many professional horsemen like myself. This select group of people were there to share information and experiences; make connections; and create consistency in programs for athletes and coaches. What a huge task! My first thought was that there was a lot of history and past stories with agendas I had yet to discover.

As I observed this group of people, it reminded me of sitting on my fence watching my own herd of horses meander, play, lead, follow, munch, run and doze in their own community. Within a herd there can be a shuffling for position, the search for power and the alpha members of the herd are making sure everyone knows who is in charge.

On any given hour of any given day, one particular horse could be the alpha. In the next hour it could be another. The leadership changes constantly, as horses are needed for their skills in different areas. It's not as simple as the lead mare leading the horses to food and the lead stallion fighting off invaders or chasing the stragglers.

Horses who live in the same herd for a long time develop strong relationships. I could see the same herd dynamics with the people in the room: the friends, enemies, 'frenemies', the besties. I could tell who the loners were by the ones that stayed by themselves, showing their strength like the stallion off in the distance observing the group. I saw who were the most social, rambunctious ones who liked to kick up their heels a bit and get noticed. Horses bond together for protection and a new horse coming into the herd can have a lot of anxiety over the fear of being cornered.

I was the new addition to this herd and I had a lot to learn. Yet after two days of meetings with this group of highly qualified individuals, I was asked if I would put my name forward as Chairman of this committee. I am sure at that moment my heart stopped! This was my first time even sitting in on meetings of any kind. Already they wanted me to lead it? At first, I was honoured and then I became terrified. Remember my dream? That tells you I said 'yes'. Here's the struggle that came first. The talk from my inner voice kicked in. That monkey that likes to sit on my shoulder and chatter at me whenever I get excited about new opportunities.

At the meeting break, I left the room and paced the hallways. Hands sweating. Doubt and fear permeating my thoughts. My biggest cheerleader paced the hallways with me as I rambled on concerning all my past beliefs about not being good enough and all the reasons why I shouldn't do this. I thought, "What do you know about being a leader?"

I felt like I had become my mare Odie. She was a shy horse who stood back watching the rest of the group run to the people for treats and massages. Only when the crowd had cleared did she feel confident enough to come forward. Odie was a good student when I rode her. She loved to learn. Taking her into new situations and unfamiliar territory always took some convincing. What I realized is that Odie needed clarity and with clarity you know where you are and where you want to go. Just like me.

It reminded me that learning to love and accept ourselves at a deep level allows each of us to contribute our best. There was no longer the need for the flashlight warning from across the pasture that I saw in my dream. I became lighter and the world became brighter.

Then it finally dawned on me:

MY HORSES HAD ALREADY TAUGHT ME HOW TO BE A LEADER!

One of the first lessons that I learned was to choose your battles. The horse stood at the far end of the arena. His head lowered and his nostrils flaring like a bull in a bullfight. He stomped his feet and kicked the dirt away with his forelegs. I was not a worthy opponent as I lay in the dirt unable to move. The pain riddled my body as my back muscles spasmed.

You see moments before, I was having a discussion with this beast about going past a window that he thought was frightful. As a horse trainer, I did all the right things. I bent him away from what he was spooking at. I sat deep into the saddle to secure my seat. Gave him a little cluck with my voice for encouragement.

The horse did not belong to me. This was a potential mount for one of my students. Safety for my riders is my number one requirement and talent of the horse, second. So, I was persistent in my request to get close to whatever was scaring this horse at the end of the ring. Lap one, didn't make it. Lap two, not this time either. Lap three, again he balked. As this continued round after round, I became frustrated. I held my breath. I reached back to his belly with my whip and tapped ever so gently. Well, gently was too much for this horse.

He exploded underneath me and proceeded to buck wildly around the arena. I do not know how long the rodeo lasted. The next thing I knew I was on my back gasping for air. I felt through my body to see where the damage was. I raised my head and looked for the horse.

He was at the far end of the arena and had an eagle eye on me.

Horses are usually gentle creatures, so I didn't feel any imminent danger. Boy was I wrong. He started to run at me. Ears pinned back. Head lowered. He headed right for me, I curled up in a ball protecting my head from the impending impact. His hoof stomped down on my leg. I had never felt any pain so excruciating in my life. People arrived at my aid and stopped him. That one pass was enough. He didn't continue but the damage was done.

That horse made a huge impression on me. Literally! The next morning, I woke up to see a full colourful hoofprint on my inner thigh.

He left his mark not only on my body but in my mind. A difficult lesson learned. If I had negotiated better would it have ended in a more mutually beneficial relationship? I wasn't sure but I did have this question – what am I willing to risk to be right?

What I realized from this experience is that you must choose your battles. This was my first lesson in LEADERSHIP. Some arguments are not worth winning!

Horses bring their personalities to their position in the herd the same way that people bring who they are to their leadership. Leadership presence is a concept that appears to have a shared understanding. We recognize some people as being leaders due to their attitude as opposed to their corporate or economic status. When you are being authentically yourself with your own unique character traits, there is a radiating effect that reaches out and inspires people.

Let me share more....

Horses have taught me to be authentic and remind me all the time when I am working with them that energy truly does precede you. If I am in a bad mood, I am greeted with a horse that pins his ears back and turns away from me not wanting to hear what I have to say.

The energy you bring to the situation will be felt immediately by the horse. There is no hiding your emotions. If you are not authentic, the horses will not have anything to do with you. This would be the same as a leader walking into a meeting and thinking 'I'm really irritated by these people, but I am going to show up anyway and they will never know.' Well they may not know exactly where it is coming from but they will still feel the negative energy, the same as the horse does.

Horses teach us about the impact we are making and how their nature requires us to show up with integrity and honesty. They teach us about the impact we have on others – whether or not what we say, is really what we mean.

In fact, horses will constantly test their human students to see who is the leader, the horse or the human, not because they are 'vying for power' or 'needing to see who is boss' but because the safety of the herd depends upon it.

The immense power of the collective is accessed not through what we would conventionally coin as 'strength', ie, toughness, might and ferocity but instead through its sensitivity, empathy, listening and quiet presence. I choose to be that person – with a quiet, calm, grounding disposition. Just as in a herd of horses, occasionally one horse proves essential to the other's sense of well-being. Yet, looks for the most part like they are doing absolutely nothing. You may not have noticed when a person is there but without lifting a hoof or engaging in drama, her presence grounds and balances the group. That is who I am. That is what they saw in me.

Mark Rashid writes in *Horses Never Lie: The Heart of Passive Leadership*, "she is chosen by members of the herd as the one they want to follow." This is "a horse that leads by example, not force," a horse that epitomizes "quiet consistency."

I believe that if you propose to create an authentic community, you have to head in the general direction that no single leader knows everything. You want to ensure that people's true talents, motivations and true feelings are acknowledged.

Imagine what it is like to not judge either and just be present. That is one of the basic reasons why people love being around horses. They don't try to fix each other or advise a fellow horse. They genuinely care for each other and allow each other to follow their own path.

Horses have taught me to embrace new habits and be flexible. There is little gain to be made if I approach a horse with an agenda on how I think the day or ride will go. They seem to always have another plan. Horses give direct, unaltered and immediate feedback to what you are asking. Wouldn't it be great if people were able to do that as well? I have learned to ask a single question of board members in many different ways. Changing the question allows us to arrive at a different or more collaborative space. We, horses and humans, are not always ready for the next step. As a trainer and volunteer board member, I have to recognize when the confidence is not quite there to follow through.

Horses are mirrors. They'll show you back whatever you show them.

Horses can't lie and if you understand their language, you will have access to this amazing world. Horses communicate with remarkable accuracy through nuances of posture by the flick of an ear or holding the head high, low or to the side. The gesture of stomping their feet or swishing their tails will tell you a lot about how they are feeling. The sounds they make are also distinctive. My horse Blackwatch always calls out to the other horses when he enters the competitive arena. He is telling the others who he is and the way in which he will lead.

I am ever so grateful for that first opportunity to chair that coaching committee. I was unaware that this one decision I made on that day would lead my life down so many paths. It led on a journey of over 40 years of serving equestrian coaching in Canada. It has opened up a world of possibilities in so many fields of training, coaching, speaking and writing. It is the reason that I specialize in coaching leaders today.

When following leaders, or being one yourself, use this analogy to get the most out of the situation. Put yourself in the horse's place – which herd-mate would you choose to follow? The one who runs at you when you are in your weakest moment. The one who chases you away from the hay-pile or the one who leads you to the water and lets you drink.

I've always seen the best in people. It is the single most important trait that makes an exceptional leader. If you are unsure of the answers to difficult questions be calm, clear and creative in any given situation. When this happens, the entire community (herd) benefits.

IGNITE ACTION STEPS

• I invite you to look at the authentic community that a horse herd shows us and how we can do it ourselves.

• We can walk together sharing leadership when the time is right. Each person can bring their own authentic talents to the community and recognize that in each other.

• We can hold space and support each other in times of need and joy.

• We can accept each other. There is no need to judge, criticize or blame.

• We thrive in the present moment and are at peace with each other and nature. We can move from one moment to the next in harmony and compassion.

• We can work together with the goal of serving humanity for peace and in doing so learn a bit, no, a lot, about ourselves along the way.

• I invite you, the reader, to be that best kind of horse/human with me

Trish Mrakawa
Leadership Coach at Trish Mrakawa Coaching
www.trishmrakawa.com

RUSTI L LEHAY

"When you needed light, someone was there.
Now be the light to guide others out of their dark spaces."

In discovering and learning how to maintain a voice of reason, regardless of challenging scenarios, I have found difficult situations can turn around quickly, as long as one person remains level and adult in their tone and word choices. I hope you embrace the light within you to join me in inviting people to become the best versions of themselves, especially when blame or tensions run high, whether that be in board rooms or within an interpersonal workplace or in family dynamics.

LEADING WITH WORDS, WORDS LEAD ME

I once spent a day in solitary confinement. Two burly female guards behind full body plexiglass shields arrived to escort, well, to prod me towards the warden's office. They flanked me with prison-grade bear-spray, safety cap on, ready with their thumbs on the quick release caps if I was unruly. I protested the food. They saw me as causing a riot.

I am a foodie after all.

The situation was a mock training exercise for prison guards and their protocols. Soon women would arrive from all around Canada, either moving from overcrowded prisons or to relocate them closer to family support. I served as chair of the Women's Mentoring Group for our city's new Federally Sentenced Women's Institution. Our whole committee volunteered to be their practice inmates for a day.

The convicted women arrived and this foreign life I only pretended to live for a day became real through the women I visited. I was matched up with R who was up for attempted murder after her partner unpleasantly caused the demise of her beloved cat. We first visited once a week in the prison and then twice a week when she was granted day parole. We went for walks in the river valley and she was amazed at how I knew all the paths and where to find the isolated parts which were almost like being out of the city. She once said it felt good to turn her face into the rain because no one would then know she was crying.

That was the first difference I learned; tears in her world meant she might be vulnerable to dangerous predatory people. Tears in my adult relationships were safe and an honest display of vulnerability. Between the sobbing, exchanging heartfelt truths often led me and the other person into a better place of understanding. R and I often talked about the disparity of our lives and what led her down the path she was on and what led me down mine. It was mostly all talk until the day I was helping her find a clinic that, for some reason, was defying my normally high functioning internal GPS. I flagged down a police car to ask for help. I thanked the officer for the directions and turned around. R was gone. Like a ghost in the movies where the main character removes their attention for a moment and then looks back stunned to find… nothing.

I stood in the middle of the street. I had signed her release for the day. Moments of panic enveloped me as the police car drove to the corner, turned and disappeared out of sight. Unsure, I returned to the sidewalk. R craned her neck out from behind a power box, "Psst." Walking over to her, she hissed, "Are you crazy? If anyone sees me talking to the cops, I'm blackballed a snitch, not to be trusted. I lose my street cred." She further explained that the police might hurt her to extract information. She was genuinely afraid.

My experience is and always has been the police officers are there to help and protect. Her experience was to hide out of sight and avoid them at all costs. After that, we stuck to walking in the river valleys where we both enjoyed privacy. She opened up. Her stories made my life look like an idyllic country childhood despite the alcoholism and abuse, then a somewhat trying marriage (later annulled), followed by the luxury of returning to college and university as a mature student.

After my two terms as chair for the Women's Mentoring Group, I somehow ended up serving on five other boards all during a two-year span. Call me crazy but they were all busy at different times or had steady smaller jobs spaced evenly throughout the year.

Common across all of these boards was the personalities. The strong, the quiet, the pushy, the controllers, the talkers, dreamers, the criers, table pounders, door slammers, chair turners and the doers. The stories I could tell about the criers and the door slammers would fill a book. If I could just get one of the speakers to return to adult mode, the others would follow. Executive Directors would often comment along the lines, "Rusti can calm down a room often before the storm and especially after." To put it crudely, once both people engage in trading shit, it becomes a shit-show. If one person stops throwing shit (communicates in adult mode) the other one looks like a shit and returns to adult mode as well.

I must credit my honed 'communication skills' to an excellent transformational dialogue coach, who just happens to be my sister. She introduced me to Transactional Analysis (TA). A very simplified example is that we all vary our speaking within three main tones of voice: Adult, Parent, Child, Adult to adult, parent to child, child to adult, and parent to adult. Now imagine what happens when you throw in some adjectives: A condescending parental tone of voice and wording spoken from a spouse to an intimate partner can lead to tension unless the intimate partner manages to remain adult in tone and word choices. If the intimate partner falls into rebellious teenager, whiny child or sarcastic adult, the fight is usually on.

You might say I cut my teeth on learning how to stay adult without whining/poor me, petulant victim, angry ex-partner when my last intimate relationship failed. Instead I practiced ethical adult, problem-solving adult and consciously uncoupling adult. Now that required a lot of practice and every negotiation conversation had me nervous. All the board interpersonal dynamics, even though tense, were a much easier arena to hone these skills. Being a good listener and pausing before responding also helps. Listening and speaking into what others need to hear has possibly always come naturally to me. In that, I have been told, I'm able to lead people out of dark spaces.

For instance, when I returned to college, I served as a listener to someone needing friend who called herself Anonymous. I'd already done seven years of counselling and healing work when I sat in that hallway as a mature student with a bunch of teens soon to be in their 20s. Of all the conversation topics zinging around, one is indelibly written on my psyche. The impact led to a lifelong friendship. I'd mentioned the rampant sexual abuse that ran through our family like a drought-ravaged grass fire. Notes then appeared in my locker. Signed by Anonymous, this person wanted to speak as freely as me about childhood abuse. I read between the lines. She was still caught in shame and silence. She wanted to know how I could be so open, so free, so light. So I'd leave a note, the top half of the letters, 'Dear Anonymous', barely sticking out.

I wrote, "You were innocent. It is time to let go of the shame and embrace yourself as the sweet child you were. You were a victim then. Call the Sexual Assault Centre Crisis Line." I still know the number of the Sexual Assault Crisis Line thirty years later. I used it enough. People were there for me and now I was able to return the favour. I didn't yet have the belief the pen is mightier than the therapist. It might have been her words that showed me the potential. They were poetically heart-wrenching. Somewhere late in the first year, she started signing with an artistic J.

It was likely J who won me the Student Life Leadership Award. Her poetry inspired me to approach the Student Life administrative department to support a creative arts publication inviting students to submit art, prose and poetry for publication. All the submissions were judged on merit before learning the names of the submitters. We only found out after the editorial committee decided, though I recognized some of the anonymous poetry as J's and abstained from voting when her work came up with the selection committee. The admin department kept a database of titles and names for us.

We all need something, somebody to hang onto and notes created a bond between us. Early in the second year she started signing her full name. Anonymous ended and we became friends. It's almost time to celebrate 30 years of knowing each other and update what we've been up to. We celebrated our 15-year anniversary by painting wind goddess bookends.

Looking at myself, I don't see a leader and yet others see me as such. Other than short stints as a chair of a board I certainly don't lead groups to action. Then I question myself again, as I have led blocked writers to their muse with students who say they will follow me anywhere. I also encourage those afraid to write to pick up a pen and offer tips on how easy it is to order about the 26 gods of the keyboard.

One by one I've led. I didn't always know it. If I examine closely, there have been micro moments of leadership and several I have only found out after the fact. Like 22 years later.

Amy attended a writing class with me in 1996. We had both enrolled in Women's Words Week. She sat beside me, quiet, reserved, eyes that pierced with an intense gaze then darted away. When she was drawn out to share, she shared wounds so deep, she cut straight into our listening.

Many of us never had to fight our own brain like she had and we were in awe. Email was new then, so I asked her for her snail mail address. I wrote to her of how much I enjoyed her writing, bringing more words to the page and asked her to please let me know when she publishes.

Jumping to 2018, after coaching, teaching, writing, facilitating other writers for years, that same instructor who taught the class back when I had originally met Amy, offered a three-week course. I gave myself the gift to go just for me, 2 1/2 hours every day. Being a student allowed me to share my own words from the assigned 10 or 20 minute writing time. Charles, another writer would ask how did I write so much. The instructor, with her quirky sense of humor, then quipped, "She writes with both hands on each side of her journal."

Using the time and space in that class, my words flowed. For me it was years of practice. Near the end of those three weeks, the instructor brought in a guest to speak about her writing and publishing journey.

It was Amy. I've seen her over the years at writers' events, picked up her first book and here she was again. She was no longer quiet about how her words led her out of mental illness; desperate scribbles on scraps of paper under her hospital mattress that a nurse found and typed up for her. That class we shared in 1996 was her first time out on her own doing 'normal' and she tells the class how encouraged she was when sharing her words. She then points at me. "Rusti was in that class with me. She wrote me a letter I received after. I don't know how many times I've moved but I still have that letter and I can tell you exactly where it is in my home."

Better than any of my stories, Amy's experience proves my belief that the pen IS mightier than the sword. I just know words have been my way to find myself and how often words have been my salvation. Some people joke how they are a recovering perfectionist. Never addicted to any substance, never having drank coffee, never having been drunk, if I am a recovering anything, it's a doubter. Over and over again, I have doubted my own authority, my own wisdom from my days on this planet. Now, as the mirror tells the shocking truth that the baby of a family of six does indeed age, it seems wisdom from my own mistakes is the only reward. I have not planned well for the winter of my life much like the silly squirrel in Aesop's Fables who didn't store nuts for the long cold season. It's time to risk a little more of myself with a broader audience. I'm planning to stay warm in my winter years through my drive to help others, especially younger women, to see different choices earlier than I did. Maybe not find themselves alone at this stage but if they so desire, be enjoying a well-stocked storehouse of love and sustenance to nourish them for many winters.

If you are like me and do not yet see yourself as a leader of many, I invite you to look for the one-on-one chances to lead others. The person who needs a smile or a word of encouragement or the person who needs an attitude adjustment. This brings me to the final ignite moment I will share on this theme.

I once went to the gym for nine years working out beside Sandra. She and I both loved the gauntlet, a machine with downward escalator stairs that we voluntarily chose to climb up and up and up at varying speeds. I know, crazy. We would take turns and she had her favourite bike. She rode that thing every day leaving a puddle on either side of her on the floor. I never really knew anything more about her outside of her obsession for cardio, that monarch bike and our shared love for the gauntlet.

One day, she storms into the change room muttering epithets I cannot repeat. She was disparaging a patron. Muttering "I'll never be able to ride my bike again. That 'animal' has soiled it." I was shocked and speechless, never having encountered such vehement and blatant racism. I shamefully raced out of the room and, ashamed, I made a vow I would never be speechless again.

I have had two chances to keep that vow. A friend and I were visiting our favourite rocky mountain tourist town when another traveller scans us up and down and stops us to chat, to admire the mountains. Then she does it: "It's a pity these (insert slang for Asians) have to ruin it for us…"

I interrupt before she can go any further. I might have even said it through gritted teeth, "These mountains are here for everyone's enjoyment and we are clearly not part of your 'us'. You can go back where you came from." I grab my friend's arm and we stride away, with both my friend's and the racist's mouths agape, albeit for different reasons. My friend quizzed me how I came up with the retort that fast and, when I stopped shaking, I told her about Sandra.

Second chance came with higher risk. A client was talking about four guys with no way to latch their large Ikea purchase to the roof of their small car. He was trying to describe them by their ethnicity asking another man in the meeting what sect they were from if they wrapped their turbans a certain way. His colleague was speechless or just not deigning to answer and my client kept on asking as if the joke depended on it.

Though not as instant, I did pipe up. "Eric the story is no longer funny. It might have been if you'd just said, 'Four guys are reaching their arms up out of all four windows holding on to the box on the roof of the car.' Ethnicity has nothing to do with it. It's just four guys. It's funny wondering if they make it home or do they get a ticket for an unsafe load. End of story."

Maybe instead of a leader, I am more of an advocate for kindness with words and using words wisely, because they can hurt more than sticks and stones. The bruises words leave are invisible and internal. Words can heal. Words lead me. I lead with words. Where can they take you? How can you lead using yours?

IGNITE ACTION STEPS

In situations when other people are raising their voice or speaking in offensive tones such as condescending adult, controlling parent, rebellious teenager, whiny child, you can stay in a neutral tone, using adult language. You will find it's almost like magic, as you create a space for the other person, or people, to return to an adult communication style with you. (see references for more ideas)

Practice and role-play with spouses or partners. Be childlike with each other when you are in fun mode. Promise each other to take turns being level and for one to be that tipping point back to level if one of you loses your cool. Ask for a redo on conversations as needed.

Practice it in customer service scenarios. You will be surprised at how much more you can accomplish when you modulate your voice to adult tones and throw a little adult toned humour. It even works on the phone with customer service! Smiles can be heard over the phone; it changes your voice.

Practice it with your children, speaking to them like adults in training. It really brings them back quickly when we model the tone of voice that keeps the respect flying back and forth. Aiming for mutually respectful and life-giving interactions is the goal and the reward.

Rusti L Lehay
Empathic Word Doula / Inspirational Speaker @ Word Quest
www.rustillehay.ca

ALISON JESSICA WEIHE

"My purpose is bigger than my past."

My hope is that in reading my story you will feel less alone in your vulnerabilities and more inspired to step into your light. Owning our stories can be hard. Embracing our vulnerabilities can be risky. But only when we are brave enough to explore the darkness will we discover the infinite power of our light.

FINDING JESSICA

When I began writing this chapter for the Ignite series, my initial reaction was 'Can I really do this right now?' But somehow deep within me I realized that voice of 'You're not good enough' is the same voice that has plagued me my whole life… I decided the voice – that says you CAN – finally needs to be heard. This is the essence of my story – it's searingly raw and honest but also joyful and triumphant.

Taught from an early age to be humble at all costs, it held me back at times from being my best self. I was always plagued by what people thought. Always trying to fit in. Always wanting to be liked. It has ruled my entire life. That's why reading Marianne Williamson *(who Nelson Mandela famously quoted)* resonated so deeply, "Our deepest fear is not that we are inadequate. Our deepest fear is that we are powerful beyond measure."

So, when I stepped up to write my story, I was finally stepping into the light, emerging from the murky shadows of self-doubt and constant approval-seeking. But even after I had submitted a rough draft of my story, I got cold feet and spoke to the editors. I was so scared of being exposed. That old familiar voice, "What will people think?" rose up and gripped me by the throat. "Some people perceive my life to be perfect. Will this make them think less of me...?"

Marianne Williamson wasn't saving me... So, I spoke to my husband the next morning and he said firmly, with absolute clarity, "You are an amazing woman and I think the world needs to hear your story. Maybe your story can help others..."

Brene Brown in her remarkable work on vulnerability talks about the people that matter, matter... My husband and my family are everything to me. If others judged, did they matter?

So where does my story begin? It begins with a privileged but turbulent childhood where emotional eating numbed my pain from a home that was sometimes volatile, erratic and unpredictable. I loved my father fiercely. He was a powerfully charismatic man and a remarkable philanthropist. However, depression was a cruel and uninvited member of my family, not just an occasional guest. The highs were enticing, the lows were devastating and dark. My gentle mother did not know what to do to make it better. Her sadness was palpable. A pregnant silence in our home signified a lull before the storm. No one at school knew about this double life. Not a soul. My father was a pillar of society and an inspiration to many, although he struggled personally. He really wanted to make the world a better place. But he fought his own battles in private. We were his fearful audience. Things are not always as they seem...

Being the plump one in an incredibly sporty and academic family didn't help. I felt like I must somehow have been delivered to the wrong address. While my siblings sought refuge and excelled in sports, I buried myself in books and a love of animals.

I had decades of brooding isolation as I picked my way through my twenties and thirties, only to find my stride in my forties and fifties. Now, I have reached an amazing space where I have somehow created a life of abundance, wholeness and happiness.

I am the happiest I've ever been. I am now a transformational and leadership coach. An accredited Image Consultant, who specializes in personal branding, an aspiring writer and speaker. I am also way more FUN as a wife, partner, mom and friend. But it wasn't an easy road to get here.

There are still days when I grapple with old patterns that threaten to paralyse and taunt my fragile confidence.

I was fortunate to become a successful entrepreneur – against all odds, having started a company with my husband 20 years ago. When we began, everyone said, "What do Alison and her husband know about running a business... give them three months..." Nobody thought we would succeed. Nobody. Neither of us had a business background. But we had drive, determination and passion. The company grew from 3 to 150 employees. We won numerous awards and were featured on television and in magazines. However, my real story is not about my entrepreneurial journey, it is about my path to wholeness. That, I think, is a far more interesting story.

On the surface of it, I looked like I 'had it all...' A wonderful home, a beautiful family, a successful company. But the real picture was not as pretty. Inside was a complex woman, so full of self-doubt, a people pleaser, a chameleon who wanted to fit in at all costs. Deep down I had a fear of food. In my twenties and thirties, after years of yo-yo dieting, flirting on the fringes of anorexia and a decade of erratic and hidden bulimia, I was finally stable in my weight and 'OKAY'. I met a tall and gentle man who everyone loved. He was highly intelligent, humble and open, no intrigue, no drama. Calm. Ironically, neither of us had been the shining stars in our families. We were kindred spirits. We loved nature, animals, design and architecture. He was the kindest man I had ever met. We married and settled down. I couldn't believe how blessed I was. His family loved and adopted me as their own. We had two delightful children. My husband was an incredible father. I finally let people get close to me and I became less guarded. But I was still wary of food. As a result, I avoided cooking, I ate spartanly and I paraded myself as health-conscious. I was simply doing the best I could to juggle all the balls in the air, as a driven entrepreneur, wife, business partner and mother.

In my late forties the company was doing well, the kids were enjoying school and we were very involved in school projects and industry shows. Life was busy. I thought I had it all figured out.

Then in 2010, my world crashed. We had a massive internal company fraud. It was a woman we all trusted and liked. I had given her special holidays and nurtured her growth and development. We uncovered eight years of fraudulent transactions. It was the ultimate betrayal. This person had come through an established employment agency. We found out much later, she had a previous track record for fraud. Gambling was her addiction. Skillful embezzlement fed it. Even the prosecutor said she was one of the

282 / Alison Jessica Weihe

most manipulative defrauders he had ever come across in 15 years. We were brought to our knees and had to rebuild staff morale throughout the company. I was emotionally broken. I was the main witness in the court case. My hair fell out in chunks from the shock and stress.

At the same time, I learnt that my husband was dabbling in an online world I was not aware of. I felt a second wave of betrayal and utterly confused. For three weeks we hardly spoke. We had always had a companionable, easy relationship. Now there were just terse, tense sentences between us.

Here is where it gets really interesting. We went to several different counsellors. Yes, us. The apparently perfectly happy couple. In doing so, we picked our way through the fragments and shards of pain to the truth. What was uncovered took my breath away.

What came out in a slow, contorted journey was that my kind, gentle husband was feeling incredibly isolated and alone in the aftermath of the fraud and the subsequent court case. He felt responsible and ashamed as he had been the main one approving transactions. All of his dyslexic childhood demons of making mistakes had returned to haunt him.

He became quiet, grey and withdrawn. He had no male friends close enough to confide in. He had always been a bit of a loner. I was his best friend. But I was dealing with my own internal struggles, taking sleeping pills to get me through the next day, facing a hostile staff who felt that we had let them down and fearing for their own futures. To deal with that, I drugged myself at night and dragged myself through the days. He sought solace and escape in an online world that would not judge him.

A technical genius, with a brilliant mind, his self-esteem was rock-bottom. He reached out to a world that would not diminish him. Ironically, he spoke glowingly about me. He was not trying to find another wife. Merely too numbed to talk about the real pain of what the fraud had done to him.

So, things are not always as they seem … THAT has been my greatest lesson.

We slowly rebuilt our relationship based on far deeper values, just as we rebuilt the company with new and innovative systems. My husband did some serious soul-work and so did I. A lot has changed. We started being more open and vulnerable and moved through the pain. I have earned my husband's respect and he continues to earn mine. Now, when people see us together, they think it is a second marriage. After 25 years, romance, intimacy and a deeply spiritual connection have become the foundation of an extraordinary relationship.

But something shifted during this terrible period – and that was ME.

I changed. I stopped being complacent. I stopped taking my marriage for granted. Something moved in my soul. In the course of counselling, I was confronted by my own role in it all... a moment of reckoning kicked in... I signed up with a personal trainer. I hated it for the first year – an entire year. I moaned under my breath, berating my lot.

I had done loads of self-development work. Buckets full of conferences, seminars, workshops and retreats about self-acceptance. But I had never ever worked on my relationship with my body other than punishing it with strict diets and mental castigation.

In that first year something shifted. I started to like myself more, to feel better. I started to run and swim. I added Pilates and yoga. I looked in the mirror and saw a different woman, lighter in both body and spirit. I started to regain my sense of humour. My husband became my biggest supporter, not only because he was proud of me and my evolution but because I was more loving. Frumpy, baggy dresses were replaced with fitted, feminine embellished fabric. The complex brooding Alison had become more fun. Lighter. Funnier.

One weekend about four years ago when we were going to a beautiful country retreat, my husband said, "I think we should leave Alison at home" – 'Alison' being the driven, focused serious one, always worrying about clients and deadlines. As we turned out of the driveway into the dappled light of a spring afternoon, he repeats, "Maybe we should just take Jessica and leave Alison behind." Jessica is my middle name. In that moment, Jessica was born. Jessica turned out to be way more fun than Alison that weekend. Now we always take Jessica on holiday and date nights. Jessica doesn't care nearly as much what other people think! Named after my much-loved Granny Jess who was still playing tennis at 80, Jessica delights in being sensuous and playful. She loves life.

Some people were bemused when they heard about Jessica. My husband would proudly tell friends that he had a mistress called Jessica but then after a swift intake of breath, would quickly add that his wife was also his mistress. As I get older, I seem to like Jessica more and more. Jessica is still ethical, with all those values my gentle spiritual mother instilled in me. But she is way more fun!

After Jessica was born, another major shift happened. I was running regular half marathons and I started to see food as fuel, as energy for endurance, as food for my soul. Then something else changed. I started to enjoy cooking and getting creative with flavours and adapting recipes. Now I celebrate food as a language of love. I never ever weigh myself. I naturally and instinctively eat healthily but have no war with food, no enemies with calories. I really enjoy delicious, healthy food. I still believe that you reflect what you consume. Now I run shorter distances but still do water aerobics, swimming, yoga and Pilates. Oh and dancing... Jessica loves to dance!

Finally, I feel WHOLE. I've stopped beating myself up for never being good enough and just started celebrating life. It's changed everything. My relationship with our children, my relationship with myself. And most powerfully with my husband. My husband is my proudest supporter and soul traveller. We discuss everything. No emotions are off limits. We never fight. We debate; we share opinions; we continue to grow in this complex, delightful journey of life. The fact that my husband wants me to tell our story is testament to the evolved, conscious, incredibly wise man he is today.

Going through counselling, took us on a deep journey of growth and understanding, to find one another again, to hear one another's perspectives, and we now have an incredibly deep soulful connection. Also, a humility to not judge others' journeys. Because you never truly know what's happening until you dive deep and listen. Truly listen.

My journey has given me the gift of deep compassion. My awareness to wholeness has changed the tapestry of my soul. I have more balance. I have humour. I delight in the small stuff, the birds outside my window, my adoring dogs, my wonderful friendships, collaborative staff, supportive family, delightful, intelligent children and above all my remarkable husband who helped me find my way home and find 'Jessica'.

Finding our inner spirit and knowing our true selves, leads us to our greatest experiences. Don't be afraid to look into the crevices of your life. You may not like what you see at first but the light will illuminate the learning and the love that is meant to shine. You can be a beacon for others as you turn up your light. See beyond your own labels and become your greatest self.

IGNITE ACTION STEPS

On Transformation: Change is scary. Discipline is hard. Get support, whether it is getting a personal trainer, going to free classes at the gym, joining a non-threatening walking/running club. Find a friend to just walk with you. Just start. But don't give up – it takes three months or more to form new habits and patterns. ACTIVITY helps regulate healthy eating. *Doing sports and activities can be your most powerful, most permanent instrument of change.*

On Finding 'your' Jessica / Expanding your Identity: We tend to cling to established patterns of living. Change is scary. Try a new brighter colour or a different style of clothing. Change your hairstyle. Or makeup. Shift something. Above all, be curious. Sometimes creating a 'Jessica', gives you PERMISSION to expand your identity. Sometimes our childhood patterning represses us from thinking it's okay to have FUN. That you have to suffer to be noble. That is why I needed 'Jessica' – to set me free from my own voices of judgement.

On Relationships: Be willing to be curious, not to be right. Be willing to be open and to learn. There are many organizations globally that have wonderful programs that deepen one's understanding of relationships and one's own triggers, drivers and patterns. If you are looking for counselling, don't be dismayed if you do not 'gel' with the first counsellor you see. Don't give up. Search until you find someone that resonates with your truth, that provides you with compassion and insight, that really listens. Counselling can help uncover what is truly serving you, what is holding you back or even worse, paralysing you. Be prepared to stop blame and judgement. Say, "What can I DO to contribute to changing and deepening of the relationship?" – with others, with myself? One of my greatest lessons is that you can only truly help others when YOU are whole. If you can model wholeness for your family you can liberate them from the patterns of the past. *(See resources at the back of the book for more support.)*

The more we listen with grace and compassion, the more we change the world. It is my deepest desire that *you too are powerful beyond measure*. If my story resonates with you in any way, please reach out to me and connect as I enjoy supporting others in their own journey towards the light. Let's create a kinder world together.

Alison Jessica Weihe
Transformation and Leadership Coach
www.luminousleadership.co.za

KRISTINA MÄND-LAKHIANI

"Learn to let go!"

How well do you know yourself? Your darkest corners? Your deepest feelings? I hope that in reading this story you might have a glimpse into those parts of your life, where resistance rules the game. Whether it is a painful kind of resistance, like fear, worry, sadness, regret; or a much more agreeable kind, such as desire, pride, holding on to people and things. We'll do a little exercise in letting go at the end, but first, let's pull back the curtain, let a little light in and see what lies in the darkest corners of those worries and insecurities.

POINTLESS SACRIFICE

Have you ever wondered why certain unpleasant events happen to you? Sometimes, it takes patience and persistence to come to the point when everything suddenly starts to make sense – as if the final piece falls into the puzzle and you see the big picture. And unfortunately, sometimes it takes years of patience, persistence and faith that things happen for a reason and everything is going to be fine.

It took me over three years to finally learn my lessons and get out of the dark. I believe that many of us keep on getting the same lessons over and over again. Sometimes disguised in quite different experiences, until we

288 / Kristina Mänd-Lakhiani

finally get the point – a paradigm shift, a new look at reality, a new set of internal beliefs.

About ten years ago I got into a business partnership with a friend. Or, to be precise, I got into a business relationship and became friends with my partner.

We had a lot in common. Similar backgrounds, similar life experiences, our children were similar ages and became best friends. So, naturally, we clicked very quickly. This was the first independent business for both of us (I had helped with my husband's business before, but did not feel the ownership there).

However, it wasn't simply our first very own business. It was a bit of a miracle in fact. Here's why. We were both born in the Soviet Union and had gone through Soviet education. Doing business was outside our model of reality. Entrepreneurship of any kind was strictly illegal in the USSR. We were raised to be perfect cogs in a huge communist machine, rather than self-sufficient, independent individuals capable of creating enterprises on our own.

For me, entrepreneurs were like unicorns – magical creatures never to be seen in real life. Yet here we were – two magical unicorns starting our very own business.

I don't think either of us realised how much we needed to learn and discover on our way to success. But we did it. We succeeded. In a few short years we had made our first million dollars. I was proud of my business partner and proud of myself. I felt as if I had proven myself capable, worthy of both love and respect.

Our lives were magnificent. We were traveling the world, meeting exciting, successful people, attending grand events and going to the best parties. Our families and households back in Malaysia were being taken care of by maids, chauffeurs and nannies.

The height of our success was marked by celebrating (in cat outfits) at a marvelous party on Necker island. It was Sir Richard Branson's private island in the Caribbean, with many of the most successful entrepreneurs and Sir Richard himself.

But, our triumph was not very long-lived. In 2014, a war broke out between the two countries – Russia and Ukraine, which made up 80% of our market. Both countries were plunged into economic crises and both currencies, the Ruble and the Hryvna,, started plummeting.

I remember a holiday campaign we were running in December that year. We wanted to be loyal to our customers and decided to fix the prices in

Roubles. It was a four-day campaign and by Thursday we were selling our goods for one fourth of the price it had been on Monday.

It was a scary time for us. It would have been scary for anyone, but we were relatively new in business. We had had it super easy till then. We were the golden kids to whom success came faster than we were ready for. We learned to live a good life and giving it up was not part of our plan.

It was hard to deal with the economic meltdown and dark times in the business. But it was even harder to deal with the emotional impact this meltdown had on me – the loss of my confidence, the doubt that crept in, "Was I really that great?" The internal worry if I could make it to the other side of the dark.

Unfortunately, by that time, our friendship was not doing well. It had started eroding a few years earlier for reasons completely non-business related.

Although the reasons were elsewhere, it was mostly the business that endured the brunt of the burden. Interactions continued to worsen as the relationship between the two partners and founders diminished.

I remember wondering in the mornings if our partnership made sense at all. I felt burdened and unhappy, constantly irritated at my business partner, dreading our work time together. It just stopped making sense to me from a purely human point of view. I kept asking myself, "Aren't we supposed to be happy in life? Why am I in this relationship? What am I staying in it for?"

Then the terror would creep up on me. "How can I break it off?" We have a business together, twenty people working for us, authors, partners and a quarter million customers. I had a moral obligation to stay in business. There was a kind of a sacrifice I had to make for a greater good, or so I thought.

But the deeper reason was much less glamorous. I was afraid that I cannot do it on my own. After all, I was born into a system designed to have me be a perfect cog, not a magical unicorn who starts her own businesses. In my mind I was absolutely sure that I would die as an entrepreneur the moment I was left alone.

But the business was not doing good and we needed to do something urgently. In the beginning of 2015, our panic was turning into paranoia. We let go of half of our people (I had the honourable task of breaking the news to the team). We stopped our advertising to save money and then lost our biggest partner.

I knew we could not go on like this. While we struggled and fought to keep our business alive, deep inside, I felt that there was a better way. I've always had issues with resistance. I believe in flowing. So I said to myself: "I'd rather go bankrupt but enjoy the ride, than fight for life with my teeth gritted."

Yet, this was not an option for us. I knew I could afford to lose everything, so playing big and risking big was absolutely natural to me, but my business partner was in a much less favourable position. I was married and the business I had started with my husband was doing great. I also had a huge family to support me. My business partner was a single mother fending for herself with no one to help her.

So we had to keep gritting our teeth. There was no 'playing big', no 'have it all' or 'lose it all'. There was no option to radically reinvent ourselves. We had to keep doing what we had been doing for years and do it despite the painful resistance of economic crisis, the bad business decisions and the nightmarish personal relationship I had with my partner.

I remember a meeting we were having in March of that terrible year. It was just me and my business partner, since we had let go of most of our employees. She was quiet. Silent, in fact. I was trying to suggest some action steps, needing her opinion, a discussion, a decision. But she was just silent. Not a word was coming out of her mouth.

I couldn't bear it any longer and asked what was the matter. Her answer was like a knife being jammed between the ribs: "I'm tired of pulling us through this all alone. I want to see how you manage without me."

Not only did we have hard times in the economy and our business, my partner had zero respect for me and my contribution in our common endeavour!

I was shocked, I was crushed, I was done.

When I got home, I sat down with my laptop and started writing a letter to my partner. I told her how much I was hurt by her words, how it was unfair, and all the usual accusations and complaints. At the end of the letter I wrote: "If this is how you feel, isn't it better for us to part ways?"

As I wrote that phrase, I realized it was the first time I vocalised the feeling I had been having inside me for the past few years. I stopped and stared at it. Was I really ready to part ways? Was I ready to do it alone? Was I ready for a nasty business-divorce (I knew it would not be nice).

Or was it an empty threat? A manipulative tactic? A way to get attention?

I looked at my letter for half an hour, knowing that I would only press the "Send" button if I could honestly say that I'm ready to part ways. Only if I know with 100% certainty that this is what I wanted.

When I did, finally, press the "Send" button, I didn't have a shadow of a doubt. I was certain. But more than that, I felt relief.

I immediately felt like sharing the good news. The horrors and worries of economic crisis, near bankruptcy and uncertainty were suddenly gone – evaporated like a dark cloud after rain. What a surprising relief it was?! I stopped resisting, I started flowing.

I still remember the next morning. I came into the bathroom to brush my teeth, looked at myself in the mirror and I felt as if I had wings behind my back. I was excited. I was elevated. I was not worried or scared about continuing this journey alone. I was excited to see how I would express myself, now that I felt unburdened and unhindered. Freed from having to make compromises for the sake of keeping a frail and painful balance with an incompatible business partner.

I was on my own now. And I was so free. Finally, I could be myself without feeling guilty or afraid of judgement. I felt my wings unfolding, as I leaned into the future.

Whether I'd stay alone in this journey was yet to be discovered. It was difficult when I broke the news of our separation to the team. Our most valuable team member, a woman who had been with us from the start and knew everything about the business, Liuba, was a close friend of my business partner and I was very nervous telling her the news.

I told Liuba that she had the freedom to either stay with me or go work with my partner. Fortunately for me, she chose to stay. Liuba is still my most trusted team member and a few weeks ago she confessed: "While you guys were bickering and sacrificing yourselves to the business, the team was suffering. You couldn't fool us. We all felt uneasy because the two of you didn't like each other. What a relief it was when you finally separated! It was like heaven after hell!"

So what was my sacrifice for?

Have you ever sacrificed yourself for "the greater good"? Have you sacrificed yourself in a dysfunctional business partnership? Have you stayed in a dead relationship "for the sake of kids or family"? Have you ever put up a 'good' face and suppressed your pain and emotions so as to not hurt the feelings of those around you?

If you sacrifice yourself for any grand idea, please stop and think again!

As His Holiness Dalai Lama once told me when I asked him about this dilemma: "Who can you help, Kristina, if you are not happy?" I will remind you, that your happiness matters and the only way you can lead others is if you courageously lead yourself first.

IGNITE ACTION STEPS

I certainly have huge respect for the sacrifice in the heroic sense of this phenomenon. When our forefathers sacrificed their lives for the right ideals and a brighter future. When rescuers sacrifice themselves to save the lives of ordinary people.

However, when we talk about sacrifice in everyday life, we usually have to deal with mundane (and often cowardly) compromising of our own wants, needs and values in fear of breaking a fragile peace, throwing things out of balance or causing a conflict.

While finding the way to your true self, recognising your values, finding your voice and courage to stand for what is important to you is a process, which cannot be covered in such a short format, I want to suggest the first step as a possible ignition point...

Learn to let go.

Sacrifice is resistance. Happiness is flow. In the words of Dalai Lama, you cannot help anyone if you are not happy. So, naturally, I want to suggest an exercise for you about letting go.

Here's what you do, a little meditation:

• Get comfortable, close your eyes, take a deep breath and relax.
• Think of any area of your life where you feel resistance. It may be a painful resistance - fear, worry, sadness, frustration, regret. Or a more pleasurable kind of resistance - strong desire, impatience, righteousness, holding on to something dear.
• Think of this feeling, locate it in your body and then tell yourself: "Let go!"
• Just take a deep breath, relax (physically) and say: "Let go!"
• Let go of everything that causes you pain... and everything that brings you that intense pleasure. Just let it all go!

And be happy.

Kristina Mänd-Lakhiani
Cofounder of Mindvalley
@kristinamand

A tremendous thank you goes to those who are working in the background, editing, supporting, and encouraging the authors. They are some of most genuine and heart-centered people I know. Their devotion to the vision of IGNITE, their integrity and the message they aspire to convey, is at the highest caliber possible. They too want you to find your ignite moment and flourish. They each believe in you and that's what makes them so outstanding. Their dream is for your dreams to come true.

Upcoming Books in THE IGNITE SERIES

If you feel you have had an IGNITE moment and a story you would like to share, please apply at www.igniteyou.life/apply. We look forward to all the applications.

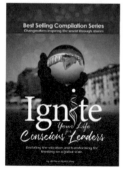

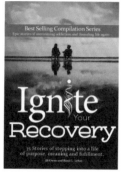

BOOKS AND RESOURCES MEANINGFUL TO THE IGNITE YOUR FEMALE LEADERSHIP AUTHORS

Alison Weihe

The Mankind Project for Men: A sacred space for men to share their journeys ~ mankindproject.org
Women Within: A sacred, gentle space for women to begin exploring their lives and their relationships ~ womanwithin.org
The More to Life Programme: Practical and profound tools for effective living. ~ moretolife.org
The Art of Living Programme, to support living happily and deepening one's purpose ~ www.artofliving.org/za-en
Vipassana, a worldwide organization for profound silent meditation retreats ~ www.dhamma.org/en-US/index

Helle Brodie

The Entrepreneur Roller Coaster by Darren Hardy, Darren Hardy

Sandra Smart

Talent Dynamics ~ talent-dynamics.com/profile-test
Ignition! ~ www.ignition.rocks
16 Personalities ~ www.16personalities.com/free-personality-test
Enneagram ~ enneagramtest.net
Human Metrics ~ www.humanmetrics.com/cgi-win/jtypes2.asp
Disc ~ www.123test.com/disc-personality-test
Myers Briggs ~ www.myersbriggs.org/my-mbti-personality-type/mbti-basics/home.htm?bhcp=1

Trish Mrakawa

Horses Never Lie: The Heart of Passive Leadership, Mark Rashid

Dr. Judy Gianni

Confessions of a Sneaky Organic Cook, Jane Kinderlehrer *– Fruits and Vegetable Juices* by Dr. Norman Walker

Rusti L Lehay

Transactional Analysis (Parent, Adult, Child) ~ www.businessballs.com